The Slaughter

The Slaughter

An
American
Atrocity

by
Carroll Case

THIS IS A PRIMARY TITLE BOOK
PUBLISHED BY FBC, INC.

Published in the United States
by FBC, Incorporated.

ISBN 0-9666499-0-7

SECOND PRINTING

PRINTED IN THE UNITED STATES OF AMERICA
by Quebecor - Kingsport

www.TheSlaughter.com

To Christy and Rebecca, my children,
who never wavered in their support and faith during
a thirteen-year investigation.

Acknowledgments

My gratitude

- to Ernest Herndon who is tough and honest and
    knows the meaning of words.
- to Charles Dunagin who, from the beginning, gave
    encouragement.
- to Charles Breeland, a military expert who shared his
    knowledge.
- to Cyrus Hoagland, retired FBI, for his expertise.
- to John Case, my brother, who never let me give up.
- to Lisa Ohler, my editor, who came late in the project
    but brought intelligence and great skill.
- to Rusty Denman, who said from the outset that the
    American people had a right to hear this story,
    and set about to make that happen.
- to Suzanne, my wife, who not only turned longhand into
    type, but with love and confidence, helped me sur-
    vive the long days and nights when the words
    would not come.

To all the above, I am truly grateful.

You never know when your time is coming.
Like birds suddenly caught in a trap,
like fish caught in a net,
we are trapped at some evil moment
when we least expect it.

Ecclesiastes 9:12
(GOOD NEWS BIBLE)

Contents

Part I:

The
Slaughter

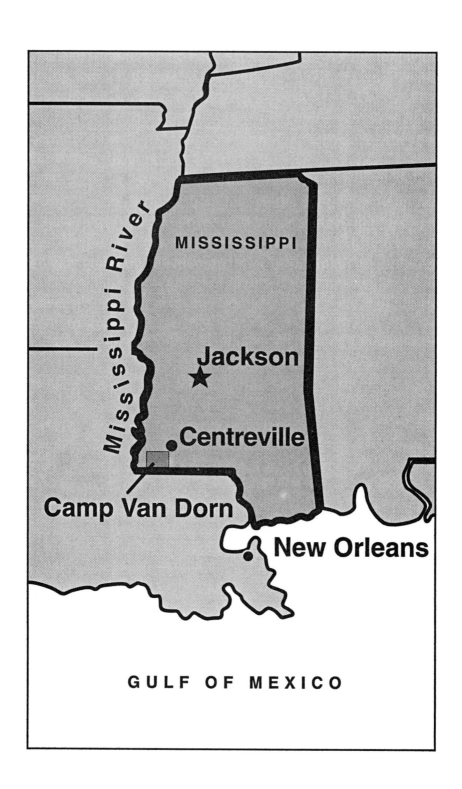

Mississippi River

MISSISSIPPI

Jackson

Centreville

Camp Van Dorn

New Orleans

GULF OF MEXICO

DURING THE YEARS I spent growing up and living in south Mississippi, I had heard hushed rumors of a mass killing of black soldiers on a nearby Army base during World War II. I simply dismissed it as southern folklore. But an unexpected encounter with an eyewitness—and 13 subsequent years of research on the subject—convinced me of the following shocking fact: in the fall of 1943, at Camp Van Dorn, an Army base in southwestern Mississippi, over a thousand black soldiers from the 364th Infantry were slaughtered. The perpetrators were not local white racists, but the United States Army itself.

The catalyst to start my search for the truth was an eyewitness confession that came out of nowhere. It was the early 1980s, and I was president of First Federal Savings and Loan in McComb, Mississippi. I had delegated the responsibility of hiring maintenance services to the institution's long-time secretary. It was nothing unusual for her to report that, for one reason or another, she was displeased with someone she had hired. She would ask me for permission to terminate their employment and, after hearing her grievances, I would agree. After a run of unsuccessful maintenance men, she came to me convinced that she had found a solution. "I would like to hire someone that, I believe, will do an outstanding job for us," she began, explaining that he was a retired white man in his mid–60s. She said that he did not need the money but wanted a little job to occupy his time. She elaborated, "He has recently moved back to McComb from Pennsylvania. I remember him as a veteran of World War II, and he served on the police force here in McComb before he moved out of state." She spoke of what a handsome man this now portly senior citizen once had been. "He always looked so striking in his uniform," she commented. We agreed to give him a try.

Over the next two years I got to know Bill Martzall quite well. He was always punctual, fastidious and dependable. He was a very private person. The two of us had regular early morning chats over coffee in the lounge, since we usually arrived for work a couple of hours before anyone else reported. Our conversations were casual, ranging from the weather to discussions about the Amish in Pennsylvania. But after a while the private person began to open up, and gradually he talked more about himself.

On a July morning in 1985, the two of us sat drinking our coffee. I asked him about his past police work and how he was originally attracted to that line of work. He told me that he had served as a military policeman in the Army. I cannot remember the exact question I asked, but I inquired if he had ever used deadly force in his police work. I remember vividly how he reacted to the question. His face flushed and the veins in his neck pulsated. "Do you mean in civilian life or in the military?" he asked me.

"Either," I responded.

There was a long, very long, uncomfortable silence. He had already placed his coffee cup down and was cradling his head in his hands.

"Mr. Case," he said, looking up, "a man can carry a heavy burden for just so long, then he has to put it down. I need to put it down if you will listen." He did not wait for my response. Something hidden in the reservoirs of his memory for 42 years pressed against the barriers of repression he had forged for himself. This time the flood gates opened, and his bloody secret poured out.

"During the Second World War, I served as an MP at Camp Van Dorn over at Centreville," he said. "At first my duty was a lot of fun. It was exciting being on a new Army base, and we were all young—lots of energy, you know. Good-looking women, civilian women, from McComb and surrounding towns, came onto the base every day to work. Then, of course, there were the new recruits coming in from all over the United States. We had problems to come up—hell, we're talking about over 60,000 soldiers at the base. There were problems, but nothing major." I listened with interest to what he was relating, but I had no idea at that point that he was about to become a credible witness to the vague story I had first heard in the 1940s.

He continued, "It all changed when the 364th Infantry hit the base in the summer of '43. The 364th was all niggers, close to 3,000 of them. Two months before they shipped out to Van Dorn, they had been in a lot of trouble in Phoenix, Arizona—racial problems, they told us. They had killed some MPs. We're talking about some mean sons of bitches. Even before the train bringing them in crossed over the state line, they were bragging about how they were going to take over the base and all of Centreville, for that matter." I sat motionless, afraid I would interrupt his thoughts by some unnecessary movement.

I had no reason to worry. He was on a roll now, and words were pouring out. "Things started tightening up, as tight as a drum, even before they arrived. They put on more MPs to help us out, and we started preparing for trouble. When their train got to Van Dorn, we cordoned off the area before they unloaded. Man, were they cocky and arrogant. They told us right quick that they were going to change things in the South and that we could kiss their ass. Can you imagine niggers talking to whites like that, especially MPs?" He was asking a question but neither expected nor wanted an answer. He went on without a pause, "I don't know what the rest of the MPs thought, but I knew right then we were going to be bustin' some heads."

Martzall described how the trouble started from the day the 364th arrived. "They walked down the streets of Centreville, talking about how they wanted some white pussy," he said. "Back in those days, small towns in Mississippi were completely segregated. There were sidewalks where even the local niggers were not allowed to walk. But when the 364th came into town, they walked on any damn sidewalk they wanted to. The local sheriff had to kill one of them to get their attention.

On July 3rd that same year, they caused a bad disturbance on the base. A large number of white women had been brought in for a Fourth of July dance. Before the dance could start, members of the 364th began pouring into the white service club where the dance was taking place. They overran the club, breaking in windows and side doors. We were called out and had to disperse the crowd. The scary part was, those niggers in the 364th showed no fear. If you ask me, I'd say they came straight from the pits of hell." Martzall continued, "Then we got word that they had caught a pregnant white woman and sliced open her belly with a knife, took the baby out and stomped it."

Martzall never knew who gave the final order, but he did remember that he was riding the perimeter of the base one day in the late fall of 1943 when the MPs got the news. "We were riding on weapons carriers and were armed with 45 caliber machine guns. We were told to wait until dark and to report to the black camp. It was located near the Engineering Division close to the railroad. They said we needed to take care of some business. Some other troops armed to the teeth joined us." For the first time, he paused for a long drink from his coffee cup. "We pulled up to the black camp and ordered the 364th out into this area. I remember that one of the nigger soldiers threw a brick and hit one of the MPs in the eye. I don't know if he lost his eye or not because all hell broke loose. We were ordered to let them have it. We had the whole area sealed off—it was like shooting fish in a barrel. We opened fire on everything that moved, shot into the barracks, shot them out of trees where some of them were climbing, trying to hide... we shot every nigger we could find. The screaming, yelling and begging was horrible." Martzall had spilled his secret almost without stopping.

In complete shock, I asked, "Didn't they have weapons?"

"Hell no. They couldn't shoot back—we had all the firing pins removed from their rifles."

"So they were defenseless?"

"Yes. But if ever anybody had it coming, they did."

I could not believe what I was hearing. "Bill," I asked, "how many soldiers did y'all shoot?"

"They told me over a thousand," he said, as matter-of-factly as if I had asked him the time of morning.

"What did you do with the bodies?"

"We were ordered out of the area after the shooting. I was told they were hauled off that same night by train."

"Where?" I asked.

"I don't know. We were placed in isolation for a while. You know, like quarantine."

"Do you mean y'all killed all the blacks in the 364th?"

"Hell, no. You're talking about nearly 3,000."

"What happened to the ones that were left?"

Bill raised his shoulders in a shrug. "I couldn't answer that," he said, "I never saw another member of the 364th after that night."

For a few minutes we sat in silence, then I spoke. "Bill," I said, "What you have just told me—is it off the record? Because if it isn't, I would like to do some research."

"Research?" he snapped. "What I have just told you is what happened."

"Yes, I know, but I would like to find some official account of this."

"You will never find it."

"Would you object to my trying?"

"I don't care what you do," he said. "I was a soldier in the United States Army and I was following orders."

"Let me make sure I understand. You were ordered by your superiors to shoot and kill hundreds or maybe even a thousand blacks?"

"I was given the order to shoot to kill, and we did."

"Could you give me the name of any other MP that did what you did?"

"No way. I've spilled my guts, but I'll never mention any-one else's name, ever."

The back door of the office opened, and someone started down the steps. It was time to go to work.

This was the conversation that launched the investigation into the alleged Camp Van Dorn massacre. Was Martzall telling the truth? I decided to find out.

I CONTACTED a friend of mine, a reporter for the local news-paper. Early in my career, I had worked for the Jackson and Vicksburg papers. For the past couple of years he and I had collaborated on some articles, investigating stories and exploring the rich culture of southwest Mississippi. My decision to tell him the Van Dorn story was based on several factors, not the least of which was that I had developed complete confidence in him. He had skillfully reported corruption in city and county government. His unbiased, well-researched account of hot issues relied on the facts, with a total absence of personal emotion. Another factor was that he had now acquired such a reputation with hunting and fishing articles that, at his very mention of crappie biting, good ol' boys would flood the narrow roadways trying to get their boats to water. His part-time job of serving as a rural mail carrier had put him on a firstname basis with county folks in three counties—Wilkinson County being one of them. That is where Van Dorn was located and where the incident supposedly occurred. I knew that if anyone could get the people of that area to talk without raising their suspicions, it was he.

When I related Bill Martzall's account to him, he listened without interruption.

After I finished he asked, "Did Martzall agree to go on record?"

"He didn't object," I answered, "but he asked me not to mention him by name as long as he was alive. He said because of his wife."

I decided to approach the investigation in the following manner. First, I would need to check on Martzall's credibility, then I would begin requesting official Army records beginning with all the morning reports from Van Dorn in 1943. The morning reports would tell me, among other things, who and how many soldiers were present during daily roll call. My friend would try to set up interviews with someone who had served at the Army base either in a civilian or military capacity during 1943.

We agreed to spread the word that we were preparing a nostalgic *"remember when..."* article on Camp Van Dorn. I would make no mention of any information gleaned from Bill Martzall. Any hint on our part of an alleged atrocity might plant an idea in the minds of the people we interviewed, and I didn't want that.

Luther Williams and Williams' brother-in-law, W.M. Ewell, were the first two people he found that had agreed to talk to us. Both of the men were lifelong residents of Centreville, Mississippi. As we rode toward Centreville, I asked my friend about the men.

"Williams," he said, "is a county supervisor—knows everyone. You know," he continued, "next to the sheriff, supervisors are the most important men in the county."

As we reached the outskirts of Centreville, he turned his head toward me. "I doubt very seriously these men will have any information about what we are looking for," then he added, "but who knows?"

There was nothing fancy about the home of Luther Williams. It was a modest brick, ranch-style structure with a neatly groomed yard. As we pulled into his driveway, we saw two late model automobiles and a pickup rigged for hauling dogs. Obviously, Williams was a hunter. Before we could get out of our vehicle, Luther Williams stepped outside the back door and invited us in. The politician was friendly and cordial. He was an average-sized man wearing a pair of khakis and a plaid shirt. His thin red hair was combed straight back, and hair oil glistened from his balding spots.

"You boys come on in and make yourselves to home." He introduced us to Ewell. W.M. Ewell was a larger man, the cattle rancher type. His snow white hair was full and neatly combed. A leather-tooled belt held up his pants, and his western shirt had pearl snaps on the pocket. His brown Laredo boots were polished. It was a cinch that the western hat on the floor next to the La-Z-Boy belonged to him.

We sat in a living room filled with bric-a-brac and crocheted doilies. Pictures of family members hung way above eye level on the walls. There was a little small talk at first, and we talked briefly about local politics. Luther's wife interrupted, bringing in a tray of coffee and cookies. She pulled the living room door closed as she left the room. Luther finally settled back in an easy chair and strummed his fingers on the overstuffed arms.

"Now, what can we do for you boys?" he asked directly.

I wondered how many times he had asked that question to a constituent visiting him needing a culvert, a bit of gravel or some other favor. My friend was digging around in his camera bag but looked up, "We wanted to talk to you about Camp Van Dorn—you know, the good ol' days."

Luther nodded his head, "That was a long time ago."

Ewell agreed. "Where, exactly, would you like to start?"

I answered, "Your most vivid memory."

Williams glanced over at Ewell and immediately responded, "Well, that's easy enough. The most vivid memory I have is the night that they killed all those niggers. It don't get any more vivid than that."

My friend and I glanced at each other in disbelief. His skill as a reporter quickly took over, "Well, that certainly sounds interesting. Tell us about that." And as simple as that, the proverbial Pandora's box was opened, and the story that we had feared, but not expected, jumped out.

Luther began. "I was not a soldier on the base; I worked in the Fire Department as a civilian. I also had a close relationship with some of the officers that liked to quail hunt. I had the dogs and knew the fields, so I got to know them quite well."

My friend reached for his notepad and asked permission to take notes. Luther agreed and continued, "I heard enough talk from the officers to know that there was a lot of trouble brewing on the base." Ewell interrupted, "Yeah. I knew it too," he said.

"Were you a civilian also?" we asked.

"Yeah. I worked in the laundry, but we knew something was up."

Luther picked up there. "Not only did we know it, but the whole town of Centreville knew it. Things were about to bust loose in town."

"What was causing the problem?" we probed.

"A bunch of niggers that had been sent to the base from out west. Troublemakers." Then Luther added, "If *they* [meaning the Army] hadn't taken care of it, then *we* [meaning the local citizens] would have. Everybody that owned a shot gun was coming to town. We didn't have a choice."

"What were they doing?" I asked.

"Taking over the town, the streets, the sidewalks, slurring our women, trying to destroy our way of life."

Ewell added, "Something had to be done."

Luther broke into a satisfied smile, "And they took care of the matter."

"Who?" my friend and and I asked in unison.

"The MPs and some soldiers on the base."

"When was that?" I asked, "I mean, what year?"

Luther shrugged, "Either '42 or '43. I can't remember."

Ewell said, "'43 I believe, I'm almost sure it was '43."

Luther began telling the story. "There were riots at first. The Fire Department was called out because they were afraid the niggers would burn the base down. That night there was more trouble. The MPs and niggers got into it, some of our trucks were over near the railroad, and that's when the lid blew off. I've never seen or heard so much shooting. I headed for cover, looking for a place to hide. I got down in a ditch underneath a culvert. When it was all over, blood was running down the ditch I was in. It was running pretty deep. I remember it was on my pants' legs."

Ewell joined in, "We could hear the shooting over at the laundry. It was the next morning when they brought in the bloody towels, sheets and mattress covers. I've never seen so many in my life, at least eight or ten of those big laundry carts stacked as high as you could see. I asked where they all came from. I was told from over at the 364th."

Luther continued. "The next day I saw a sight I will never forget as long as I live. They had this makeshift morgue, and I saw the bodies—hundreds and hundreds of bodies stacked up like hogs, almost as high as the ceiling."

"What happened to the bodies?" I asked. "Were they sent home?"

Luther looked at Ewell for support, then slowly answered, "I really don't know. I heard they hauled them away on a train, stacked them up like pulpwood and hauled them away."

We visited with Luther and Ewell for nearly three hours, going back into the recollections and asking questions, trying to get more bits and pieces. Before we left, we asked the two men if we could someday use their statements. Both agreed. Luther's last words to us were, "You can ask any man in Wilkinson County about me. I'm a truthful man, and I know what I saw with my own eyes."

My friend and I talked about what we had heard all the way back to McComb. Something caught my attention—Bill Martzall had said they shot into the barracks of the 364th. Maybe that explained the towels and bloody mattress covers.

If what we had heard were true, the federal government had a lot to explain.

I set about canvassing nearby counties for clues, returning to the town of Centreville and the overgrown grounds of the long-abandoned Army base, now private land. I poured over countless old newspapers and documents, and I made a formal request to the Archives of the United States Army for information pertinent to the incident. Yet I received a surprising response: many of the records were missing or, in some cases, never existed. There were 20 companies which contained the more than 3,000 men in the 364th. No morning reports exist for 7 companies, approximately one-third, for the entire period of time in question. The phrase "government cover-up" started to feel all too applicable.

We wrote a double-page feature, a *"what if?"* article hinting at the possibility of the incident without going into all of the details we had heard from the eyewitnesses, in an effort to elicit more information. The night before the story broke, my friend said, "If we open this box, whatever jumps out can't ever be put back in." After the article appeared in the newspaper, I received a barrage of unsolicited calls and letters from people confirming the atrocity. Somehow the word spread from this small paper in south Mississippi, and I was being contacted by people from as far away as California. Interestingly, letters from individuals thousands of miles apart reported the incident using the very same descriptive terms, imagery and circumstances.

Disturbing incidents surfaced which never showed up in any of the Army's official documentation. One such contact was from a man named Shorty Coile. His brother, Private Paul C. Coile, Co. 'B' 163 Engr Combat BTW, was a white soldier who had been stationed at Camp Van Dorn just prior to the time of the massacre. Paul had written a letter dated June 25th, 1943 to his aunt Mary. A part of it reads, "Listen, I want you to know something that no one else knows. There have been a few riots in the camp between the Negroes and whites and I want you to know that there have been about 20 or 25 Negroes shot and killed. They have had 5 or 10 shots right through the head. And we are going to give them hell when they come around us." But a few days before the letter arrived, Private Paul Coile died in what the family was told was a drowning, on July 11, 1943. As Shorty explained, this was very hard for the family to believe, since his brother was renowned as an expert swimmer. As Shorty related, "The attendant at the funeral home tried to get me not to open the casket, but I had to see him. What I saw will haunt me until the day I die." His brother's body had been mutilated and disemboweled, and his genitals had been cut off. A member of the honor guard who accompanied the body told Shorty that he could not discuss any of the details of his brother's death. He said he had known Paul on the base and considered him an Army buddy, and he promised to tell Shorty what really happened after the war was over. Shorty never heard from the honor guard member again.

Soon the gravity of my personal situation—the hornet's nest I had dared to stir up—struck very close to home. The newspaper article triggered serious death threats. One anonymous phone call warned, "We are going to kill you and your family if you write any more of that nigger mess in the paper." My office was mysteriously burglarized, and field notes and research pertaining to the investigation were stolen; an ominous calling card—the passport of what I later learned was a fictitious person—was left behind to intimidate me. Apparently many people were highly displeased at what I had begun to uncover.

I made the decision to leave the area and move to Jackson to head the Mississippi Arts Commission. During the next few years that followed, I was concerned that I would not be able to finish my research and write the Van Dorn story. On three occasions I tried to give the story away in the hope that someone would complete the work. My first attempt was to give my information to Will Campbell, a friend and southern writer whom I trusted implicitly. We talked in a tiny cabin, deep in his daddy's woods. "It's your story," he told me, "and one day you will write it."

My second attempt to get the story told was when I contacted a television reporter for a Jackson, Mississippi station. He converted some of the material into a three-segment evening news piece. Although he received an outstanding award for his work, it only received statewide coverage. My final attempt was in 1989 when a federal judge's son, who had heard about my story, brought Ronald Lee Ridenhour to talk with me.

Ron Ridenhour was a soldier who helped expose the My Lai massacre in Vietnam. We talked about my research and he asked if he, too, could look at my materials and help with my investigation. I agreed and loaned him some important documents such as morning reports, letters and taped interviews.

In 1994 I received a phone call that would lead to vital evidence. There is something unsettling about a telephone call that wakes you in the middle of the night, especially if you have a daughter away at college. My first thought was a fear that something had happened to Rebecca. She was playing tennis for the University, and they were always traveling back and forth to tournaments. An unfamiliar voice when I answered only intensified my feeling of uneasiness.

"Is this Carroll Case?" he asked.

"Yes." I grew more concerned.

"You have an interest in Camp Van Dorn?"

"Yeah." By now my concern for Rebecca had shifted to the threatening night calls I had received in 1985. "What do you want?" I asked bluntly.

"My name is Neil McMillen, and I am a history professor. Someone at the Secretary of State's office told me of some research you did on an alleged massacre that occurred on that base."

"That's correct," I answered, wondering where this conversation was going.

"I discovered some documents in the Archives at Suitland, Maryland, where the modern military records are kept," he said.

"What type of documents?" I asked.

"Some classified material that has recently been declassified."

Now the professor had my full attention. I had been told by the United States Army in 1985 that there was no classified information on the 364th Infantry Division. McMillen and I talked for about an hour. He explained that he was doing research not on Van Dorn, but on the black soldier's role in World War II. He asked for my help in setting up some interviews with local black veterans who had served in that war. He also asked me to tell him about my research and what I had uncovered over the past nine years. McMillen promised to send me the recently discovered documents.

The documents arrived three days later. I couldn't believe my eyes.

There were twelve pages of information enclosed in the packet, including a cover letter from the NAACP Legal Defense and Educational Fund, Inc., dated June 30, 1943, and emotional affidavits and letters from desperate black soldiers who were members of the 364th Infantry: Corporal Clarence Jones (dated June 15, 1943), Private Irwin C. Wiley (dated June 1, 1943), and Corporal Anthony J. Smirely (dated May 30 and May 31, 1943). These documents were obtained under the Freedom of Information Act. They are both photocopied in their original form at the end of Part I and transcribed here for legibility exactly as they were written.

N.A.A.C.P. LEGAL DEFENSE AND EDUCATIONAL FUND, INC.
69 FIFTH AVENUE, NEW YORK

TELEPHONE: ALGONQUIN 4-3551

June 30, 1943

Hon. Truman Gibson
Acting Civilian Aide to Secretary of War
War Department
Washington, D.C.

Dear Mr. Gibson:

Enclosed herewith please find copy

of affidavit of Corporal Clarence Jones relating

to conditions at Camp Van Dorn, Centerville, Mis-

sissippi.

Very truly yours,

Milton R. Konvitz
Assistant Special Counsel

MK: GS
Enc.

STATE OF GEORGIA
COUNTY OF FULTON

In person appeared before the undersigned officer, authorized to administer
oaths, Clarence Jones, who being duly sworn, says: First, I am 20 years
of age and live at 262 Piedmont Avenue, N.E., Atlanta, Georgia. I was
inducted into the military service February 6, 1941, at Atlanta, Georgia
and at present am Corporal in Headquarter Company, 1st Battalion, 364th Infantry, stationed at Camp Van Dorn, at Centerville, Miss.

I am now absent without leave, in Atlanta, having left the Camp on
June 3, at 12:00 o'clock, because of the cruel treatment which the members
of our Regiment received from the Military Police and civilian authorities
at Centerville.

As soon as our Regiment 364th Infantry became stationed at Centerville,
the Military Police and Civilian Police and other civilian authorities began to abuse and beat up our men whenever we went into the town of Centerville; that not knowing that it was the custom in Centerville for whites
to walk on one side of the street and colored on the other, we happened to
walk on the wrong side; and also not knowing the one Drug Store in the town
where colored people were allowed to go, some of us, by mistake, went into
the wrong one with the result that some of our men were handled roughly by
civilian men and Military Police and beaten up, although we offered no re-
sistance; that practically every time we went to town some of us were set
upon by Military Police and other officers and beaten without cause; that
we complained to this treatment to our Commanding Officer but they did not
do anything about it because they themselves were subject to the authority
of the old post commander, Col. Guthrie; that on or about the 28th or 29th
of May, 1943, a colored soldier of Company A, 364th Infantry, was shot and
killed in the town of Centerville by one of the civilian law officers, and
as far as the deponent knows, nothing was done about it.

Deponent further states that the 364th Infantry in which he serves is composed very largely of men from the north and had just come from Phoenix, Ariz, around the 22nd of May, last; that the local people as well as the Military Police did all they could to keep the colored soldiers from having anything to do with the local colored people, saying that "the northern Niggers would spoil the local colored people;" That most of the colored soldiers of that Regiment remained away from the town except to pass through to go to Baton Rouge, La., or other places, and they remained always in fear of being beaten up if they stayed in Centerville any length of time.

The deponent further says that he left his post of duty for the sole reason of being able to report to some outside authority the hard and un-bearable things that the colored soldiers of the 364th Infantry at Camp Van Dorn, Miss., had to put up with, and that as soon as he has made known those conditions to somebody who can bring them to the attention of the higher military authorities, he is going to return to his Company and Re-giment; that when he left without permission he did not then, and does not now, intend to desert from the Army, and intends to return to it, but he does hope that something will be done to make it easier for colored soldiers to serve their country at Camp Van Dorn, Miss. as well as every other place where the military authority sees fit to send them.

                                        Signed Cpl. Clarence Jones

Sworn to and subscribed before me
this 15 day of June, 1943.

S/ W. J. Shaw
Notary Public Fulton Co., Georgia
Atlanta, Ga.

My commission expires 8/14/44

Camp Van Dorn
Mississippi
June 1, 1943

TO WHOM IT MAY CONCERN:

This is not only a letter of protest against the brutal treatment of soldiers of color in the south, but it is also a plea to the people of America to do that which is in their power to put an end to such wholesale desecration of the Constitution of the United States.

Sunday afternoon, May 30, 1943, a soldier, a member of the 364th Infantry Regiment (Colored), now stationed at Cap Van Dorn, Mississippi, was brutally murdered in a town called Centreville, approximately four miles from camp, by a civilian sheriff, a resident of the town. From the sworn testimonies of several eyewitnesses to the crime, the following information was revealed, and is being published for the benefit of those who might be inclined to believe the articles which are published in the behalf of the southern white gentry.

It was learned that five colored soldiers, while making a tour of the town of Centreville, were accosted by two Military Police, who ordered one of them to button his shirt sleeve. The soldier informed the MP that the button had become detached, and that he had not been able to replace it. Whereupon, the two MPs leaped from their car, brandishing black-jacks, and one of them proceeded to attack the soldier who had no button on his shirt sleeve. The remaining soldiers persuaded the other MP to let the men fight it out, and "let the best man win." But the MP, obviously getting the worse of the battle, noticed the sheriff of the town, Mr. Knighten, coming up with his two deputies and called, "Mr. Knighten, shoot this nigger." The soldier then straightened up, and said, "No, you won't shoot me." Whereupon, Knighten drew his revolver, saying, "The hell I won't", and firing point-blank at the soldier, struck him fully in the chest. The sheriff then turned to the MP and asked, "Any more niggers you want killed?". Meanwhile, the deputies put two of the other soldiers to flight with well aimed blows to the head with a sap-stick, but took the other two to the guard house.

Obviously, the unsavory reputation of the 364th Infantry Regiment has preceded them to this station, due mainly to the fact that this is the same Regiment which figured so prominently in the Thanksgiving Day riot in Phoenix, Arizona, and it is also quite obvious that the civilian authorities of this locale have heard of this so-called belligerent outfit, and have taken it upon themselves to whip them into submission, and to subjugate them as they have done other Negro outfits in the past.

Of a certainty, the War Department is cognizant of circumstances so prevalent here in the south, particularly in the case of the Negro troops stationed here. The question uppermost in the minds of the members of this organization is, "Could the War Department be collaborating with the civilian authorities of the south in subjugating this regiment which has caused such a disturbance in the past few months, by knowingly sending them to a place where racial conflict is inevitable due to the stubbornness of both factors?" If such is the case, then we, the soldiers of color might just as well lay down our arms, for the fight in which we are so willingly sacrificing our lives is already lost.

Leading papers of the south are already branding this regiment as troublemakers, and have even gone so far as to petition the War Department for a transfer of this regiment to a northern station due to the fact that we are responsible for fomenting race riots among the Negro troops, and the white civilians in nearby Centreville. Such allegedly instigation of race riots on our part is a gross misstatement. We merely ask that we are given the same opportunity to find recreation among our people, and be accorded the same treatment given other members of the armed forces, regardless of race, creed or color.

Credit must be given to one man in particular, Colonel John F. Goodman, Commanding Officer, 364th Infantry, who, regardless of personal safety, and thinking only of the well being of his men, walked calmly into the face of flying bullets fired from the guns of Military Police sent to our Regimental area in order to quell the disturbance created by our men when news of the wanton slaying of one of their men reached the camp, and forced the MPs to cease firing on the defenseless men. Through the daring and forethought of Colonel Goodman, and several of his subordinates, only was soldier was injured, and he, not seriously.

It was Colonel Goodman, who took this regiment under his wing during the Phoenix Thanksgiving Day disturbance, and guided them through a maize of criticisms, accusations, and extremely low morale, to respectability in the eyes of the Phoenix residents. The memory of Colonel Goodman will be admired and cherished by every member of the 364th Infantry long after this present world conflict has become a thing of the past, for, before the very eyes of his superior officer and other officers, obviously of the south, ordered a soldier, one extremely sun-tanned, to remove his shirt and undergarment, and to ascend the platform on which he was standing and without further ado, put his arms around the soldier, and said, "My children, for to me, you are my children, color doesn't mean a damn to me, and I love every one of you". And with tears in his eyes, he said, "I am not much of a Christian, but I want each one of you to say the Lord's Prayer along with me".

When the prayer was ended, the soldier on the platform wept shamelessly at the sincerity of this man whom all have grown to love, and to trust, and who would willingly follow him into the very bowels of hell, if needs be.

As Colonel Goodman issued orders to the Company Commanders to take charge of their troops, many a hardened soldier came to attention as tears welled in his eyes, which was, in itself a great tribute and an acknowledgement of devotion and respect to a man who through his love and understanding of the Negro soldier, averted one of the most disasterous encounters between the Negro soldier, and the white Military Police that was ever anticipated.

NOTE: Permission be hereby granted to those concerned to include, exclude, or alter in any way the contents of this letter, which will serve to render it suitable for publication.

S/ Private Irvin C. Wiley
Service Company, 364th Inf.
Camp Van Dorn, Mississippi

Co.   364th Infantry
Camp Van Dorn, Miss.
May 30th, 1943

Mr. E. Washington Rhodes
Editor, Philadelphia Tribune
Philadelphia, Pennsylvania

Dear Sir.-

I am a native of Philadelphia, residing at 5916 Arch St.
in West Philly. I enlisted in the Army in May, 1942. After
coming to the 364th Infantry, in Arizona last September, I have
been wondering--Why did I join the Army? Instead of building
morale, it's taken it away.

Last Thanksgiving, this Regiment made a bad name for itself
by inciting a riot. The news of this affair was in every news-
paper--white and colored--that I have read.

Now, the regiment has been moved down here in the deep South.
The land of the white man. The place where the colored man,
soldier or civilian, hasn't the slightest chance for an even
break. Hardly had this Regiment been here 47 hrs before the
"White Supremacy" took its first toe-hold. The men here, some
having homes and families in a close vicinity were rounded up
by white MPs and civilian. authorities and sent back to camp.
When duty hours are over, other soldiers are allowed anywhere,
but not the colored ones. How do the so-called white over-lords
expect us to win a war for them? If some of these malfunctions
of the people could be corrected, I believe that it would be
better off all-around.

There is one thing I can say, and I wish that others would
take heed to it and that is--the white officers of our Regiment
are about the best there are. Our commanding officer, Colonel
John F. Goodman, is a champion of the colored soldier. A better
Regimental Commander would be hard to find.

Mr. Rhodes, I appeal to you for some kind of investigation
of this matter and hope that the negro-hating man of the United
States can be made to see the light.

I have heard of what may happen if I write, but I am not
afraid of the consequences if my story can bring to life the
truth of the matter. Therefore I sign this

329 words

Corporal Anthony J. Smirely, Jr.
Co. H. 364th Infantry
Camp Van Dorn, Mississippi

Co. H. 364th Infantry
Cam[ ]an Dorn, Miss.
May 31st, 1943

Mr. E. Washington Rhodes
Editor, Philadelphia Tribune
Philadelphia, Pennsylvania

Dear Sir.-

I have written to you before, but the latest news is to much
for me to bear.

Yesterday, Sunday, a day of holiness and good wishes, a soldier
of this regiment was shot and killed by an MP (white, of course).
We aren't even safe in the Post Area. From the white section of the
camp, came four (4) armored scout cars, each with about ten MPs
armed to the teeth. We were absolutely defenseless against these
men. All rifles and amnution had previously been taken up.

Tonight, just an hour ago, one of my fellow-soldier friends
came back from an intended over-night pass. He had been beaten
about the head by the white MPs, who are now recognized Negro-
haters.

What do these people want of us? Do they want us to leave their
"lovely South?" I would gladly give them their wish. What have
we done to them? Just because we soldiers are living better than
some of the poorer classes of whites, is no reason why they should
try and humble us. They should know by now that that is beyond hope.
I think, and I do believe that I speak for the majority of my race,
that we, the Negroes, are just ordinary people, trying to make a
decent living and trying to make the world so that we can do it.
We don't try to be the Masters of any other race--why do they try
to master us? All I ask for is an even break.

Being in this camp is just like being in prison. The inmates
of Leavenworth are better off than we are. If we dare venture off
the Post, we are subject to come back on a stretcher. (Living _in_
camp isn't much better, as the incident of yesterday will prove.)
A man can't even go out to visit his wife, less he be beaten and
invalided for few days. _Yet_, the army is stressing absenteeism.
They don't want you to be incapicitated in any way when it comes
to drill time. What the hell can a man do? If he asks others not
of his organization for help he is reprimanded for going over their
heads. By writing to you, a newspaper man of fearless outspokeness,
is the only way that we can hope for any consideration. If I fail
in what I am undertaking now, I might as well reserve a berth in Hell,
for that is what it will be here.

Mr. Rhodes, I beg of you to _please_, from my heart, please do
something for the fellows and myself whom are among the unfortunate
to be in this State of blood--Negro blood--that is constantly flowing
in the streets.

Hopefully, I am
Corporal Anthony J. Smirely, Jr.
Co. H, 364th Infantry
Camp Van Dorn, Mississippi

Finally the tragedy had a human face, and names, as I read the letters of these men. They describe the brewing crisis as it was being experienced firsthand, and their pleas for help are heart-wrenching. The Army considered Corporal Clarence Jones AWOL—but in his opinion, he ran for help.

I WAS NOT PREPARED for what else the packet contained... a declassified confidential memorandum for the Deputy Chief of Staff, written by none other than the Inspector General of the United States Army, Major General Virgil L. Peterson. It was written on June 8, 1943 in the tumultuous period leading up to the slaughter. After reading it carefully and analyzing it—both what was said and just as importantly what was not said—I understood why it had been kept secret and hidden from the public for almost 50 years. Even though I had heard countless grisly eyewitness accounts of the incident itself, watched the videotaped interviews over and over and seen the expression in their eyes as they described it in graphic detail, something about reading this report's cold, dispassionate military language gave me chills. This situation taking place on one base in south Mississippi had the attention of the highest levels in the military. No wonder an event of this magnitude could have been so effectively covered up.

Again, the document is transcribed exactly as written.

CONFIDENTIAL

WPCSA 333 (6-9-43)   COPY - MCE

IG 333.9-364th Infantry (4)   8 June 1943

MEMORANDUM for the Deputy Chief of Staff

SUBJECT: 364th Infantry, Camp Van Dorn, Missississippi

1.   Pursuant to your instructions I have had an officer on duty
in my office investigate the report of an imminent race riot in the
364th Infantry at Camp Van Dorn, Mississippi. The officer who conducted
the investigation, Colonel J. R. Burney, reports the following pertinent
facts and circumstances ascertained as a result of his investigation:

a. The 364th Infantry arrived at Camp Van Dorn on Wednesday,
26 May and Friday, 28 May, from its former station at Phoenix, Arizona.
Beginning with the first arrival of these troops, reports from a number
of sources establish the fact that there was a general bragging on the
part of the men to the effect that they were going to "take over" Camp
Van Dorn, the town of Centerville, and the state of Mississippi. These
statements were so general and so persistent as to cause serious alarm
on the part of the civilian population in the nearby community. (It
appears that these remarks were also very distrubing to the colored troops
already in the camp.)

b. Following the arrival of the 364th Infantry, a series of
events have taken place at Camp Van Dorn which indicate that these boasts
were not entirely idle threats. On Thursday, 27 May, one day after the
arrival of the first contingent, a group of men from this organization
while visiting the colored service club in the camp, were boisterous,
refused to obey the rules of conduct in effect, namely removal of caps,
wearing of complete uniform, avoiding indecent language, and the introduction of beer into the club. It also took about an hour for the hostess
and the noncommissioned officers in charge to clear the club of these men
after the prescribed closing time on this particular night.

c. On Friday night, 28 May, a group of several hundred
colored soldiers, the majority of whom are known to have been from the
364th Infantry, broke into one of the camp exchanges, rifled the stock
and damaged the fixtures to the extent of several hundred dollars. The
exchange had been temporarily closed by the exchange officer a short time
before because of the profane, disrespectful and threatening conduct of

CONFIDENTIAL

CONFIDENTIAL

the men. The culprits excaped into the nearby barrack areas prior to the arrival of the military police.

d. On Saturday night, 29 May, a number of men from the 364th Infantry visited Centreville and marched around the town in formation, using indecent, and profane language in the presence of all encountered. This group (approximately 74 men) was arrested by the civil police, consisting of the town marshal and a number of deputized citizens armed with shotguns. Upon arrival of the military police officer, this group, upon his orders, immediately dispersed and returned to camp.

e. On Sunday afternoon, 30 May, a member of Company A, 364th Infantry, Private William Walker ASN 36170964, was accosted outside the reservation by a military policeman because the soldier was improperly uniformed and had no pass. Following a brief argument, Private Walker assaulted the military police and was attempting to take his pistol when the county sheriff arrived on the scene. The sheriff reports that upon his arrival the military police was on his back in a "jeep" with the colored soldier on top of him. Private Walker, noticing the arrival of the sheriff, jumped out of the car and made a lunge for him. Upon refusing to halt when ordered to do so, the soldier was shot and killed by the sheriff. Information of this incident was immediately transmitted to the 364th Infantry and to its Commanding Officer, Colonel John F. Goodman.

f. Colonel Goodman at once dispatched all officers to their respective organizations and he, with members of his staff, proceeded to the barracks area of Company A, the company to which the slain soldier, Private Walker, had been assigned. Colonel Goodman reports that upon his arrival he found the entire company milling around, swearing, cursing, and threatening to break into the supply room for rifles and ammunition. Seeing the situation was becoming serious, Colonel Goodman ordered the firing pins removed from all rifles and that an officer guard be placed over all supply rooms in the regiment. The situation at Company A was kept under control by the officers, but in Company C a group of men stormed the supply room and obtained a number of rifles before the arrival of the company officers. (All of these rifles except two had been found prior to the arrival of Colonel Burney at Camp Van Dorn. The two missing rifles had not been located at the time of his departure from the camp on Thursday, 3 June).

g. A short time later a crowd of several hundred members of the regiment assembled near the regimental exchange. A riot squad (colored) from the Military Police Detachment of the camp was forced to fire into this group in an attempt to stand them off. Private Raymond

CONFIDENTIAL

CONFIDENTIAL

Johnson, ASN 34066051, Company C, 364th Infantry, was wounded by this gunfire. The timely arrival of Colonel Goodman and his Cahplain, (Captain) Elmer P. Gibson (colored), was perhaps the only thing preventing serious bloodshed at this point. Colonel Goodman was able to quiet this group and following a talk by him to the assembled battalions, the entire regiment was marched to the company areas where it has been confined since.

      h. During the period Thursday, 28 May to 3 June (the date the investigation was completed), there have been a number of instances reported of unprovoked attacks on individual white soldiers passing near the 364th area; instances of bottles being thrown at passing cars, and insulting and offensive shouting from these barrack areas to officers and others driving by.

      i. Prior to the arrival of the 364th Infantry, the colored troops in the camp had been well-behaved, and all such incidents which have occurred were in the nature of individual offenses. It appears that other colored troops in the camp almost uniformly deplore the conduct of the men of this organization and the few from other organizations who have joined them in their riotous conduct.

      2. The events which took place in the 364th Infantry, especially on Sunday, 30 May, had ominous possibilities. It is apparent that the situation was held in check almost entirely through the personal efforts of the regimental commander, Colonel Goodman.

      3. During the course of the investigation, a conference was held with the Mayor of Centreville at which the sheriff and the deputy sheriff of Wilkerson County, the town marshal and numerous representative citizens of Centreville and surrounding communities were present. These citizens are very much exercised over the situation, have armed themselves so as to protect their lives and property, and are definite in their insistence that the 364th Infantry be transferred to another station.

      4. Upon Colonel Burney's return from Camp Van Dorn and at your suggestion, he, in a personal conference, presented the facts established as a result of his investigation to General McNair. The solutions to the problem of this regiment were discussed at length. General McNair is of the opinion that the worst possible solution would be to transfer this organization to another station, this being not only what the local citizens want, but quite possibly, in his opinion, is the motive behind some of the disturbances engaged in by the members of the organizations since its arrival in Mississippi. On the other hand, he is of the opinion that the best solution is to confine the organization to the limits of its regimental area and to deprive it of all privileges until such time

CONFIDENTIAL

as it will disclose its real trouble-makers and has demonstrated its worthiness to enjoy the rights of other organizations. Furthermore, he is prepared to assure the citizens of Centreville and other local communities near Camp Van Dorn that no member of this organization will be permitted to enter these towns until such time as the citizens themselves request that the ban be lifted. In addition, he plans or prescribing a training program for this organization which will keep the men exceedingly busy, a program which may require additional officers who will be provided if necessary.

5. In considering the decision of General McNair in this matter, it should be recalled that this organization, while stationed at Phoenix, Arizona, engaged in two serious breaches of military discipline which were the subject of a previous investigation by officers from my office. On one of the occasions approximately 500 men of the regiment engaged in a disturbance that had all the earmarks of a mutiny, an affair in which the men refused to disperse when ordered to do so by the regimental commander. No disciplinary action was taken against the offenders in this instance. The second event took place on Thanksgiving night 1942 when approximately 100 men from the regiment engaged in a shooting affray with a detachment of colored military police, within the city limits of Phoenix, in which one officer, one enlisted man, and one civilian were killed, and 12 enlisted men were severely wounded by the gunfire. Sixteen of the ringleaders in this affair were tried by a general court-martial, each receiving a sentence of fifty years confinement. Following these events the regiment received a new regimental commander. Colonel Goodman, the present commander, and a new executive officer. In addition a new and up-to-date camp with all possible convenience and recreational facilities was built for the regiment. The sentiment among the enlisted men appears to be that the regiment, other than the 16 men tried, profited much by the conduct of the malcontents during these instances. No serious disturbances have been reported in this regiment since Thanksgiving last year until its arrival at Camp Van Dorn.

6. However, the similarity of the events now taking place in this organization to those which took place in Phoenix, indicates that the corrective action taken has been wholly ineffective; that the regiment will still resort to mob action to show its disapproval of conditions which are accepted by other troops and that it is a dangerous and thoroughly undisciplined outfit. The situation in my opinion warrants such prompt, vigorous and effective action as will reasonably insure that neither the regiment or small groups thereof will hereafter participate in or encourage disturbances of this nature. The breaking up and disbandment of this regiment by the transfer of individuals or small groups will insure that the organization as a unit or a large portion thereof will not again participate in similar disturbances. However, such a procedure would result in the guilty ringleaders and offenders going unpunished for their recent mutinous conduct and would permit and probably encourage them to create unrest and promote in the colored units to which they would be assigned mutinous conduct on their part.

CONFIDENTIAL

CONFIDENTIAL

7. Subsequent to the Phoenix occurrence the regimental commander took steps to eliminate, from the regiment, ringleaders that were fomenting unrest. About fifty men were transferred and the regimental commander was of the opinion that effective action had been taken. The recent occurrence establishes that such assumption on his part was incorrect, and that action by constituted authorities to that end was ineffective and will probably continue to be so in the future.

8. In my opinion the only way which ringleaders may be known is for the regiment as a whole to be placed in such a disciplinary state that it will make known the remaining ringleaders and trouble-makers within the unit. The action proposed by General McNair while drastic and yet untried in the 364th should result in bringing definitely home to the sounder thinking members of the unit that the ringleaders must be disclosed, that all tendencies toward mutinous conduct must be suppressed and controlled by them. Further, it will bring home to other colored organizations where unrest is prevalent and mutinous conduct is smoldering that the Army is prepared to take vigorous, disciplinary action to suppress sucy conduct. The recent marked increase in disturbances wherein colored personnel is involved, indicates that such a notification would not only be timely but appropriate.

9. A decision as to the appropriate action to be taken in this case should be made with the understanding that the citizens of Centreville and adjacent communities will probably vigorously protest through their Congressmen the non-removal of this regiment from Camp Van Dorn, since as previously stated they are highly disturbed by the present situation and feel the need of defending their lives and property by extreme measures even to the extent of openly carrying arms. Further, it is probable that colored newspapers and national organizations will protest the disciplinary measures taken against this regiment.

10. Notwithstanding the protest that may be made, I concur in the action proposed by General McNair with the possible exception of giving assurance to the citizens of Centreville that members of the 364th will not be permitted to visit that town or other communities within the vicinity until the citizens so request, since his other actions may result in such a purging and disciplining of this unit that military authorities will realize that a further restriction of its personnel would be unjust and unnecessary. Further, if the situation is cured, he should be in a position to express approval and recognition of the action of the better element within the regiment by restoring it to a normal status.

VIRGIL L. PETERSON,
Major General,
The Inspector General.

CONFIDENTIAL

The fact that such a high-ranking official in the Army, the one-and-only Inspector General himself, took the time and effort to file such an extensive report about a single infantry unit of soldiers in southern Mississippi in the middle of World War II, is incredible. It proves how serious a problem the Army considered the 364th to be.

After reading the document, something became apparent to me. The terms Inspector General Peterson used to describe the 364th were startlingly derogatory: "dangerous," "thoroughly undisciplined," "trouble-makers," "malcontents," "ringleaders," "culprits," guilty of "mutinous conduct," needing "purging." For a military report, it is extremely bold, emotive, even inflammatory language, especially coming from such a high level. Once he did this, their fate was sealed. As soon as someone at a top level of authority makes such strong statements about subordinates, those at the basic street level of enforcement would feel complete freedom and sanction to get away with anything. Behavior is exaggerated down the line almost to an exponential degree. A rank-and-file MP on the base would have no fear of repercussions dealing with troops branded from above with such negative characterizations.

The Inspector General's report must also be scrutinized in light of its historical context. To ascertain what took place on a night in 1943 on Camp Van Dorn in Centreville, Mississippi, one must understand what was taking place on military bases throughout the United States during that time. My research revealed a collage of racial violence involving black troops during World War II. There were hundreds of disturbances at military bases across the country. The incidents were not confined to any one geographic area. Facilities at military bases were segregated, and the conditions of the white soldier were far better than those of the black soldier. The 364th would have included black men from all across the country, including those from large cities who were used to relatively progressive civil rights and for whom segregation was a thing of the past. Those who had experienced relative equality were thrown together with those who hadn't, and all were forced to live in the segregated environment of an Army base. The bases themselves were often located in the most segregated regions of the country. As the black soldiers faced the prospect of dying for their country, the rumblings for freedom grew. They began to ask the question, why should we travel across the earth and fight for freedoms that our people don't have at home?

The Army felt the situation was so serious that it threatened the unity of the war effort. By 1942, it had become a major concern not only of the Army's top brass but also of the War Department. Sometimes the violence that erupted pitted the black soldiers against military police. Sometimes the soldiers were in conflict with local law enforcement or civilians. These disturbances ranged from minor conflicts to serious riots. Confrontations were commonplace from the beginning, and black inductees lived in a state of fear during training.

It is not surprising that many of these incidents were picked up by the news services and began appearing in major newspapers. The enemy then used this as propaganda against the United States. On March 28, 1942, a black-owned New York newspaper, *The Amsterdam Star News*, reported the black soldiers' plight in the following manner: "They cherish a deep resentment against the vicious race persecution which they and their forebears have long endured. They feel that they are soon to go overseas to fight for freedom over there. When their comparative new-found freedom is challenged by southern military police and prejudiced superiors, they fight for freedom over here."

Swept up in wartime paranoia, military intelligence (G2)

suspected that outside agitators—Japanese, German and Communist, together with the black press—were contributing to the disorders, but there was no proof. The Army instead concluded that location of troops, poorly trained military police and a lack of equal facilities were the contributing factors. They recommended, as part of the solution, two important changes: 1) The movement and stationing of black troops in areas differing from their home environment should be kept at a minimum; and 2) steps should be taken to muzzle the black press. These recommendations reached General McNair, the General of the Army's Ground Forces.

Racial disturbances reached alarming numbers by late 1942. The War Council said the problem was so out of control that the War Department could not handle it, and that Secretary Stinson should take it to the commander-in-chief, the President. By 1943 the situation had only intensified. In the summer of that year, riots of rebellion against authority and disregard for discipline escalated. What the young black men of the 364th considered to be crying out for justice and equal treatment was, in the eyes of the Inspector General of the Army, "dangerous," "thoroughly undisciplined," resorting to "mob action" ... "mutinous."

It is tempting to jump to the conclusion that the massacre at Van Dorn was an atrocious act executed by prejudiced white southerners and soldiers. Many of the Centreville townspeople and law officials of 1943 held what could be considered extreme racist views, and Private William Walker, shot and killed by the sheriff, could be called a direct casualty of that. Indeed, in my own present-day investigation, many of the eyewitnesses freely used the abhorrent word "nigger" in dialogue. But in fact this was not a southern thing. It was an Army thing. The United States Army faced problems of immense magnitude with the 364th. In the Army's state of panic, they felt if disobedience occurred, a domino effect would take place, not only with the entire 364th but also with the thousands of other black soldiers stationed at Van Dorn. They believed the news would spread like wildfire to other military bases where black soldiers were stationed. The Army would stop at nothing to prevent this from happening. They had no tolerance for any variance from the norm. They considered it a threat to their authority, something to be dealt with swiftly, efficiently and harshly, especially during wartime. They had carte blanche to do what they deemed necessary, and they exercised that right.

At Camp Van Dorn, the 364th was placed under extremely harsh disciplinary orders and unbelievable restrictions. The idea was that the only way "ringleaders" could be identified was for the entire regiment to be placed in such a "drastic" disciplinary state, to shake out and make known those within the unit who were causing the trouble. This was clearly stated in the Inspector General's report. But the very harsh sentence of 50 years hard labor for the "ringleaders" back in Phoenix had not been enough of a deterrent. The report goes on to say, "The corrective action taken [a 50-year prison sentence] has been wholly ineffective... the Regiment will still resort to mob action to show its disapproval of conditions which are accepted by other troops... it is a dangerous and thoroughly undisciplined outfit." In his report, he rationalizes that 50 years at hard labor hadn't worked. Their initial attempt to ferret out the "trouble-makers" hadn't worked. Improving the segregated facilities in Phoenix hadn't worked. Splitting them up and transferring them to other units wouldn't work. And, as evidenced by new disturbances such as the one Paul Coile described, extreme disciplinary measures at Van Dorn weren't working. What option was left? The unstated one: a final and effective solution.

Soon another disturbing fact surfaced during my research. The Inspector General's report was dated June 8, 1943. Here we have this very strong, lengthy, detailed report about a serious situation with "ominous possibilities." Yet there is no written record of what happened next, no word of how it was resolved. Nothing. The Inspector General's files on this matter—from June 8, 1943 until the 364th was unexpectedly shipped out several months later—are missing.

I was able to track down the member of the honor guard who had promised to give Shorty Coile the details of his brother's death, but not, he said, until after the war was over. By now he was in his 80s, and he had remained in the military until his retirement. I told him who I was and that I wanted to ask him a few questions about Paul Coile's death and also about Camp Van Dorn. Before I was able to tell him that I was in possession of a letter Paul had written to the Coile family, he became irate and began screaming into the phone. When I was able to say that I had the letter, he became even more angry and bellowed, "What are you trying to dig up? All that happened over 50 years ago!"

In early 1998 Ron Ridenhour and I again compared notes on the investigation. He said at that time he had a sworn affidavit from a soldier who falsified Army payrolls and the morning reports.

In May of 1998, Ron died of a heart attack while playing handball in New Orleans, Louisiana. In our last conversation shortly before his death, Ron and I reiterated our belief that this story was one the American people needed to hear, and that I needed to tell it soon.

The following is what I believe took place at Camp Van Dorn, Mississippi in 1943. We have examined the United States Army's official account of what happened to the 364th while stationed at Camp Van Dorn from May 1943 to December 1943. We also know there are missing records and reports from June 8th to December 1943. This is the story the Army has not told.

The fate of the star-crossed 364th was determined in Phoenix, Arizona before they boarded the troop trains headed for the Deep South. While stationed in Phoenix, the 364th became involved in at least two major "breaches of military discipline." In the first, which Inspector General Peterson labeled as having "all the earmarks of a mutiny," approximately 500 members of the 364th allegedly refused to obey orders of a regimental commander. The Inspector General points out they got away that time without punishment. In the second disturbance, occurring on Thanksgiving night of 1942, approximately 100 men took part in a shootout with a detachment of military police. There were 15 casualties; the dead included an officer, an enlisted man and a civilian. The Army decided to teach them a lesson. 16 men of the 364th were tried by general court martial and sentenced to 50 years hard labor. Trying to appease the rest of the men of the 364th, the Army attempted to bribe them into good behavior by building new recreation facilities on the base. Still, the determined 364th refused to accept the unequal treatment they continued to receive under existing military conditions.

The Army needed a solution, and fast. Even though their own experts had recommended that black troops not be located away from their own geographic areas, the Army decided that the 364th would intentionally be sent to the very heart of Dixie. If the 364th made a miraculous recovery, they would be retrained at Van Dorn and shipped overseas. Those that did not knuckle under would never leave alive, and the Army could use the racially scarred state of Mississippi as a scapegoat.

The soldiers of the 364th suspected at least part of the plan. They knew that they were being sent to Dixie for punishment. As described in the Inspector General's report, they boasted that they would take over the base, the town, and even the state of Mississippi.

The Army knew that the citizens of Centreville, population 1,200, would be terrified when the first contingent hit town. Centreville had a completely different code of behavior. The local blacks tipped their hats to white women and men and said "Yassah" and "Nawsuh." Even the sidewalks were segregated.

The situation on the Van Dorn base itself was ripe for disaster. There were already several thousand black soldiers successfully training for combat, and another 30,000 white soldiers, some of whom had already seen active duty and were being retrained to be sent overseas. Many reacted with outrage when what they considered the "uppity" 364th got off the trains on May 26th and 28th and began demanding equal treatment at the Post Exchange.

On Sunday, May 30th the local sheriff shot and killed one of the members of the 364th in the streets of Centreville. The situation arose when an MP stopped the soldier and ordered him back to base because a button on his uniform was missing. After his death, riots ensued. One described by Paul Coile occurred sometime before June 25th, 1943, and 20 to 25 black soldiers were shot and killed. There is no record of this in the official report. There is official documentation of a subsequent incident, a major disturbance in July that involved over 3,000 soldiers, although there are holes in the account. According to the report, the soldiers were shooting wildly with weapons, although we know from past reports that the firing pins had been removed from the weapons of the 364th. A white colonel of the 364th went on record estimating that there were 3,000 participants in that riot. The fearsome 99th Infantry Division, the "Battle Babies," had to be called in to stop it. Amazingly, we are told "officially" that no one was killed or wounded in this confrontation. One must remember that this major clash occurred after the extreme disciplinary orders had been handed down and instituted, as recommended in the Inspector General's report of June 8th.

At this very tense and critical moment, the Army panicked with this realization: the 99th Division, famous for its bravery, leadership and stabilizing influence, was on alert and was about to be shipped overseas. The ramifications were ominous...the 364th would be the largest single infantry unit left at Camp Van Dorn. The Army then turned to its final solution.

They infiltrated the 364th with intelligence operatives, basically the same procedure the Army had used in Phoenix. The operatives again identified the ringleaders *and*, this time, all others who were sympathetic to what the Army considered to be the rebellious activities of troublemakers. Very carefully they sorted out the good guys from the bad. They divided and segregated the two groups, and orders were cut for those who could be salvaged to be shipped out on a moment's notice. Due to the secrecy of wartime movements, this was not unusual or noteworthy.

The unfortunate ones were quarantined to barracks. More extreme punishment and disciplinary actions were imposed on them. Their final riot took place on a night in the late fall of 1943. For the first time, white MPs were called in, and a special riot squad armed with 45 caliber pistols and machine guns took charge. This is the incident which Bill Martzall participated in. They shot everything that moved, until nothing did; not one defenseless soldier got away. When the shooting stopped, over 1,200 members of the 364th were slaughtered. Their bodies were loaded on boxcars and stacked inside like pulpwood. They were hauled off by train to the south gate of the base where they were buried and limed in long trenches dug by bulldozers.

Following this bloodbath, records were not only altered but destroyed. The Army notified the next-of-kin of the victims, saying that the soldiers were killed in the line of duty. It was easy to explain that the bodies were not recoverable, and no further explanation was necessary. Foul play was never suspected during wartime. This was World War II— before the public cynicism resulting from Vietnam and Watergate—and no one would think to question the government or the military. Families who had sent their sons off to fight *the good war* feared but almost expected the telegram from the War Department stating, "We regret to inform you..." The soldiers killed in the 364th were from all over the country. It would be highly unlikely that a family member in Duluth, Minnesota would talk to another slain soldier's family in Seattle, Washington in 1943 and become suspicious. Even if there were more than one soldier from the same city, such as New York or Chicago, the odds of the families questioning the deaths would be slim.

The remaining members of the 364th were suddenly shipped out, not overseas as originally planned, but to remote islands off the coast of Alaska where they remained until the war was over.

Over the 13 years of the Van Dorn odyssey, I have listened to the story of the slaughter retold a thousand times. I have honed inaccuracies, extrapolation, and contradictions. I have cemented details in my mind and avoided exaggeration. As Will Campbell said to me, "If you tell the truth about what actually happened, you will have to leave home like I did." Despite all the difficulties in my journey to uncover this horrible incident, I knew it needed telling, somehow. The words Corporal Anthony Smirely, Jr. of the 364th wrote in his letter come to mind: "I have heard of what may happen if I write, but I am not afraid of the consequences if my story can bring to life the truth of the matter."

After the material came from Neil McMillen in 1994, I had some missing pieces to the puzzle and started writing *The Evangeline File*, a fact-based fictional account of the slaughter and my struggle to uncover it. I had to get the story out for people to read. It is such a terrible, ugly tragedy, and there is an innate human hesitance to admit what actually happened. By putting it in a vehicle of fiction, it somehow makes it easier to face the truth. My ultimate goal is to finally tell the story so that wrongs can be righted and justice be done.

It is my tribute to the soldiers who are buried in the red clay hills of Mississippi

Documents

2 ᴍᴀʏ 1943

N. A. A. C. P. LEGAL DEFENSE AND EDUCATIONAL FUND, INC.

69 FIFTH AVENUE, NEW YORK

TELEPHONE: ALgonquin 4-3551

June 30, 1943

Hon. Truman Gibson
Acting Civilian Aide to Secretary of War
War Department
Washington, D. C.

Dear Mr. Gibson:

Enclosed herewith please find copy

of affidavit of Corporal Clarence Jones relating

to conditions at Camp Van Dorn, Centerville, Mis-

sissippi.

Very truly yours,

Milton R. Konvitz
Assistant Special Counsel

MK:CS
Enc.

STATE OF GEORGIA
COUNTY OF FULTON

In person appeared before the undersigned officer, authorized to adminster

oaths, Clarence Jones, who being duly sworn, says: First, I am 20 years

of age and live at 262 Piedmont Avenue, N. E., Atlanta, Georgia. I was

inducted into the military service February 6, 1941, at Atlanta, Georgia,

and at present am Corporal in Headquarter Company, 1st Battalion, 364th In-

fantry, stationed at Camp Van Dorn, at Centerville, Miss.

I am now absent without leave, in Atlanta, having left the Camp on

June 3, at 12:00 o'clock, because of the cruel treatment which the members

of our Regiment received from the Military Police and civilian authorities

at Centerville.

As soon as our Regiment 364th Infantry became stationed at Centerville,

the Military Police and Civilian Police and other civilian authorities be-

gan to abuse and beat up our men whenever we went into the town of Center-

ville; that not knowing that it was the custom in Centerville for whites

to walk on one side of the street and colored on the other, we happened to

walk on the wrong side, and also not knowing the one Drug Store in the town

where colored people were allowed to go, some of us, by mistake, went into

the wrong one with the result that some of our men were handled roughly by

civilian men and Military Police and beaten up, although we offered no re-

sistance; that practically every time we went to town some of us were set

upon by Military Police and other officers and beaten without cause; that

we complained to this treatment to our Commanding Officer but they did not

do anything about it because they themselves were subject to the authority

of the old post commander, Col. Guthrie; that on or about the 28th or 29th

of May, 1943, a colored soldier of Company A, 364th Infantry, was shot and

killed in the town of Centerville by one of the civilian law officers, and

as far as the deponent knows, nothing was done about it.

Deponent further states that the 364th Infantry in which he serves

is composed very largely of men from the north and had just come from
Phoenix, Ariz, around the 22nd of May, last; that the local people as
well as the Military Police did all they could to keep the colored soldiers
from having anything to do with the local colored people, saying that "the
northern Ni.gers would spoil the local colored people;" That most of the
colored soldiers of that Regiment remained away from the town except to
pass through to go to Baton Rouge, La. or other places, and they remained
always in fear of being beaten up if they stayed in Centerville any length
of time. "

The deponent further says that he left his post of duty for the sole
reason of being able to report to some outside authority the hard and un-
bearable things that the colored soldiers of the 364th Infantry at Camp
Van Dorn, Miss., had to put up with, and that as soon as he has made known
these conditions to somebody who can bring them to the attention of the
higher military authorities, he is going to return to his Company and Regiment; that when he left without permission he did not then, and does not
now, intend to desert from the Army, and intends to return to it, but he
does hope that something will be done to make it easier for colored soldiers
to serve their country at Camp Van Dorn, Miss. as well as every other place
where the military authority sees fit to send them.

Signed Cpl. Clarence Jones

Sworn to and subscribed before me
this 15 day of June, 1943.

S/ W. J. Shaw
Notary Public Fulton Co., Georgia
Atlanta, Ga.

My commission expires 8/14/44

Camp Van Dorn
Mississippi
June 1, 1943

TO WHOM IT MAY CONCERN:

This is not only a letter of protest against the brutal treatment of soldiers of color in the south, but it is also a plea to the people of America to do that which is in their power to put an end to such wholesale desecration of the Constitution of the United States.

Sunday afternoon, May 30, 1943, a soldier, a member of the 364th Infantry Regiment (Colored), now stationed at Camp Van Dorn, Mississippi, was brutally murdered at a town called Centreville, approximately four miles from camp, by a civilian sheriff, a resident of the town. From the sworn testimonies of several eyewitnesses to the crime, the following information was revealed, and is being published for the benefit of those who might be inclined to believe the articles which are published in the behalf of the southern white gentry.

It was learned that five colored soldiers, while making a tour of the town of Centreville, were accosted by two Military Police, who ordered one of them to button his shirt sleeve. The soldier informed the M.P. that the button had become detached, and that he had not been able to replace it. Whereupon, the two M.P.'s leaped from their car, brandishing black-jacks, and one of them proceeded to attack the soldier who had no button on his shirt sleeve. The remaining soldiers persuaded the other M.P. to let the men fight it out, and "let the best man win". But the M.P. obviously getting the worse of the battle, noticed the sheriff of the town, Mr. Knighten, coming up with his two deputies and called, "Mr. Knighten, shoot this nigger". The soldier then straightened up, and said, "No, you won't shoot me". Whereupon, Knighten drew his revolver, saying, "The hell I won't", and firing point-blank at the soldier, struck him fully in the chest. The sheriff then turned to the M.P. and asked, "Any more niggers you want killed?". Meanwhile, the deputies put two of the other soldiers to flight with well aimed blows to the head with a "sap-stick, but took the other two to the guard house.

Obviously, the unsavory reputation of the 364th Infantry Regiment has preceded them to this station, due mainly to the fact that this is the same Regiment which figured so prominently in the Thanksgiving Day riot in Phoenix, Arizona, and it is also quite obvious that the civilian authorities of this locale have heard of this so-called belligerent outfit, and have taken it upon themselves to whip them into submission, and to subjugate them as they have done other Negro outfits in the past.

Of a certainty, the War Department is cognizant of circumstances so prevalent here in the south, particularly in the case of the Negro troops stationed here. The question uppermost in the minds of the members of this organization is, "Could the War Department be collaborating with the civilian authorities of the south in subjugating this regiment which has caused such a disturbance in the past few months, by knowingly sending them to a place where racial conflict is inevitable due to the stubbornness of both factors? If such is the case, then we, the soldiers of color might just as well lay down our arms, for the fight in which we are so willingly sacrificing our lives is already lost.

Leading papers of the south are already branding this regiment as troublemakers, and have even gone so far as to petition the War Department for a transfer of this regiment to a northern station due to the fact that we are responsible for fomenting race riots among the Negro troops, and the white civilians in nearby Centreville. Such allegedly instigation of race riots on our part is a gross misstatement. We merely ask that we are given the same opportunity to find recreation among our people, and be accorded the same treatment given other members of the armed forces, regardless of race, creed or color.

Credit must be given to one man in particular, Colonel John F. Goodman, Commanding Officer, 364th Infantry, who, regardless of personal safety, and thinking only of the well being of his men, walked calmly into the face of flying bullets fired from the guns of Military Police sent to our Regimental area in order to quell the disturbance created by our men when news of the wanton slaying of one of their men reached the camp, and forced the M.P.s to cease firing on the defenseless men. Through the daring and forethought of Colonel Goodman, and several of his subordinates, only was soldier was injured, and he, not seriously.

It was Colonel Goodman, who took this regiment under his wing during the Phoenix Thanksgiving Day disturbance, and guided them through a maize of criticisms, accusations, and extremely low morale, to respectability in the eyes of the Phoenix residents. The memory of Colonel Goodman will be admired and cherished by every member of the 364th Infantry long after this present world conflict has become a thing of the past, for, before the very eyes of his superior officer and other officers, obviously of the south, ordered a soldier, one extremely sun-tanned, to remove his shirt and undergarment, and to ascend the platform on which he was standing and without further ado, put his arms around the soldier, and said, "My children, for to me, you are my children, color doesn't mean a damn to me, and I love every one of you". And with tears in his eyes, he said, "I am not much of a Christain, but I want each one of you to say the Lord's Prayer along with me".

When the prayer was ended, the soldier on the platform wept shamelessly at the sincerity of this man whom all have grown to love, and to trust, and who would willingly follow him into the very bowels of hell, if needs be.

As Colonel Goodman issued orders to the Company Commanders to take charge of their troops, many a hardened soldier came to attention as tears welled in his eyes, which was, in itself a great tribute and an acknowledgement of devotion and respect to a man who through his love and understanding of the Negro soldier, averted one of the most disasterous encounters between the Negro soldier, and the white Military Police that was ever anticipated.

NOTE: Permission is hereby granted to those concerned to include, exclude, or alter in any way the contents of this letter, which will serve to render it suitable for publication.

S/ Private Irvin C. Wiley
Service Company, 364th Inf.
Camp Van Dorn, Mississippi

P
Y

Co. C 364th Infantry
Camp Van Dorn, Miss.
May 30th, 1943

Mr. E. Washington Rhodes
Editor, Philadelphia Tribune
Philadelphia, Pennsylvania

Dear Sir,-

I am a native of Philadelphia, residing at 5916 Arch St.
in West Philly. I enlisted in the Army in May, 1942. After
coming to the 364th Infantry, in Arizona last September, I have
been wondering--Why did I join the Army? Instead of building
morale, it's taking it away.

Last Thanksgiving, this Regiment made a bad name for itself
by inciting a riot. The news of this affair was in every news-
paper--white and colored--that I have read.

Now, the regiment has been moved down here in the deep South.
The land of the white man. The place where the colored man,
soldier or civilian, hasn't the slightest chance for an even
break. Hardly had this Regiment been here 47 hrs before the
"White Supremacy" took its first toe-hold. The men here, some
having homes and families in a close vicinity were rounded up
by white M.P.'S and civilian. authorities and sent back to camp.
When duty hours are over, other soldiers are allowed anywhere,
but not the colored ones. How do the so-called white over-lords
expect us to win a war for them? If some of these malfunctions
of the people could be corrected, I believe that it would be
better off all-around.

There is one thing I can say, and I wish that others would
take heed to it and that is--the white officers of our Regiment
are about the best there are. Our commanding officer, Colonel
John F. Goodman, is a champion of the colored soldier. A better
Regimental Commander would be hard to find.

Mr. Rhodes, I appeal to you for some kind of investigation
of this matter and hope that the negro-hating man of United
States can be made to see the light.

I have heard of what may happen if I write, but I am not
afraid of the consequences if my story can bring to life the
truth of the matter. Therefore I sign this

329 words

Corporal Anthony J. Smirely,Jr.
Co. H. 364th Infantry
Camp Van Dorn, Mississippi

Co. H. 364th Infantry
Camp Van Dorn, Miss.
May 1st, 1943

Mr. E. Washington Rhodes
Editor, Philadelphia Tribune
Philadelphia, Pennsylvania

Dear Sir:-

I have written to you before, but the latest news is to much for me to bear.

Yesterday, Sunday, a day of holiness and good wishes, a soldier of this regiment was shot and killed by a M.P. (white, of course). We aren't even safe in the Post Area. From the white section of the camp, came four (4) armored scout cars, each with about ten M.P.'s armed to the teeth. We were absolutely defenseless against these men. All rifles and amnution had previously been taken up.

Tonight, just an hour ago, one of my fellow-soldier friends came back from an intended over-night pass. He had been beaten about the head by the white M.P.'s, who are now recognized Negro-haters.

What do these people want of us? Do they want us to leave their "lovely South?" I would gladly give them their wish. What have we done to them? Just because we soldiers are living better than some of the poorer classes of whites, is no reason why they should try and humble us. They should know by now that that is beyond hope. I think, and I do believe that I speak for the majority of my race, that we, the Negroes, are just ordinary people, trying to make a decent living and trying to make the world so that we can do it. We don't try to be the Masters of any other race--why do they try to master us? All I ask for is an even break.

Being in this camp is just like being in prison. The inmates of Leavenworth are better off than we are. If we dare venture off the Post, we are subject to come back on a stretcher. (Living in camp isn't much better, as the incident of yesterday will prove.) A man can't even go out to visit his wife, less he be beaten and invalided for few days. Yet, the army is stressing absenteeism. They don't want you to be incapiitated in any way when it comes to drill time. What the hell can a man do? If he asks others not of his organization for help he is reprimanded for going over their heads. By writing to you, a newspaper man of fearless outspokeness, is the only way that we can hope for any consideration. If I fail in what I am undertaking now, I might as well reserve a berth in Hell for that is what it will be here.

Mr. Rhodes, I beg of you to please, from my heart, please do something for the fellows and myself whom are among the unfortunate to be in this State of blood--Negro blood--that is constantly flowing in the streets.

Hopefully, I am
Corporal Anthony J. Smirely, Jr.
Co. H, 364th Infantry
Camp Van Dorn, Mississippi

CONFIDENTIAL

COPY - MCE

WTCSA 333 (6-9-43)

IG 333.9-364th Infantry (4)   8 June 1943

MEMORANDUM for the Deputy Chief of Staff

SUBJECT: 364th Infantry, Camp Van Dorn, Missississippi.

   1.   Pursuant to your instructions I have had an officer on duty
in my office investigate the report of an imminent race riot in the
364th Infantry at Camp Van Dorn, Mississippi. The officer who conducted
the investigation, Colonel J. R. Burney, reports the following pertinent
facts and circumstances ascertained as a result of his investigation:

   a.   The 364th Infantry arrived at Camp Van Dorn on Wednesday,
26 May and Friday, 28 May, from its former station at Phoenix, Arizona.
Beginning with the first arrival of these troops, reports from a number
of sources establish the fact that there was a general bragging on the
part of the men to the effect that they were going to "take over" Camp
Van Dorn, the town of Centerville, and the state of Mississippi. These
statements were so general and so persistent as to cause serious alarm
on the part of the civilian population in the nearby community. (It
appears that these remarks were also very distrubing to the colored troops
already in the camp.)

   b.   Following the arrival of the 364th Infantry, a series of
events have taken place at Camp Van Dorn which indicate that these boasts
were not entirely idle threats. On Thursday, 27 May, one day after the
arrival of the first contingent, a group of men from this organization
while visiting the colored service club in the camp, were boisterous,
refused to obey the rules of conduct in effect, namely removal of caps,
wearing of complete uniform, avoiding indecent language, and the introduction of beer into the club. It also took about an hour for the hostess
and the noncommissioned officers in charge to clear the club of these men
after the prescribed closing time on this particular night.

   c.   On Friday night, 28 May, a group of several hundred
colored soldiers, the majority of whom are known to have been from the
364th Infantry, broke into one of the camp exchanges, rifled the stock
and damaged the fixtures to the extent of several hundred dollars. The
exchange had been temporarily closed by the exchange officer a short time
before because of the profane, disrespectful and threatening conduct of

CONFIDENTIAL

CONFIDENTIAL

the men. The culprits escaped into the nearby barrack areas prior to the arrival of the military police.

d. On Saturday night, 29 May, a number of men from the 364th Infantry visited Centreville and marched around the town in formation, using indecent, and profane language in the presence of all encountered. This group (approximately 74 men) was arrested by the civil police, consisting of the town marshal and a number of deputised citizens armed with shotguns. Upon arrival of the military police officer, this group, upon his orders, immediately dispersed and returned to camp.

e. On Sunday afternoon, 30 May, a member of Company A, 364th Infantry, Private William Walker ASN 36170964, was accosted outside the reservation by a military policeman because the soldier was improperly uniformed and had no pass. Following a brief argument, Private Walker assaulted the military police and was attempting to take his pistol when the county sheriff arrived on the scene. The sheriff reports that upon his arrival the military police was on his back in a "jeep" with the colored soldier on top of him. Private Walker, noticing the arrival of the sheriff, jumped out of the car and made a lunge for him. Upon refusing to halt when ordered to do so, the soldier was shot and killed by the sheriff. Information of this incident was immediately transmitted to the 364th Infantry and to its Commanding Officer, Colonel John F. Goodman.

f. Colonel Goodman at once dispatched all officers to their respective organizations and he, with members of his staff, proceeded to the barracks area of Company A, the company to which the slain soldier, Private Walker, had been assigned. Colonel Goodman reports that upon his arrival he found the entire company milling around, swearing, cursing, and threatening to break into the supply room for rifles and ammunition. Seeing the situation was becoming serious, Colonel Goodman ordered the firing pins removed from all rifles and that an officer guard be placed over all supply rooms in the regiment. The situation at Company A was kept under control by the officers, but in Company C a group of men stormed the supply room and obtained a number of rifles before the arrival of the company officers. (All of these rifles except two had been found prior to the arrival of Colonel Burney at Camp Van Dorn. The two missing rifles had not been located at the time of his departure from the camp on Thursday, 3 June).

g. A short time later a crowd of several hundred members of the regiment assembled near the regimental exchange. A riot squad (colored) from the Military Police Detachment of the camp was forced to fire into this group in an attempt to stand them off. Private Raymond

CONFIDENTIAL

Johnson, ASN 34066051, Company C, 364th Infantry, was wounded by this
gunfire. The timely arrival of Colonel Goodman and his Cahplain,
(Captain) Elmer P. Gibson (colored), was perhaps the only thing preventing serious bloodshed at this point. Colonel Goodman was able to quiet
this group and following a talk by him to the assembled battalions, the
entire regiment was marched to the company areas where it has been confined
since.

    h. During the period Thursday, 28 May to 3 June (the date
the investigation was completed), there have been a number of instances
reported of unprovoked attacks on inidvidual white soldiers passing near
the 364th area; instances of bottles being thrown at passing cars, and
insulting and offensive shouting from these barrack areas to officers and
others driving by.

    i. Prior to the arrival of the 364th Infantry, the colored
troops in the camp had been well-behaved, and all such incidents which
have occurred were in the nature of individual offenses. It appears that
other colored troops in the camp almost uniformly deplore the conduct of
the men of this organization and the few from other organizations who
have joined them in their riotous conduct.

    2. The events which took place in the 364th Infantry, especially
on Sunday, 30 May, had ominous possibilities. It is apparent that the
situation was held in check almost entirely through the personal efforts
of the regimental commander, Colonel Goodman.

    3. During the course of the investigation, a conference was held
with the Mayor of Centreville at which the sheriff and the deputy sheriff
of Wilkerson County, the town marshal and numerous representative citizens
of Centreville and surrounding communities were present. These citizens
are very much exercised over the situation, have armed themselves so as
to protect their lives and property, and are definite in their insistence
that the 364th Infantry be transferred to another station.

    4. Upon Colonel Burney's return from Camp Van Dorn and at your
suggestion, he, in a personal conference, presented the facts established
as a result of his investigation to General McNair. The solutions to the
problem of this regiment were discussed at length. General McNair is of
the opinion that the worst possible solution would be to transfer this
organization to another station, this being not only what the local
citizens want, but quite possibly, in his opinion, is the motive behind
some of the distrubances engaged in by the members of the organizations
since its arrival in Mississippi. On the other hand, he is of the opinion
that the best solution is to confine the organization to the limits of
its regimental area and to deprive it of all privileges until such time

as it will disclose its real trouble-makers and has demonstrated its worthiness to enjoy the rights of other organizations. Furthermore, he is prepared to assure the citizens of Centreville and other local communities near Camp Van Dorn that no member of this organization will be permitted to enter these towns until such time as the citizens themselves request that the ban be lifted. In addition, he plans or prescribing a training program for this organization which will keep the men exceedingly busy, a program which may require additional officers who will be provided if necessary.

5. In considering the decision of General McNair in this matter, it should be recalled that this organization, while stationed at Phoenix, Arizona, engaged in two serious breaches of military discipline which were the subject of a previous investigation by officers from my office. On one of the occasions approximately 500 men of the regiment engaged in a disturbance that had all the earmarks of a mutiny, an affair in which the men refused to disperse when ordered to do so by the regimental commander. No disciplinary action was taken against the offenders in this instance. The second event took place on Thanksgiving night 1942 when approximately 100 men from the regiment engaged in a shooting affray with a detachment of colored military police, within the city limits of Phoenix, in which one officer, one enlisted man, and one civilian were killed, and 12 enlisted men were severely wounded by the gunfire. Sixteen of the ringleaders in this affair were tried by a general court-martial, each receiving a sentence of fifty years confinement. Following these events the regiment received a new regimental commander. Colonel Goodman, the present commander, and a new executive officer. In addition a new and up-to-date camp with all possible convenience and recreational facilities was built for the regiment. The sentiment among the enlisted men appears to be that the regiment, other than the 16 men tried, profited much by the conduct of the malcontents during these instances. No serious disturbances have been reported in this regiment since Thanksgiving last year until its arrival at Camp Van Dorn.

6. However, the similarity of the events now taking place in this organization to those which took place in Phoenix, indicates that the corrective action taken has been wholly ineffective; that the regiment will still resort to mob action to show its disapproval of conditions which are accepted by other troops and that it is a dangerous and thoroughly undisciplined outfit. The situation in my opinion warrants such prompt, vigorous and effective action as will reasonably insure that neither the regiment or small groups thereof will hereafter participate in or encourage disturbances of this nature. The breaking up and disbandment of this regiment by the transfer of individuals or small groups will insure that the organization as a unit or a large portion thereof will not again participate in similar disturbances. However, such a procedure would result in the guilty ringleaders and offenders going unpunished for their recent mutinous conduct and would permit and probably encourage them to create unrest and promote in the colored units to which they would be assigned mutinous conduct on their part.

CONFIDENTIAL

7. Subsequent to the Phoenix occurrence the regimental commander took steps to eliminate, from the regiment, ringleaders that were fomenting unrest. About fifty men were transferred and the regimental commander was of the opinion that effective action had been taken. The recent occurrence establishes that such assumption on his part was incorrect, and that action by constituted authorities to that end was ineffective and will probably continue to be so in the future.

8. In my opinion the only way which ringleaders may be known is for the regiment as a whole to be placed in such a disciplinary state that it will make known the remaining ringleaders and trouble-makers within the unit. The action proposed by General McNair while drastic and yet untried in the 364th should result in bringing definitely home to the sounder thinking members of the unit that the ringleaders must be disclosed, that all tendencies toward mutinous conduct must be suppressed and controlled by them. Further, it will bring home to other colored organizations where unrest is prevalent and mutinous conduct is smouldering that the Army is prepared to take vigorous, disciplinary action to suppress such conduct. The recent marked increase in disturbances wherein colored personnel is involved, indicates that such a notification would not only be timely but appropriate.

9. A decision as to the appropriate action to be taken in this case should be made with the understanding that the citizens of Centreville and adjacent communities will probably vigorously protest through their Congressmen the non-removal of this regiment from Camp Van Dorn, since as previously stated they are highly disturbed by the present situation and feel the need of defending their lives and property by extreme measures even to the extent of openly carrying arms. Further, it is probable that colored newspapers and national organizations will protest the disciplinary measures taken against this regiment.

10. Notwithstanding the protest that may be made, I concur in the action proposed by General McNair with the possible exception of giving assurance to the citizens of Centreville that members of the 364th will not be permitted to visit that town or other communities within the vicinity until the citizens so request, since his other actions may result in such a purging and disciplining of this unit that military authorities will realise that a further restriction of its personnel would be unjust and unnecessary. Further, if the situation is cured, he should be in a position to express approval and recognition of the action of the better element within the regiment by restoring it to a normal status.

VIRGIL L. PETERSON,
Major General,
The Inspector General.

Part II:

The Evangeline File

The characters in this book are fictional;
however, the story is inspired by actual events.

PROLOGUE

By the summer of 1964 the town of Camellia City, Mississippi had begun to alienate itself from the rest of the nation. Her citizens, southerners to the core, embraced a prejudice that was no more deliberate than the blooming of the camellias in the spring. It was this summer that the civil rights movement came to a head in south Mississippi. The conflict between government intervention, states' rights and the threat of losing the southern way of life was acted out on the streets for all the country to see. The government was determined that blacks would integrate the schools, lunch counters and public transit systems of the South, and, in retaliation, scores of Negro churches, homes and buses were blown up and burned out.

In the years that would follow, Camellia City became the dynamite capital of the world, and the number of unsolved murders in Topisaw County would be the highest for any rural area in the United States. However, all of the atrocities of the sixties combined could not compare to the horror that occurred during World War II on a military base located outside of Camellia City. The incident took place in the fall of 1943 and, for over 50 years, it was one of the closest kept secrets of the nation's history.

On an Easter morning in 1985, Clay Brady came home from the University of Mississippi to bury his mother. He would be graduating in less than a month with a degree in Journalism. When he said goodbye to his brother at the gravesite, he was determined to leave Camellia City forever. He had no desire to return.

CHAPTER ONE

RANCEY JAMES and the Albino sat inside a white Cadillac in a Wal-Mart parking lot and made final plans to kill newspaper editor Vassar Lawrence.

"I'm gonna give her one more call—just to scare the hell out of her before we do it," Rancey said. "She's been warned, so now, as far as I'm concerned, she deserves what she's getting."

"Tell her about the straight razor," the Albino suggested, "women have a horror of being cut. It's the vanity thing, you know."

"You gonna kill her with a razor?"

"No. I'll slash her up a little to get the information you need, and then I'll pop a couple of caps in the back of her brain."

The two men talked more about the time and place until they were satisfied that the details were flawless. Then the Albino got out of the car, and Rancey left for the truck stop to eat an early lunch.

Rancey was what people in the South call a double-barrelled Dixie Darlin', a name for rednecks with money. They usually built gaudy, extravagant homes and bought expensive cars to compensate for a lack of education and culture. He was wearing a gray felt hat, a dingy white dress shirt, summer sport coat, polyester pants, a white patent leather belt and a pair of two-toned loafers. In his front pocket was a roll of hundred dollar bills and, in his back pocket, a snub-nosed .38 revolver. Rancey was raised dirt poor on a farm in Topisaw County. At night the men of the family could piss off the door steps if they liked. During the day, yellow-legged chickens strutted leisurely on the front porch of the sharecropper's rent house.

For a Saturday morning there were not many cars outside the truck stop when Rancey pulled in. He chose a booth close to a window so that he could keep an eye on his car parked outside. Brushing some crumbs from the table with his hand, he dragged his finger through a butter patty and stuck it in his mouth. As he waited for a waitress, he lit up a Winston, sucked the smoke deep into his lungs and exhaled slowly through his nose. Having smoked for over 62 years, he was confident that cigarettes had not hurt him except for a persistent cough that he called a bad cold. Doctors and lawyers, in his opinion, didn't know crap. When a waitress walked by, Rancey reached out and stopped her. "Hon," he said, "bring me a hot roast beef sandwich, French fries and a cup of coffee." Picking up the ash tray he added, "And a clean one of these. This son of a bitch is dirty."

Rancey began his underworld career after being discharged from the Army in the late forties. He fenced stolen jewelry and ran whores. As the Exalted Cyclops of the Ku Klux Klan in the sixties, he stockpiled firearms and explosives. It was brutality, murder and drugs that had made him a wealthy man. Camellia City's most visible racist was the connection if a person needed someone beaten, burned out or killed.

For the professional hit jobs he used Feret Du Boise—a.k.a. the Albino. Smothering his food in catsup, he thought about the earlier conversation he had with Du Boise. He hoped he hadn't forgotten anything important. His memory wasn't as good as it once was. By now the Albino should be passing through Manchac on his way back to New Orleans. He was sure he had told him the time, the place and had given him the front money. Deep down he hated the assassin. Du Boise was arrogant, expensive and always demanded 75% up front. But he had the reputation for being the best that money could buy.

"Bring me another cup of coffee," he bellowed, with a mouthful of food, to a waitress at another table, "this one's cold." Looking out of the window, Rancey saw Toxie Hux climbing out of his pickup. As Toxie walked toward the restaurant, he spit on the sidewalk. His long greasy hair needed combing. He was wearing a black sleeveless muscle shirt, jeans and a pair of steel-toed biker boots. Toxie Hux was a bully by the time he was nine years old. He dropped out of school in the seventh grade and graduated from bully to bad in the beer joints of Topisaw County. He had a long police record before he hooked up with Rancey James. Toxie was exactly what Rancey was looking for—he didn't ask too many questions. For years Rancey had loaned money to the blacks, paid their bail when they got in jail, sold them dope and bought their stolen merchandise. If someone owed him money, Toxie was sent to collect it. If someone got out of line, Toxie took care of it. As he told Rancey, "It ain't nothin' as fun as bustin' a nigger's head." If a beating didn't solve the problem, other measures were taken. Burning them out was like fighting to Toxie. He thrived on it.

He slid into the booth across from Rancey. "You want something to eat?" Rancey asked.

"Naw. I ain't hungry, but I could use a cup of coffee."

Rancey motioned for the waitress, then asked, "You find Sugar Red this morning?"

"Yeah. I found him all right."

"Any problems?"

"I didn't have no problems. He had a few." Toxie's lips parted in a smile.

"How's that?"

"Had to get his attention. He started with that jive ass shit and I knocked the livin' hell out of him. I told him that if he ever tried to hold out on you again that they would find his black ass floatin' in the river."

Rancey grinned with approval. "Did you get the money?"

"Yeah. And a little extra for the trouble."

CHAPTER TWO

CLAY BRADY sat at his computer working on an article in the newsroom of the *States Times* in Jackson, Mississippi. The 33-year-old investigative reporter was dressed in a blue denim shirt, chinos and a pair of Cole Haan loafers. His sleeves were rolled up to his elbows, his shirt was unbuttoned at the neck and his tie hung loosely. He was young, classically handsome and athletic. His work cubicle reflected a visual representation of his persona. There was a New Orleans Jazz Festival schedule and an aerial photo of a wilderness area in Arkansas that he planned to backpack in the fall. In a small shadowbox was a silver pin that had held his knee together after a high school football injury. On his desk was a canoe paddle, a souvenir from a near fatal river trip. Close to his computer was a snapshot of Captain Ted Brady, his father; Carl, his brother; and nine-year-old Clay, standing in front of a Christmas tree. The two boys were caught with an expression of youthful innocence, totally unaware of the tragedy that lay ahead for the family. In the white margin of the Polaroid was the inscription, "Christmas, 1972. Camellia City, Ms.," in his mother's handwriting.

Clay picked up a pencil and drummed it nervously on the corner of his desk as he tried to find the words that would put magic in his article. His quest for perfection had left him discouraged when he had not won top awards in the recent southern newspaper competition. He was beginning to question his writing skills. It was easier than acknowledging the fact that his writing, like his personal life, had gotten into a rut.

The telephone beside him rang. He picked up the receiver, cradling it between his chin and shoulder, and continued working.

"Newsroom. Brady."

"Clay, this is Vassar Lawrence. I'm the editor of the *Camellia City Chronicle*. Do you have a minute to talk?"

"Sure, go ahead."

"Your editor, Ed Williams, is a friend of mine. I have read some of your articles, and I admire your work. You're beginning to make quite a name for yourself."

"Thank you. I can use that this morning."

"I understand that you're a native of Camellia City. I was wondering if you've given any thought to coming back home?"

Clay chuckled. "Actually, I've worked very hard to get away from there."

"Clay, I've discovered something that I think would be of great interest to you."

"A story?"

"The story of a lifetime, but I'm afraid to talk about it on the telephone. I'll be happy to come to Jackson, but I'd rather you'd come to Camellia City."

Clay was interested. "When would you like to set this up?"

"As soon as possible." He sensed urgency in her voice.

Looking at his calendar, he said, "I can come down on Saturday morning."

"That's perfect. I'll see you in my office at the *Chronicle* at eleven."

Clay reflected on their conversation as he put the finishing touches on his article. Why would the editor of a small, very conservative newspaper be calling an aggressive investigative reporter? If something important had come up, Vassar should be able to get to the bottom of it herself. She had the reputation of being more than a decent reporter. Before leaving on assignment, he placed his finished article in the basket on Ed Williams' desk.

ON SATURDAY an unseasonably warm February wind blew against Clay's Jeep Cherokee as he took the Camellia City exit off Interstate 55. He turned right on Walker Boulevard and followed it until he saw the *Chronicle* building off to the right, hidden in a cluster of moss-covered oaks. Inside the building, a receptionist greeted him and led him past workspaces with empty desks and dividers. Stopping at Vassar's office, she announced, "Ms. Lawrence, Clay Brady is here to see you," before she smiled and walked away.

The office was impressive, with mahogany and leather furniture, oriental rugs, brass accessories and lush green plants. A wall of floor-to-ceiling windows bathed the room with light and illuminated regional water colors and paintings. Vassar stood up from behind a desk that was covered with a computer, books and newspapers. The 59-year-old executive was well dressed, thin and attractive. Her high cheekbones and naturally gray hair added to her striking appearance. Walking over to Clay, she removed her reading glasses and extended her hand in his direction. She wasn't prepared for the young reporter that stood so militarily erect before her. Somehow she had expected the *yes, I'm a journalist* look— short guy with wire-rimmed glasses, shaggy hair and, maybe even a beard.

"Thank you for coming, Clay," she said, "please have a seat." She gestured toward a chair, poured him a cup of coffee and sat in the chair next to him, and for a few moments they exchanged pleasantries.

"I know you are wondering why I asked you to come down," she said finally.

"Yes, I am," Clay responded.

"I've gotten into something way over my head. About six months ago I stumbled across something quite by accident, became suspicious and started looking into it. I did not talk to anyone about what I was doing." Vassar paused and took a deep breath. "A week ago I received a threatening telephone call, and the caller said enough to let me know he knew exactly what I was trying to uncover."

"Did you recognize the voice?"

"I've heard it before, but no, I couldn't recognize it. It was a man's voice."

"Exactly what did he say?"

"He said that if I didn't stop asking certain questions, he would kill me. Last night I saw someone standing in the shadows near my house. I live alone and I'm terrified."

"Have you told the police about the phone call and the prowler?"

"No, I haven't."

"Why not?" Clay asked incredulously.

"I don't trust them."

"Are you telling me that you have a reason to distrust the police?"

"Yes."

"You must be on to something very sensitive."

"It's more than sensitive, Clay. I've only scratched the surface. I need your help. I realize that it is rare for a person to leave the state's largest newspaper to come to a small one unless it involves a real opportunity—usually a top management position."

"Yes, you're right."

"I want to tell you before we go into this any further that

the purpose of our meeting this morning is to try to persuade you to come to work for me at the *Chronicle*."

"Why do you want me?"

Vassar picked up a folder and handed it to him, "Because Ed Williams told me you're the best investigative reporter he's ever hired, and besides, I know a lot about you," she said.

Clay opened the folder—Vassar had done her homework. It was all there: his early years in Camellia City, his football scholarship to Ole Miss and his employment with the *Milwaukee Journal* and the *States Times*. Then there was the personal data: a notation that his father had been killed in Vietnam and that his mother had died almost two decades later. A section on his brother was underlined: "Carl Brady, 44 years of age, only living family member, a detective with the New Orleans Police Department." On a separate page there was even mention of a speeding ticket and of Brian Cothern, a friend and tennis partner.

Clay looked up at the editor. She was smiling. "I even know your present salary," she said. "Did I leave anything out?"

"Yes. You left out why you took the liberty to do a background check."

"Because I had to know everything about you before our meeting today."

"Perhaps I could help you on a consulting basis. Even though Camellia City was once my home, it is not a place I would want to come back to."

"Wait until you hear my offer, and then you can think about it." Clay did not protest and Vassar continued, "First, I will double your present salary for a period of two years, plus insurance, the whole package. To protect you, if something should happen to me, I'll put that in writing." She smiled engagingly, "I've never offered anyone an employment contract before."

Clay returned her smile, "You're doing very well, so far."

"Second, I will give you all the information I have gathered on the story and turn it over to you. After it breaks I'm sure you will have book offers and a position on any newspaper in the country if you want it." Vassar could tell she had the young reporter's attention. "Finally," she said, "you will be brought in under the guise of feature editor. There is one stipulation—no one, absolutely no one, is to know what you will be working on."

Clay was stunned. That kind of salary, plus a story, made it more than attractive. Trying not to show his enthusiasm, he said to her, "So far you have been vague about what you have discovered. Surely there's something else you can tell me."

"I'd rather not say any more about that here. I'll tell you what I can at lunch."

"Tell me about the *Chronicle*," Clay said, changing the subject.

"Sure, let me show you around." He was taking the bait, and Vassar knew it.

She turned off the lights in her office and locked the door. Stopping at the newsroom down the hall, she knocked softly and poked her head inside a partially opened door. "Parker, I know you are busy, but there is someone here I'd like you to meet."

A casually dressed, immaculately groomed reporter stood up and flashed a brilliant smile before extending his hand. "Hello," he said, coming from behind a desk to greet Clay, "I'm Parker Phillips. Nice to meet you."

Vassar picked up the introductions. "Parker, this is Clay Brady from the *States Times*. I'm showing him around our paper this morning and reacquainting him with Camellia City. He used to live here."

Parker was nodding. "I remember you. You played football for Robert E. Lee Academy, and we went to the University together."

"Ole Miss?"

"That's right. I was on minority scholarship and you were on football scholarship."

Vassar was enjoying the repartee between these two bright young men. "I don't remember running into you there," Clay said.

"No, you wouldn't have remembered me," Parker laughed, "I didn't make many fraternity functions."

They laughed together and Clay was surprised to feel such a strong rapport. He had no black friends at the *States Times* and didn't want any. This guy seemed different. "Parker," Vassar said, "I'm leaving for today. If anything comes up you can reach me at home later this afternoon."

As they continued their tour, Vassar explained to Clay that Parker Phillips was one of the *Chronicle*'s best reporters and that he worked most Saturdays. They walked past the empty advertising department.

"Where is everyone? I thought you were a daily."

"No, we print a paper six days a week—we skip Saturdays."

"What's your circulation?"

"About 15,000."

"Pretty impressive for a rural area."

"Well, we would always like more."

"What's the town's population?"

"About 12,000, but we cover most of three counties."

Vassar opened a gray steel door to the press room. "We're proud of this," she said, pointing to a brand new press.

"It's a Webb Newsking, isn't it?"

"You bet. It's really made a difference in our operation."

"What can it do?"

"At full capacity, about 30,000 impressions an hour." The editor reached down and picked up an extra paper out of

Friday's run. "This is our product," she said, handing it to him.

Clay examined it, "I like it, good quality."

"This is our morgue," Vassar said as she opened another door. The distinct smell of musty old newsprint rushed out of the room. When she turned on the lights, Clay could see rows of shelves stacked with single newspapers, photographs and bound yearly volumes.

"Don't you store on computers and microfilm?" Clay asked as they walked through the stacks.

"Yes, but we still keep copies."

Along the back wall he noticed another door. Pointing to it, he asked, "More morgue?"

"No, that goes to the publisher's office."

"Publisher's office?"

"Yes."

"Your publisher has to go through the morgue to get to his office?"

"No, he has his own private entrance inside a garage at the rear of the building. His office is not accessible or visible from any other place inside."

"No windows?"

"No windows."

"Sounds very private."

"He's a very private person."

"Who is the publisher?"

"Ash Walker."

Vassar closed the door and led him to another part of the building. She showed him some new Quark software at one of the computer terminals, a spacious lounge and the office that would be his.

"I'll bet you are getting hungry," she said, glancing down at her watch. "It's past noon. I thought we would have lunch at the country club."

"Sounds great," Clay responded, "I haven't been there since

the night of my senior prom."

In the parking lot Vassar walked over to a late model Buick. "Let's go in mine," she said. As she drove toward the club, she continued her sales pitch. "As you know, it's not far to New Orleans. If you like, you can wake up on a weekend and be eating breakfast at Brennan's in less than two hours." Clay grinned, "I would like that."

She turned off the interstate onto a smaller highway, passed the Camellia City airport and then turned onto a narrow road that led to Willow Wood. They drove along the side of a challenging golf course and, at the foot of a hill, passed the tennis courts. Two men dressed in tennis whites were enjoying a windy, but pleasant, afternoon. Willow Wood was big and rambling, yet it was old and had character. Inside, a neatly dressed hostess greeted them, "Good afternoon, Ms. Lawrence, your table is ready."

The silver sparkled on the white linen tablecloth, and a vase of fresh cut flowers centered the table. A waiter came over and asked if they would like to order something to drink. "I believe we're ready for lunch," Vassar said.

"Our special for today," the waiter politely began, "is angel hair pasta with crayfish sauce, mixed vegetables, your choice of French onion soup or salad, and pecan pie for dessert."

Looking at each other, they both answered together, "Sounds wonderful."

Clay and Vassar had a long leisurely lunch and finished up with the pie and coffee. Vassar got up to pour herself another coffee from the silver service nearby and to assure herself that the two of them were alone in the big dining room. "Clay," she began, "I'm especially interested in the series you did on drugs and sexual crimes involving high ranking officers in the military."

"That was difficult reporting. I didn't expect any cooperation, and I certainly didn't get any."

"Would you say that this was an isolated example of a military cover-up?"

"No, I think they are quite good at it. The circumstances of my father's MIA status is still being covered up. Does your story have something to do with the military?"

"Yes, and the highest levels of the federal government."

Clay whistled softly, "Then it's powerful stuff."

"I think it's only fair to tell you that the players are ruthless and will go to any lengths to keep it from being uncovered. I'm concerned about my personal safety and I cannot go into any more detail until you accept my offer and come on board."

Clay smiled. "That's fair enough."

Vassar pushed her coffee cup aside and her blue eyes narrowed. "There is one other thing I can tell you. This investigation has to do with a racial atrocity. How would you feel about that?"

Clay knew she was referring to his early education at an all-white academy. "I'll be candid with you, Vassar," he said, "if this is about a white, prejudiced redneck, killing or raping a poor innocent black, then I wouldn't be interested at any price. I've been very careful to avoid stories that depend on that type of sensationalism. If you're on to something like that, then Parker can do it for you."

"It's not that simple, Clay," Vassar said quietly. "This will require the acquisition of sensitive documents and information that only a seasoned reporter can produce."

"A seasoned white reporter, you mean."

"Well, yes, if you put it that way. I doubt that a black reporter could be objective about this. But I can assure you that this project in no way reflects the trite, predictable scenario that you have just described."

Vassar knew that she had struck a nerve with her question, but she also knew that Clay's lack of sensitivity about race might be an advantage in the long run.

Their conversation turned to lighter topics, and they talked late into the afternoon. It was almost dark as they drove back toward the *Chronicle*. Clay said, "I have an unconventional way of developing a story."

"What do you mean?"

"I mean I would have to do things my own way if I accept your offer. Total freedom."

"You can have it."

She pulled into the parking lot and parked next to Clay's Cherokee. "I hope you will take my offer but, if you don't, I appreciate the fact that you came down." She reached for her purse, pulled out a business card and quickly jotted down a number. "This is my home telephone number. If you call me there, be careful. I don't think my phone is bugged, but it may be. I'll be waiting to hear from you."

Clay stopped and turned around as he opened his door. "I have one more question—what made you come to Camellia City?"

Vassar answered slowly, "A man."

Breaking into a smile, he said, "I'll let you know something soon."

Clay watched as Vassar drove away. She looked lonely and vulnerable.

Driving back to Jackson, he thought of Vassar's proposal and, for the first time in months, he felt a rush of excitement. Vassar didn't know how perfect her timing was. He was sick of Jackson. It was just a big country town, an extension of Ole Miss, with the same ole phony baloney *who do you know* bullshit. Every time he saw an ex-Chi Omega (now turned doctor's wife) driving a Lexus with a cell phone to her ear, he wanted to throw up. After four years at Ole Miss, he had enough of that to last a lifetime.

Things at the *States Times* weren't much better. The paper

that had once flourished under private ownership had become just another liberal tool of the syndicate. It could just have easily been written in Chicago or Los Angeles. It preached the same *let's give it all away* philosophy. The only good thing about the past eight years had been his relationship with Ed Williams. He was not only a good boss, but a good friend as well. More than once they had exchanged views on the crime and violence that were crippling the capital city. Citizens were being gunned down in the best shopping malls, and no neighborhood in any section of town was considered safe.

As disillusioned as Clay was with Jackson and the paper, he was even more disillusioned with himself. He was far from where he wanted to be at 33. He had planned to be a published novelist, financially secure and married to someone he loved. Instead, he had a drawer full of rejection slips, all his plastic was maxed out and he had been totally unable to commit to a monogamous relationship. Recently, he had considered a career change to get into medical sales with his friend, Brian. That seemed to be where the real money was.

Clay slowed his Cherokee and came to a stop as he approached a traffic accident on the interstate in the city limits of Jackson. He picked up his cell phone and called Susan Perkins to tell her he was running late. Susan and Clay had been going together for over a year and neither had made any kind of commitment or asked for one. They had good sex, similar interests and freedom to have their own space. They had made plans to hear Mose Allison tonight, and he wanted her to meet him at the restaurant. Still waiting in traffic, he dialed Ed Williams' number. His boss answered on the second ring.

"Ed, this is Clay."

"Hi, Tiger. What's up?"

"I had an interesting meeting with Vassar Lawrence."

"So, how did it go?"

"Pretty good. What can you tell me about her? She said the two of you go way back."

"We do. What do you want to know?"

"Anything."

"Well, she's the only female editor in Mississippi, and she runs a successful newspaper..."

"What kind of reporter is she?"

"A damn good one. Back during the civil rights movement she did some good work for a paper in Covington, Louisiana—so good, in fact, that she got on with *The Times-Picayune*. That's where I knew her. She was a real arm breaker, exposed a lot of graft and corruption in Louisiana politics, even fingered some members of the Dixie Mafia. She gained some national attention during the JFK assassination era with her stories on Clay Shaw and Jim Garrison."

"Then she knows a good story when she sees one?"

"Oh, hell yes. You're not considering going down there, are you?"

Clay did not answer. Ed continued, "Surely you know that Camellia City's a tough place. The whole damn county is bad. There have been more unsolved murders in Topisaw County than any other county in the state. Those rednecks down there play hard ball."

"Thanks, Ed. Traffic's beginning to move. I'll let you go."

When he pulled in to park at Hal and Mal's, the trendy little restaurant was already beginning to get crowded. The famous jazz musician, Mose Allison, was a native son, and when he came home his fans packed the place to enjoy his music.

Susan had a table not too far from the piano and had ordered drinks. "Before they start, I need to make a phone call," Clay said. "I'll be right back." When he reached the pay phone, he pulled Vassar's card and number from his wallet.

In a second, she answered.

"Vassar, this is Clay. I'm calling to accept your offer."

"I can't tell you how pleased that makes me. When do you think you can come?"

"How about the first Monday in March?"

"Perfect. There is a yearly social function scheduled for the Saturday night before March 1st. It's the Camellia Ball, sort of our Mardi Gras. Everybody attends, and it would be a good time to introduce you. Do you think you can make it?"

"Sure."

"Wonderful. I'll get back to you with the details. Your contract will be drawn up, stating only our financial agreement, and sent to your office by Monday. I'm glad you called with good news."

Susan motioned for him to hurry as he approached the table. "They're about to start," she said.

Mose opened with a song about Parchman, the Mississippi state penitentiary. The "Parchman Farm" lyrics were clear and cutting, "I'm puttin' that cotton in a 'leven foot sack with a twelve gauge shotgun at my back." Clay melted into his chair and sipped his Scotch and water. It had been a long day. He looked over at Susan. She was smiling, enjoying the music. He would have to tell her about his decision, but it could wait until morning.

CHAPTER THREE

IT WAS ALREADY DARK when Clay's Cherokee crossed over the Topisaw County line. All his possessions were stuffed in the back, including a rack of elk antlers that he could not leave behind. In the aluminum attaché case on the passenger seat beside him was a Nikon camera, note pads and a nine millimeter automatic.

The last few weeks at the *States Times* had been hectic. He had left the newspaper with an investigative series that he considered to be his best work. It was an in-depth report about a serial killer that had murdered his way across thirteen states. The story would have been an exclusive except for a simple twist of fate. Hours before his story hit the street, the killer, after watching a local newscast in his jail cell, became enamored with a sexy female anchor. Word was sent to her that if she would come to interview him, she could have the story for the late news. Her report lacked dimension and actually served as a boost to launch Clay's story. In the days to follow, the *States Times* enjoyed an all-time record in newspaper sales. Ed Williams was more than pleased.

Leaving on such a positive note made it a little harder for Clay to say goodbye. Ed made no effort to hide his feelings about Clay's leaving. He believed that it was a mistake. The last thing he told Clay was, "Be careful and watch your ass. I don't trust those people down there and remember, if this doesn't work out, you can always have your job back." Clay kept his promise to Vassar and made no mention of the story that awaited him.

About six miles north of Camellia City, Clay turned off the interstate and crossed over to Highway 51. Coming down a steep hill, he saw the green road sign that marked "Lake Dixie Springs." Dixie Springs, as it was called, consisted of a huge, clear, spring-fed lake nestled in the creases of two rolling hills. Acres of virgin pine surrounded the steep bluffs along the banks. 50 or more luxurious waterfront homes, a few unpretentious cabins and Larkin's Landing made it one of the most unique communities in south Mississippi. Property owners carefully kept their land in the family for generations. Occasionally, when something came on the market for sale, names on a waiting list would be consulted and the property would go to the highest bidder.

Larkin Wahl was one of the few people in Topisaw County that Clay remembered fondly. In high school they had enjoyed a special, uncomplicated friendship that Clay had never found again with another girl. Larkin had never left Dixie Springs. When other members of their graduating class left home to seek careers elsewhere, Larkin stayed behind. She had everything she ever wanted right here, Clay thought, as he pulled off the asphalt and parked near the front door of the restaurant.

A landmark in its own right, it had belonged to Larkin's family since the early forties. The white stucco building was accented with hot pink neon lights, and Clay could hear the jukebox before he even stepped out of his Cherokee. As he walked toward the Landing, he anticipated the distinct smell of fresh cut onions and fish frying. He was not disappointed. Cigarette smoke hung in layers, and the sound of caps popping off of longnecks signaled a good time. Clay walked through the dining room straight to the lounge. Behind two swinging doors were a half-dozen small tables covered with mallard green cloths. One wall was solid glass, offering a spectacular view of the lake. On the opposite wall was the bar and a fireplace. An old upright piano sat in the corner. Clay spotted a familiar face behind the bar, and, by the time he had found a stool, Harvey had already poured his drink and had it waiting for him. "Good Evening, Mr. Brady," he said, extending his hand, "it's been a long time." Harvey glanced down at the filled glass in front of him, "Johnnie Walker and water?"

Clay grinned, "You bet, how do you remember?"

"Tricks of the trade." Harvey had become one of the Landing's greatest assets. He was friendly, sensitive and well informed. At his bar you were assured the special treatment that lures a loyal following. "Are you still in Jackson?" Harvey inquired.

"No, as a matter of fact, I'm moving back to Camellia City."

"Good. Then we'll be seeing you more often?"

"You can count on that." Clay's eyes searched the room. "Where is Larkin?" he asked.

Harvey looked at his watch. "She should be here any minute, I would say."

Clay settled in and was enjoying the music when Larkin tapped him on the shoulder. She was in her middle 30s, tall and athletic, dressed in a black oversized sweater and black leggings. Her hair was neat and she wore only a hint of make-up. Her bronze tan complemented her natural beauty. "Clay Brady," she said as she slipped her arms around his neck to give him a welcoming hug, "I was just thinking about you the other day. What are you doing here?"

"I'm moving back to Camellia City."

"What? You're the one who said you'd never come back."

"I know. I didn't plan to, but I'm going to be joining the *Chronicle*."

"That's great! Bring some life to it, it's way too conservative. If they found Jimmy Hoffa's body on Main Street it wouldn't make the front page."

"It's that bad?" Clay asked jokingly.

"Pretty much. But Vassar Lawrence is very nice. She's a good friend and a good customer."

Larkin spotted one of her regulars and excused herself to greet them. "I'll be right back," she said to Clay.

Harvey smiled at Clay, "Same old Larkin," he said.

Clay repeated, "Same old Larkin."

In a moment she returned and leaned against the stool next to Clay. "What are your plans for tonight?"

"A couple of drinks, dinner and then I plan to go into town and get a room for the night. I've got to find an apartment tomorrow."

Larkin took over. "This is what you're going to do. Enjoy a couple of drinks and then come down to my house for dinner. I'm having some people over, most of them you won't know, but you'll like them. Anyway, I want you to see my new house."

"Where is it?"

"Just follow the road behind the Landing next to the water. Look for all the cars. You can't miss it." Larkin stood up and kissed Clay on the cheek. "It's so good to have you home. Now, don't hurry. Take your time with your drinks. You know my parties, they sometimes last all night." She smiled mischievously then turned and disappeared through the swinging doors.

Leaving the Landing, Clay drove down a tiny lane that followed the turns and bends of the lake. He passed cattails, lush green plants and bamboo that brushed the side of the Cherokee. When he saw the cars, he stopped. Larkin's house reminded him of some he had seen in Sausalito, California. It was made of cypress lumber, had a tin roof and there was stained glass everywhere. Antique furniture warmed the interior and art was dripping from the walls. The doors were thrown open leading to large decks overlooking the lake. There were at least a dozen people in and around the kitchen. Larkin was stirring a large black pot of gumbo. This was the way Clay loved to remember her. Larkin's friends were always welcome at her house, and there would be something special prepared for them on the stove or the giant cookers and smokers outside.

When she realized that he had arrived, she turned from the stove and yelled out, "Y'all, I want you to meet Clay Brady. He's moving down from Jackson and going to work for the *Chronicle*." She pointed to an antique oak counter from an old grocery store, "Fix yourself a drink and mingle," she said. The counter was laden with more food and booze than Clay had ever seen. As he moved around the room, he met a lawyer, an automobile dealer, an artist, and several attractive women. The group was like one large engine of energy and, as usual, Larkin was the sparkplug.

Larkin took Clay out on one of the decks where several had gathered. "I believe you have met everybody except Khaki Woodson. Khaki, this is Clay Brady." "Hi," she said and resumed her conversation. She was telling them about a shopping spree in Dallas. She was gorgeous, even in the poor light. Her blonde hair was pulled back like a Degas dancer. She was absolutely the best looking woman Clay had ever seen.

Larkin picked up a fifth of bourbon and reached for Clay's arm, "Let me show you around," she said. When they passed Khaki Woodson, Clay could smell her perfume. At the water's edge Larkin led him onto a pier that jutted out over the water. She sat down on the timbers and crossed her legs. "Sit down and tell me about yourself," she said. "We've got to catch up."

"What about your guests?"

"Oh, don't worry about them. They're at home here."

"Do you get together like this often?"

"Real often, but you know how it is on the lake. No one locks their doors, and something is always going on—usually here."

Clay laughed. "It's comforting to know that some things never change."

The lights reflected and sparkled on the water from the houses across the lake. Larkin looked at Clay, "I'd forgotten what a handsome man you really are," she said, "and that's not a pass."

"Thanks," Clay laughed.

"I'll bet there's some girl with a broken heart in Jackson tonight."

"There are a lot of girls with broken hearts in Jackson," he responded. "But what about you? How's Tony?" He was referring to a long-time sweetheart of Larkin's. "I thought you two would be married by now."

Larkin looked at Clay with an expression of bewilderment. "I can't believe you're that out of touch. Tony's dead."

"Tony Damico is dead?" Clay was apologetic. He took her hand, "I'm so sorry, Larkin. I didn't know. I would never have brought it up."

"It's okay. It really is. I had a hard time with it for a while. Ten years of my life gone," she snapped her fingers, "just like that."

Tony Damico and Larkin had been an item since high school. All of their friends assumed that the couple would marry and have a house full of little Damicos. "It was all my fault, Clay," she said. He tried to interrupt but she continued. "You know how much Dixie Springs means to me. The truth is, it means too much. If I hadn't been so attached to this place, Tony would still be alive." She handed Clay her Styrofoam cup, and he poured her another drink.

"Do you remember Charlie Tyler?" she asked.

"Yes."

"Well, Charlie and Tony and a couple of other guys put together a band. They were pretty good. Before long they were doing gigs all over south Mississippi and Louisiana. They got a chance to play in a club on Bourbon Street in New Orleans, and they took it." Clay was listening and didn't interrupt her. He was thinking that she probably needed to talk about it.

"Tony came home every weekend after they finished playing on Saturday night. I wanted them to play at the Landing, but Tony had wanderlust."

"A lot of us do," Clay interjected.

Larkin smiled for the first time. "He wanted me to move down to New Orleans, get married and get one of those neat places in the French Quarter. I don't know what he thought we would use for money, but you know Tony."

Clay laughed softly. "I'm surprised you didn't go. I don't remember you as being the most practical person in the world."

"Oh, Clay, I wish I had gone." Her mood changed as she continued, "Charlie said they finished their gig around 2:30 Sunday morning. It was August 18th. It was my birthday. Tony was driving home as usual," Larkin seemed to be reliving it all again. "30 minutes later, he was killed in a collision on the Lake Ponchartrain causeway. They said he died instantly." Larkin took a deep swallow from her cup and said, "Since then, I haven't taken life too seriously."

There was a roar of laughter from Larkin's house. "Do you need to go back?" Clay asked.

"Absolutely not. Sounds like they are having fun. Besides,

I've been doing all the talking. I want to know what happened to your love life. The last thing I heard was that you gave up a chance with the NFL to chase a Yankee skirt. Where did you go, Clay, Michigan?" The old Larkin was back, and she was probing.

"Well, you're half right," Clay admitted. "I did chase a Yankee skirt, but the NFL thing was never offered. I wasn't that good, believe me."

"So, now, after all these years, the great Clay Brady has found a little humility." Larkin was teasing.

"No, the truth is, I didn't have what it takes for the NFL."

Larkin handed Clay the bottle of bourbon. "You'd better help yourself because you're not getting off the pier until you bare all. Forget about going to Camellia City. You can have my guest room tonight and, if it's taken, you can grab a couch."

Clay loved it. Larkin and Dixie Springs were still just as he remembered them. He was more at peace than he had been in months.

Clay unscrewed the top from the bottle and turned it up. "Now what is it that you want to know?" He put his hands behind his neck and stretched out on the pier.

"The girls, Clay. I want to know about the girls."

"Larkin, I didn't date much at Ole Miss. Those girls check your bank statement and your old man's tax return."

"I heard they were all suckers for football players."

Clay knew that Larkin's hurt over Tony's death was a bitter experience but an experience that had been cushioned by the loving concern of her family and friends. She could never understand the depths of his despair. A father missing in Vietnam, a mother drinking herself to death over it, and a brother who was preoccupied with holding on, weren't much support to him when he needed them. There had been no one there for him but Brian.

Clay was, after all, a big boy when he fell in love with the dark-haired Ole Miss beauty that turned him wrong side out. It was a wild sexual attraction, of course, but she was different from the southern girls he had known, and that made it even more mysterious. Even sex with her was different. She adored him one minute and pushed him away the next. He remembered once when they had spread a blanket on the beach at Sardis Lake and he proposed. She was warm and loving, offering herself to him. Her voice was soft in his ear as she whispered how much she loved him and wanted him to touch her, caress her and make love to her. They had shared an intimacy that they would never recapture. Before they returned to the campus, she had changed her mind and given the ring back, vowing that she never wanted to see him again. Two days later she called crying and begging him to forgive her. He followed her to Milwaukee at the end of the year and took a job at the *Milwaukee Journal* to be near her. Everyone had warned him. Their worlds were too different. They were right. He received a hand-delivered note at the *Journal* coldly informing him that she was marrying an old sweetheart. Brian came to Milwaukee to move him back to Mississippi. Yes Larkin, he thought, I have also felt the bite of an ill-fated romance. But Clay Brady was not going to expose the chunk that had been ripped from his heart.

Larkin's playful poke at his ribs jolted him back to reality, "I'll bet right now you are dying to ask me about Khaki Woodson," she said.

Clay lied. "I don't care to know anything about her."

"Well, you're the first man I ever met that didn't," then with a mischievous grin, she teased, "you haven't turned funny on me, have you?"

"Hardly." They both laughed.

About midnight they ate prime rib that had been slowly cooking in a smoker on the deck. It was nearly three a.m.

before all the guests said their goodbyes and Larkin showed him to his room.

CLAY WAS AWAKENED by someone knocking on the door. He looked at his watch. It was eight a.m. The knocking grew louder. "Just a minute," he said, as he slipped on a pair of jeans and reached for a sweatshirt. When he opened the door Larkin was standing there holding out a Mimosa. "Brought you an eye popper," she said, "get your shoes on, I want to show you something." Clay splashed some water on his face, brushed his teeth and put on his loafers. She was already in the car and had the motor running when he stepped outside. In a matter of seconds Larkin's red Miata was speeding down the lakefront road. She pulled into a driveway and stopped in front of a vacant, rustic cabin. "Get out," she said. When they reached the front door Larkin pulled out a key and opened it. Inside the cabin was one large room, a small kitchenette, a couple of closets and a bath. It had a fireplace, cathedral ceiling and hardwood floors. The front windows offered a panoramic view of the lake. A wooden walkway led to a pier over the water.

"Who owns this place?"

"I do, and unless you have your heart set on an apartment, you can lease it."

"Are you serious?"

"Absolutely."

"I doubt I can afford it."

"Well, you can't live in Camellia City."

"Why?"

"Because Camellia City is tacky, Clay."

Clay laughed. "It's always been tacky."

"Yeah, a vinyl siding company has been running a TV blitz in this area, and Camellia City must be their number one target."

"Why am I not surprised?"

"You won't believe it. They have taken houses with 100-year-old heart pine lumber and covered them with plastic. And the ones that don't have vinyl siding have satellite dishes in the front yard."

"Everybody doesn't have your taste, Larkin."

"Just wait till you see it."

Looking around the cabin, Clay said, "I would love this place, but what can I do about furniture?"

"I've got an old sofa and table in a storehouse you can use. All you need to buy is a bed and I know where we can find a great one."

"You've got a deal."

Larkin sipped on her Mimosa and walked around the empty room. "We'll put a table over here, your bed over there and the sofa in front of the fireplace. We'll need to get a rug, something Native American. I see a lot of green plants over by that window." She was already decorating the place. "Let's get started," she said, "we've got a lot to do. Let's go into town and we can do our shopping." Clay agreed. With Larkin running things, he could just sit back and enjoy the ride.

Sudie Graves, the proprietor of Sudie's Antiques and Used Furniture, was one of Camellia City's free spirits. When Larkin and Clay entered her shop, she was sitting on a loveseat smoking a cigar, reading a thick romance novel. Since retiring from teaching classical Greek at LSU, she had vowed to read nothing more challenging than Danielle Steele. Sudie got up and hugged Larkin.

Larkin wasted no time, "I want you to meet Clay Brady. He's moving here from Jackson and he wants to buy that." She pointed to a gunmetal and brass bed directly in front of them. Clay walked over to the bed and examined a white price tag. Larkin saw him roll his eyes in amazement. "Don't worry. That's the asking price, not the taking price," she said.

"Right, Sudie?" Sudie did not answer. "We need a rug too. Something with a southwest flavor."

"I've got it," the owner said. "Picked it up in Taos last summer."

The rug had the right colors and was the ideal size. Larkin and Sudie haggled and finally Sudie came up with her lowest take-it-or-leave-it price. Larkin looked over at Clay. "It's a bargain, believe me." He pulled out his checkbook. "One other thing, Sudie," Larkin continued as they were leaving, "I've got to have it delivered early this afternoon."

"Brown is out on delivery, but as soon as he gets back I'll tell him to take it on up."

"Wonderful. Tell him to come by my house. I have to pick up a few things in storage to move as well."

"That's going to cost you a fifth of Scotch."

"You got it," Larkin said, walking out the door.

"I've got to call Vassar and pick up a tuxedo for the Camellia Ball before I go back up to the lake," Clay said. "Let's get something to eat and take it back with us."

Vassar was pleased to hear Clay's voice. He told her he had found a place at the lake. She said, "I have your ticket for tonight. I wish I could be here when you come by, but I was just walking out the door for a hair appointment. I live at 425 Jefferson Avenue. It will be in my mailbox."

The white Victorian house with forest green shutters made the typical southern statement. Her yard was neatly manicured. Camellia City had a network of deep concrete drainage ditches that helped control the heavy spring and winter rainfall. One of those ditches followed Vassar's property line. She had carefully masked it with azaleas and flowering hedges. Clay found his ticket in the mailbox and, on the way to pick up his tuxedo, Larkin pointed out the National Guard Armory where the ball would be held. They picked up Chinese food for lunch and a bottle of champagne.

It was six o'clock before they drove the last nail and hung the last painting. Brown had been conned into helping Larkin move and place all the furniture. His pickup had been handy for moving the monstrous plants Larkin hauled in from her decks and from the Landing. The effect was perfect. Even the elk antlers had found a home over the fireplace.

CHAPTER FOUR

CAMELLIA CITY'S BIGGEST EVENT was the Junior Auxiliary's annual Camellia Ball. It was held in the National Guard Armory, always scheduled during early spring to coincide with the blooming of the azaleas and camellias.

It was the only social event where the crème de la crème of society mixed with prominent professionals and an assortment of status-seeking newcomers. This event was not open to the general public. Attendance was carefully regulated. You had to know someone to get an invitation, a ticket. Seating assignments and table placements were indicative of one's social status. Ash Walker's table was reserved for Camellia City's aristocracy. He had the distinction of being the first crowned king of the Camellia Ball.

Elaborate gowns were purchased a year in advance from the finest shops in Atlanta, Memphis and New Orleans, and a truckload of tuxedos was brought down from Jackson for the escorts. To an outsider it was a tongue-in-cheek farce, but for the attending locals, it was the event of the year.

This year the theme of the ball was the "Arabian Nights" and, for months, cutsie little Junior Auxiliary members planned their decorations for the Armory. The centerpiece of the activity was the crowning of a king and queen whose identities were hidden until the exact moment of their arrival and announcement. The prerequisite for being exalted to royalty was threefold: being a member of the social elite, white Anglo-Saxon, and financially able to host a King's breakfast after the ball at the Willow Wood Country Club.

As guarded as Ash Walker was about his personal life, he looked forward to the Camellia Ball. Secretly he enjoyed the presentation of the past kings, the bright spotlight and waving to the crowd of applauding admirers.

Ash had taken a late afternoon nap in order to be fresh for the occasion. It would be many hours before he would get back to bed. His wife, Rita, had awakened him precisely at six p.m. as he demanded. After stepping out of the shower, he stood in front of his bathroom mirror drying himself. He meticulously combed his thinning gray hair and splashed his face with cologne. He leaned closer to the mirror and admired his reflection. He was vain and had reason to be. For a man in his 70s, he was still handsome. Cosmetic surgery and the local dermatologist kept his complexion flawless. His teeth were capped by the best dentist in Los Angeles, and there was not an ounce of fat on his aging body. He was a fastidious dresser with a physique that looked striking in clothes. He was a man of impeccable taste who knew exactly what image he wanted to project. All of his suits and even the jet black tuxedo hanging on the valet inside his bedroom were hand-tailored by Brioni.

He tied the towel around his waist and was still standing in the bathroom admiring himself when his wife Rita walked in and placed a martini next to the lavatory. Rita was his high school sweetheart and was from one of the more influential families in the county. In the early years of their marriage, she was attractive and a viable asset to her husband. By the mid-1980s, Ash Walker had become clearly entrenched as the town's power broker. There was a dark side to Ash Walker and Camellia City, but that dirty linen was carefully folded and hidden away. Many said that the only person that ever really knew Ash Walker was his childhood friend, Earl Bower.

"You had better get dressed. You know how long it takes you," Ash said gruffly, then added, "what are you wearing?"

"Does it matter?" Rita asked.

Ash ignored her comment, "Wear something black—it doesn't make you look so fat."

Ash walked over to the telephone, looked up a number and dialed it. Fats Norton, the mayor of Camellia City, answered.

"Fats, this is Ash. I just called to be the first to congratulate the new king tonight."

Fats hesitated. "I didn't think anyone was supposed to know yet." Quickly recovering he added, "but I should have guessed they would tell you."

As carefully as the Junior Auxiliary tried to protect the secret, Ash always knew who was going to be king. They cleared their decision with him. Fats nervously rambled, "Ash, you did get your invitation to the king's breakfast, I hope?"

"Yes, I did."

"I can't wait for my older daughter and her family to meet you. They drove over from Sweetwater, Texas just for this blowout."

Fats Norton was uncouth. He was important to Ash only because of the position he held in city government. Ash had gotten him elected and controlled him. Their worlds were light years apart. Fats had just taken out a second mortgage on his home to pay for the upcoming king's breakfast, but Ash's wealth far exceeded what even the bankers of Camellia City knew. His two grown daughters had been educated in the finest finishing schools of Virginia. He owned a summer home at Point Clear, Alabama, and an apartment in Manhattan. Two of his favorite personal toys included a quarter interest in a Lear Jet and a private box at the New Orleans

Superdome.

He made one more call to his answering service. "We're going to be out until morning, please take our calls." He bit into the olive from his martini and started dressing. 45 minutes later a black Mercedes carrying Ash and Rita Walker stopped briefly at the end of a long winding driveway at the security gate. Leaving the most enviable address in Camellia City, they headed for the Armory and the Camellia City Ball.

Arriving a few minutes before the coronation, Clay presented his ticket to a smartly dressed but agitated member of the auxiliary. "Let me check your seating assignment," she said, fumbling through the pages of names. When she found it her attitude completely changed, and she gave him her full attention. "Oh, Mr. Brady, I believe you're at Mr. Walker's table. Let me direct you." They walked past rows of long tables filled with people and stopped at table number one.

Vassar saw Clay first and walked over to greet him. She took him to a distinguished looking man sitting at the head of the table. "Ash Walker, I would like for you to meet Clay Brady." The two shook hands, then Ash took over. "This is my wife Rita. Clay, we've heard a lot about you, and if you're half as talented as the people in our business say you are, you will be just what the *Chronicle* needs. Let me introduce you to our table. This is Dr. Glen Darby." Another distinguished gentleman rose from his chair and shook Clay's hand. Ash proceeded around the table making introductions. "This is Khaki Woodson, a newcomer to Camellia City." Following Khaki's cue Clay showed no sign of recognition as she smiled and exchanged greetings. "Henry Hinson," Ash Walker continued, "the best CPA in Mississippi and his wife, Carolyn. Senator Stewart Sutton and Toni; and the man behind the cigar, my dear friend Whitney Davenport and Sara. Also meet Arthur Fisher. Arthur is the president of the fastest growing bank in Camellia City. His wife, Linda, is in the powder room, I believe. Everyone," Ash addressed the table, "this is the young man Vassar was telling us about earlier. She's high on him, and you all know that Vassar is not that complimentary about just anyone. She's persuaded him to leave the *States Times*, and tonight we want to welcome Clay to Camellia City and to the *Chronicle.*"

Everyone at the table was cordial, welcomed him to town and said if he needed help to get settled he should just ask. "You're among friends," Ash concluded, "have this seat here next to me and make yourself a drink." The table top was lined with booze, buckets of ice and mixers.

Ash put his arm around Clay's shoulder and moved closer to his ear. "I'm glad you could be here tonight. It's a good opportunity to meet everyone."

"The pleasure is mine, Mr. Walker."

"Clay, my enemies call me Mr. Walker. Please call me Ash." Clay smiled, "Sure, thanks."

In a louder tone Ash continued, "You're going to enjoy coming back to Camellia City. It's just the right-sized town. Have you found a place to live yet?" Clay was aware that Khaki was listening. "Yes, I did. I leased a cabin today at Dixie Springs."

"Splendid, excellent choice, just splendid." Ash poured himself another drink. Clay caught Khaki's eye briefly before she turned her attention to Ash. They were interrupted by the master of ceremonies.

"Ladies and Gentlemen, welcome to the 32nd annual Camellia Ball. Tonight we invite you to The Arabian Nights. May the gifts of Ali be bestowed on you beginning with these beauties from the East." Stepping from a long veil of nylon, three belly dancers began to entertain the crowd. When their dance concluded, the master of ceremonies introduced the 31 queens and kings of the past balls. Each had a moment in the spotlight, then, after a slight hesitation, the emcee continued, "Now, for the moment we have been waiting for..." There was a fanfare from the dance band's trumpet player and a drum roll. The spotlight panned to the opposite end of the building. Emerging from the sheets of nylon decoration was the head of a camel. Clay stared in disbelief as a long neck and then the complete live animal lumbered into the armory carrying on its back the most obese man Clay had ever seen. Fats Norton paraded to the center of the dance floor wearing a royal concoction of satin, rhinestones, and glitter. On his head was a crown two sizes too small for his head. The emcee continued the farcical performance, "King Clovis Nathaniel Norton, behold your loyal servants." It took two assistants to help the new king dismount. Thankfully, the queen was presented with a simple fanfare of trumpets.

To Clay's amazement, no one was laughing. He turned to Vassar, "This is a joke, isn't it?" She quietly responded, "I'm afraid not." Vassar touched his arm. "When the dancing starts I need to talk to you."

The band began to play. People made their way to congratulate the royal couple while others got up to dance. Clay stood up and extended his hand to Vassar. As they excused themselves from the table, Ash and Khaki were deep in conversation.

"What is it?" Clay asked as soon as they reached the dance floor.

"I received another threatening call tonight just before I left to come here. It frightened me so much that I'm still shaking inside. This time I recognized the voice."

"Was it a different person?"

"No, I was just able to place it."

"Who was it?"

"Rancey James. The name won't mean anything to you now, but he's a very dangerous man." A couple bumped into them and Clay lowered his voice, "Do you believe he's just bluffing, trying to scare you?"

"I certainly hope so. I've heard that if someone wants to kill you they don't do a lot of threatening, they just do it."

"You have told Ash, haven't you?"

Vassar stopped and stood perfectly still. She looked straight into Clay's eyes and said, "No, absolutely not, and you must not tell him either."

The song was over and she quickly added, "We can talk about this in more detail on Monday."

When Clay and Vassar returned to the table, Ash was ignoring his wife and flirting with all the ladies. Clay observed how the entire group played to Ash. He was polished, egotistical, and self-confident. Clay respectfully danced with each of the ladies at the table. They all asked if he were married. Whitney Davenport had read his stories in the *States Times* and complimented them. He asked Clay if he would be an investigative reporter with the *Chronicle*. "No," Clay told him. "I will be assisting Vassar as feature editor." Vassar was pleased with his answer.

It was almost eleven before he asked Khaki to dance. The band started one of his favorite Eric Clapton songs, and he turned to find her looking at him. "Would you like to dance?" She stood up with the grace and poise of a ballerina and walked toward the end of the table. She was wearing a silver slip gown, cut tight and low. He had forgotten how incredibly beautiful she was. She moved easily in his arms, and he brought her closer until she placed her cheek against his. "Where is Larkin?" he asked.

"Something came up at the restaurant at the last minute. She told me you leased her cabin." Khaki snuggled closer as the musicians wound down to take a break before the last set.

When they returned to the table Vassar was already leaving. She always left early to help lay out the gala in the

Sunday edition of the *Chronicle*. She turned to Clay and said, "Have fun. See you at the paper Monday morning."

A LITTLE AFTER MIDNIGHT the 32nd annual Camellia Ball came to a close. Clay made it a point to say something to each of his new friends as they left. Ash and Khaki were standing away from the group talking when Clay found them. He hesitated, not wanting to interrupt, but Ash saw him and motioned him over. "Some of us have been invited to the Country Club for breakfast. If you like, you can go as my guest." He turned to Khaki, "Or you might be like Khaki. She says she's had all the Camellia Ball she can stand for one night."

"Thanks for the invitation, but I'm going to go back to the lake. I still have some unpacking to do."

Ash and Rita disappeared into the crowd, and for the first time Clay and Khaki were alone. "I hope to see you at the lake sometime," Clay said.

"You will sometime."

"When?"

"Soon," Khaki said.

AT ELEVEN-THIRTY that same evening, Rancey James picked up the Albino in the truck stop parking lot. He had followed Rancey's instructions and parked on the dark side. It had taken less than a minute for the hit man to lock his vehicle and get into the Cadillac. He brought with him a black gear bag as carefully selected as the contents inside. The bag contained a pair of black sweats, a black watch cap, black gloves, a mini Maglite, a 22 calibre Ruger revolver with silencer, a lock pick and a straight razor.

The Albino wore no deodorant or cologne and when Rancey reached for a cigarette, he said, "Don't light it. She's not a smoker and I don't want her to smell it when she steps inside." He pulled the sweats over his dark tennis shoes and clothing as they rode and checked the time on his watch. "Is there a chance she will come home early?"

"I've been told she never does, she is supposed to go by the paper. We'll check by the *Chronicle* just to be sure," Rancey said. The Buick that belonged to Vassar was still at the *Chronicle* when they sped by. "You can relax, she's still here," Rancey said.

"I am relaxed," sneered the Albino as he methodically popped his knuckles.

But Rancey was nervous, "What if she won't talk?"

The Albino pulled a straight razor from the bag and opened it, exposing a shiny blade, "You don't worry about that. You just be at that bridge ten minutes after she gets home."

Rancey turned two blocks away from Jefferson Avenue and stopped at a narrow bridge. The Albino pulled the watch cap over his shaved head and sprang out of the car, dropped into the concrete drainage ditch that would take him to Vassar's back yard, and vanished into the night.

Rancey watched for 15 minutes before Vassar's Buick pulled up to her garage. He watched her walk to her front door and open it. The lights never came on. He counted the minutes as they dragged by—seven, eight, nine, ten, then he turned on the key to engage the starter. It hesitated. The adrenaline raced to the top of Rancey's head. "What if," he thought, but then it caught. He drove to the bridge and slowed down to stop. No cars were in sight. He looked carefully for a flash of light, the Albino's signal, but did not see it. He made the block again slowly, looking down the ditch into the darkness. This time he saw it, a quick flash of light. He brought the Cadillac to a full stop, and in an instant the Albino was sitting beside him. "Get out of here," he said. Rancey swallowed deeply and gunned the engine. They were back on the interstate before they spoke again. Rancey said, "I was beginning to get worried, afraid something went wrong."

"She held out to the very last."

Rancey watched as the Frenchman filled up the gear bag with his bloody sweat pants, razor, and gloves. He could smell the distinct odor of freshly fired gunpowder when the Albino pulled the revolver from inside his belt.

"What did she tell you?" asked Rancey.

The Albino glared at him in the darkness. "Where is the rest of my money?" he asked.

Rancey reached under the front seat of his car and pulled out an envelope. "Here. Now tell me what she said about the new man she hired."

"He's not involved. Just came to help at the paper."

"Are you sure?"

"Perfectly sure."

Rancey lit a Winston and drove to the truck stop parking lot. As the Albino got out of the car Rancey pointed to the gear bag. "What about that?" he asked.

"I'll take care of it."

"I'll be back in touch with you when I need you."

"Anytime."

Rancey was craving a piece of lemon meringue pie. Inside the truck stop restaurant he stopped at a pay phone, fished out a quarter from his pocket and dialed a number. A sleepy voice answered politely, "Ash Walker's answering service."

CHAPTER FIVE

THE METAL GARAGE DOOR at the rear of the *Chronicle* responded to Ash Walker's remote control. As it lifted, Ash pulled his Mercedes inside the bay and was closely followed by Rancey's white Cadillac. He closed the door quickly to hide the two vehicles. Ash opened the door to his office. It was in this hideaway that he conducted his clandestine and criminal activities. The room was filled with computers, fax machines, telephones and hi-tech electronic equipment. Built into a wall were cabinets for files and, in the floor, a safe filled with the spoils of fifty years of crime.

"Did you have any problems?" Ash asked Rancey as he handed him a thick envelope.

"None."

"The Albino doesn't know of my involvement, does he?"

"No, Ash, absolutely not."

"What about Clay Brady?"

"Not involved."

"Anything else that I don't already know?"

"Nothing."

"Good. You'd better leave. It will be daylight soon."

"All right," Rancey answered. "When you need something you know where to come."

Ash walked out to the bay and raised the door again for

Rancey to leave. He glanced at his watch; it was 4:30 a.m. It would be 5:30 in Washington, D.C. Picking up one of the phones, he dialed in the area code for the District of Columbia then followed it with a number he had long since memorized. Lieutenant Colonel Lee Bradford answered.

"Bradford," he said, clearing his throat, trying to wake up.

"Bradford, Ash Walker. Sorry to wake you at this hour."

"Hold on a minute and let me change phones." Ash could hear him telling his wife to hang the phone up. He picked up on the other line and waited for the click before he asked, "What have you got?"

"Vassar's been taken care of."

"What exactly did she know?"

"Just what I told you."

"Tell me again."

"She found out about the electronic transfers."

"How did she get that information?"

"Has to be a leak at the bank."

"What else?"

"She was on to Camp Middleton."

Ash was interrupted by a whistle of surprise from Bradford on the other end.

"What do you think?" Bradford asked.

"I don't think she had any hard evidence."

"You may be right. I sure hope so."

"It doesn't matter. She won't be doing any talking."

"How do you want to handle the transfers?" Bradford asked.

"They need to be sent to my bank in New Orleans, but I'll get back with you on the details."

"And the leak at your bank?"

"I'll take care of it."

"What about this new man Vassar hired?"

"Clay Brady is not involved."

"Don't underestimate him. Our initial investigation has turned up some interesting information."

"Like what?" Ash asked.

"Like he may have more than a passing interest in the military. His dad was MIA in Vietnam. He's tough, apparently can't be bought. Our sources say a big drug ring in Jackson tried to buy him off."

"Money didn't move him?"

"Didn't budge him. They put a lot of heat on him, but three weeks later he broke the story. He's very thorough. The *States Times* swears by him. Our advice is, watch him."

"I'm going to offer him the job as editor, and that will put him in my back pocket. That way I can keep an eye on him. If he doesn't accept that offer, I'll pay off his contract and get him out of town."

"The latter might be the best solution."

"You forget, Bradford, I've still got a newspaper that someone's got to run."

"What about Vassar's brother?"

"Earl Bower is a paranoid schizophrenic. His condition will never change."

"Then you are confident that this whole matter is resolved?"

"Absolutely."

"Ash, I want to know immediately if there is any problem even remotely related to the Evangeline File. This matter must not come up again during this administration." They hung up.

Next Ash called bank president Arthur Fisher. "I have a problem," he said. "Someone at the bank is leaking sensitive financial information on some of my personal accounts. I want you to find out who it is."

"Of course, I'll take care of it."

"Then I can depend on that?"

"Yes sir. You can depend on it."

Ash picked up the phone again and called another member of the conspiracy. "It's over. I want her body discovered within the hour," he said.

He stood up, took off his tuxedo jacket and hung it on the back of his chair and waited. Ash had left the king's breakfast at three a.m., had taken Rita home and told her he had to check on something at the *Chronicle*. At six a.m. the second phone in his private room rang. It was Rita. "Ash," she said, "come home at once. Something awful has happened to Vassar Lawrence. They say she's been murdered."

At 6:15 he was at Vassar's house getting the details of the murder from the police. He returned home around 8:00. That's when he called Larkin Wahl and asked her to tell Clay to come to the *Chronicle* immediately.

CHAPTER SIX

LARKIN WAS POUNDING on the cabin door. When Clay heard the knocking, he wrapped a sheet around his waist and went to the door. "What's up?" he asked, wiping the sleep from his eyes.

"Ash Walker called just a few minutes ago. He said something important has come up and he needs to see you immediately at the *Chronicle*. It sounded serious. Stop by when you come back."

"I'll do that," Clay said as he closed the door.

ASH WAS WAITING for Clay at the *Chronicle*. He looked drained, tired and worried, much different than the debonair, charming man Clay remembered from a few hours ago. On the way to Vassar's office Ash said, "Clay, the police called me with some terrible news. Vassar Lawrence is dead. The police discovered her body this morning. It appears that she has been murdered."

Clay strained to keep his composure. "Murdered?" he repeated.

"Yes, I'm afraid so. The police have not released any official details. I have been over there and plan to go back, but I wanted to see you as soon as possible and tell you."

"I'm glad you did." Clay was visibly shaken by the news.

Ash unlocked the door to Vassar's office, turned on the lights and asked Clay to sit down. Vassar's desk was still cluttered as she had left it. Ash pulled back her chair and sat behind the desk, "The *Chronicle* has suffered a great loss, and we will mourn that loss at the appropriate time. I hope you will not think I am insensitive, but, as you know, I have a newspaper that must continue to run without interruption."

Ash pulled out a drawer in Vassar's desk and removed a manilla folder. It contained Clay's employment contract. "I found this," he said, "and I must admit I was a little surprised. Vassar has worked here for many years and, to my knowledge, she never gave anyone a contract. I was equally surprised at the terms—quite frankly, your salary. I would like to talk to you about that." Clay prepared himself. This is when Ash is going to try to wiggle out of the written agreement, Clay thought. Ash quickly put his mind at ease as he continued, "We are certainly going to honor this contract. What I would like to ask you is exactly what you were told your responsibilities would be to merit this type of salary."

"Feature editor," Clay answered immediately, "as stated in the contract."

Ash moved up closer to the desk and placed his chin on his hand. He wanted to study Clay carefully when he asked the next few questions. "Did she expect you to do any reporting for the *Chronicle* in addition to your responsibilities?"

"She didn't say so, but I would expect if we were short-handed I might have been asked to pitch in."

"Did she mention that she would like for you to do any investigative reporting?"

"No, sir."

"You are an investigative reporter, aren't you?"

"I was an investigative reporter at the *States Times*."

"Did she ever mention any special projects that she was

working on that she might need your assistance to complete?"

"No, sir."

"Well, Clay, I'm a little curious as to why a man with your talents would come to the *Chronicle* or Camellia City."

"She told me that the newspaper had grown to the point that she needed some help. She said that she wanted to improve the *Chronicle*'s image. I came for the money and the opportunity to work in management."

"Forgive me for this inquisition. I'm not usually this direct with people I have just gotten to know. I haven't had any sleep, and this tragedy has really shaken me."

"I understand, sir," Clay responded politely.

Ash leaned back in his chair and folded his hands behind his head. "Clay," he said, "I'm going to have to honor your contract, and I'm a man that believes in getting all the bang I can for my bucks. I need an editor and I don't want to go outside to search for one. I've had a trip to Europe planned for some time and, even with this tragedy, I cannot change my plans. I'll be out of the country for a month. Would you consider the editor's position on a probationary basis? When I return, if we are both satisfied, the position will be yours."

Clay did not show any emotion. He sat cool and calm as he listened. Ash continued, "Martha, Vassar's secretary, is extremely knowledgeable and can almost run this paper without an editor. She would make this transition an easy matter for you. What do you say?"

"I would like to ask you a few questions first, if I may."

Ash was a little taken aback that Clay didn't immediately seize the opportunity, but he liked that. It showed that the younger man was thorough and confident. "Ask away," he said.

"How much latitude would I have in the managing of this paper?"

"As much as you want. You're not a bleeding heart liberal or a Communist are you?"

"No, not at all."

"Splendid then. If you get too far off the track, I'll tell you. You will, of course, have complete authority to hire and fire as you see fit."

"Without interference?"

Ash hesitated, then answered. "Without interference."

"Then, under those conditions, sir, I will accept your offer."

"Good." Ash opened the other folder. "I've worked on an obituary and written some information that might help you on the lead article." He handed the folder to Clay, who then read the piece in silence.

> VASSAR BOWER LAWRENCE, 59, died March 3, at her residence in Camellia City. Visitation will be from 6-8 tonight at the Chapman Funeral Home and from 10 a.m. to 12 noon Monday. Memorial services will be held at 3:00 Monday at the Camellia City Cemetery with Chapman Funeral Home in charge of arrangements.
>
> Mrs. Lawrence was born May 6, 1937, in Topisaw County. She was the daughter of Prentiss and Anna Bower. She was editor of the Camellia City *Chronicle* and had worked on papers in Covington and New Orleans before coming to the *Chronicle*.
>
> Mrs. Lawrence was a longtime member of First Baptist Church where she taught a Sunday School class. She was a member of the Garden Club, the D.A.R. and served on the Library Board.
>
> She was preceded in death by her parents and her husband, John W. Lawrence. She is survived by her brother, Earl Bower of Camellia City, and a sister-in-law, Rose Bower, also of Camellia City.

Ash told Clay that the body would be cremated. "I'll have all the details about the service Monday morning. I'll come in, have a quick meeting with the staff, and turn the paper over to you. You've got a lot of hard work ahead of you."

They shook hands, and Clay thanked Ash for the confidence and the opportunity. As he drove back toward the lake, Clay had no doubt that he could handle the challenges of the new job. He thought instead about the threats on Vassar's life. Who was Rancey James, the voice that she had recognized on the phone the night of the Camellia Ball? Even more important, what had she told her killer before she died? Had she told them why he was back in Camellia City? Was he the next target?

He found Larkin on the deck enjoying the warm spring sun. When she saw him she knew something was terribly wrong.

"Clay," she said, "what on earth has happened?"

"Vassar Lawrence has been murdered."

"Who would kill Vassar Lawrence?"

"I don't know. The police are still investigating."

Larkin sat speechless in disbelief for a few minutes and then walked over to a grill and bathed some chicken halves in barbecue sauce, "Where was she and what happened, Clay?" she asked.

"I don't know any details," Clay answered.

"How will this affect your job?" she asked.

"Ash Walker has asked me to serve as editor."

Larkin smiled, "That's a real opportunity, Clay."

"Yes. I just wish it had not come as a result of such sad circumstances. Larkin," Clay asked quietly, "do you know a man named Rancey James?"

Larkin put her basting brush down on the table and turned to him, "Know him? I should say so. He's a real lowlife, Clay. He's one of the few people I've had to ban from the Landing.

Surely you remember him. Everyone in town knows Rancey James."

"No, I don't remember him."

"Why would you ask about him?"

"Vassar mentioned his name to me last night at the Camellia Ball."

The conversation turned to the ball and Clay let it drift. While they waited for the chicken to cook they talked and watched the boats and jet skis work the lake. Larkin served a late lunch of chicken, potato salad, baked beans and French bread.

MEANWHILE, IN A rural black community outside Camellia City, Parker Phillips was meeting with a group of concerned members of the Sweet Home Missionary Baptist Church. A popular black teacher, a member of their congregation, had been fired—seemingly without cause. The group was meeting to plan a strategy for the hearing she had requested before the white school board. Parker found himself under attack because of the position the *Chronicle* had taken to support the board.

"Why have none of our pastor's 'Letters to the Editor' been published?" one of the Elders demanded.

"I can't say," Parker replied. "Perhaps they are trying to defuse this matter. 'Letters to the Editor' from either side would only stir things up."

Someone in the back said he thought it was time to stir things up. Another suggested a boycott. "White people need to be reminded that we spend money too!"

Parker tried to be the voice of reason, but to many in his community he was just a part of the establishment—too dependent on whitey to stand up for his people. Everybody there knew that Parker had never attended a NAACP meeting or worked on the voter's drive or marched behind their leaders in the parade on King's birthday. Sensing the crowd's mood, Parker's voice grew louder and more determined, "You're going to destroy everything we've worked for if you take overt action before you know the facts. Those facts will not be known until the hearing next Friday. My advice is to wait. We have made tremendous progress. With only 2% of the white vote we can elect a black sheriff in this county in the next election. Do you want to throw that away? If the white community sees you polarizing they will do the same and we will both lose."

IT WAS LATE in the afternoon when Clay drove down to his cabin. He needed some time to be alone and think. He changed into a pair of shorts and walked out on the pier to catch the last rays of the sun. He had been in southwest Mississippi less than 48 hours, and already he felt like he was on a runaway train. The reality of his situation began to settle in. There was Vassar Lawrence's murder, a nebulous story that, as far as he knew, would never come to fruition and now the responsibility of a newspaper to run. Music and laughter from Larkin's deck drifted down the lake.

CHAPTER SEVEN

C LAY'S ALARM JOLTED him out of bed before daylight on Monday. He jogged to the Landing and back, showered, dressed and was driving into Camellia City before six a.m. As he drove, a news headline on the radio caught his attention. Robert McNamara was admitting that the war in Vietnam was a mistake and that it could not have been won. The worst part was that he was promoting a new book in which he revealed that he knew, at the time, that our involvement was futile. "Thanks a lot, Bob," Clay said aloud to himself. That would not bring his dad back or any of the others who died in Vietnam. If Robert McNamara was supposed to be one of Kennedy's brightest and best, then no wonder we lost the war. Good material for an editorial, he reflected, and made a mental note to get more information off the AP wire at the *Chronicle*.

His dad's death and the mysterious, sketchy details that surrounded it was a ghost that he had learned to live with since he was ten years old. Captain Ted Brady, 5th Special Forces was inserted in the jungles near DuPrang. On May 17, 1973, his patrol was pinned down by enemy fire. Headquarters ordered Brady to make a run for it. His last communication was "I'm not going to leave my dead and wounded behind." Clay's mother received a notification that her husband was missing in action. The uncertainty took its toll on her health. She could not believe the way the government stonewalled, denied and deceived. Not until 1985 did she learn that her husband was, in fact, lost not in Vietnam but in Cambodia.

Clay remembered how she grieved, grew bitter, and finally gave up hope. McNamara's announcement was, in his opinion, the quintessence of arrogance. In disgust he turned off the radio.

Camellia City looked as though it had been poured out of a bag across Interstate 55, Highway 51 and the Illinois Central Railroad. It was founded just prior to the Civil War when a handful of lumbermen built a sawmill next to the tracks from Chicago to New Orleans. Very soon the town that sprang up around it became the largest in Topisaw County.

Clay turned off the interstate at the Walker Boulevard exit, the main artery that connected the interstate to downtown. The boulevard was lined with a diverse selection of fast food restaurants that included Taco Bell, Burger King and McDonald's. Clay remembered when he was growing up how, on Sunday mornings, greedy churchgoers would race to the Holiday Inn to be first in line to gorge on a buffet that featured southern fried chicken, okra, butterbeans and cornbread.

The brick streets of old downtown were now covered with asphalt. A first-time visitor would find little about the town that was aesthetically pleasing. Residential sections lacked architectural imagination— neo-classical homes were built on cramped lots next to bungalows. Even Wentworth, a deserted antebellum college occupying a tree-covered block in the center of town, was rotting from neglect. Industry had passed up the town due to the racist attitudes of the sixties, and businesses closed, leaving their buildings vacant and run down. Since the arrival of Wal-Mart, located in a mall close to the interstate, the downtown storefronts had become even more snaggletoothed with vacancies.

The 12,000 citizens of the town were mostly hardworking—the whites predominantly ultra-conservative, the blacks, liberal. There was also a hard core group of extremists in both races. These people were armed to the teeth, preparing for a race war that they were convinced was imminent.

Clay drove past the familiar post office, the Masonic Hall and the now-abandoned "Dixie" theater with its faded marquee. He continued past a bank, a hardware store and a bakery. Crossing the railroad he saw a brick depot and remnants of railroad shops. Across the tracks were a restored hotel, a furniture store, a supermarket and a shoe repair. When he turned on Front Street he saw the courthouse and, below it, more buildings with names like Abrams, Shamis, Serio, Tuminello and Damico painted on their storefronts. Damico's, a two-story building, was older than the others on Front Street. The bottom floor was a grocery store with living quarters above it. A tall wooden sign outside the building advertised oysters.

The no-frills Camellia Café was open on the corner of Front Street and Presley. Clay parked and went inside. A "WE SUPPORT OUR TROOPS" cardboard sign left over from Desert Storm was visible in the window. The café was a working man's food factory. Hanging baskets of plastic flowers, the dollar store variety, were the only decorations. The floors smelled of disinfectant from a pre-dawn mopping.

Tina stood behind the cash register. Her name did not describe her size. She was hostess, cashier, and waitress. "What'll it be?" she asked, pointing to the menu painted on the wall behind her. Clay settled on the special, served-anytime breakfast. Grits, eggs, country ham, red-eye gravy and homemade biscuits. "I'll have the special—eggs over easy and coffee," Clay said smiling. Tina did not look up. She punched the keys on the cash register and gave him his total. She yelled his order to the cooks behind her, took a deep drag from her cigarette and gestured with her head, "Coffee and silverware is over there on the counter. Help yourself. I'll bring your food when it's ready."

Clay found a seat among the early morning customers. There were men in business suits, construction workers, farmers, and a table of younger blue collars in tee shirts, jeans and baseball caps. As he waited for his food, he drank his coffee and soaked up the conversations of the locals. In a few minutes Tina sat a heaping platter of the special down in front of him. "Baby," she said, "if you want some cream for your coffee, I'll get it for you."

"No, thank you," Clay responded. "I drink it black."

Clay had always liked the café. There were no Styrofoam cups or plates, no plastic forks or spoons, no salt and pepper sealed between sheets of paper. It was old and quaint, just as he remembered it, so unlike the fast food places.

After leaving the restaurant, Clay drove to Third Street to see the house where he had lived for 18 years. It all looked so different to him now. The street was narrower than he remembered it and the house much smaller. The magnificent English Tudor had been raped and left naked by a former owner. The boxwood shrubs lining its slate walkways, which had been planted and nurtured by his mother, were gone. The English ivy that covered the north wall of the house had been stripped away. Even the brown trim, so characteristic of that style architecture, was now painted a garish green. Larkin was right, Camellia City was tacky.

Turning off of Third Street, he headed for the *Chronicle* to report for work. Before the 46 *Chronicle* employees gathered in the lounge, Ash Walker and Clay had a quick meeting. Ash gave Clay the keys to the building and introduced him to Martha, Vassar's executive secretary. "Martha can find anything you need," Ash said, "She can also explain our computer network." Martha was pleasant but looked worried and apprehensive. Ash continued, "The *Chronicle* is going to offer a $50,000 reward for the arrest and conviction of Vassar's killer." Ash also told Clay that he would be leaving town immediately following Vassar's memorial service. He and Rita were meeting friends in New York and then would leave directly for Europe, but if he needed to be contacted, his answering service could reach him.

When Ash was sure that all the employees were present he told them about the weekend's tragic event. Most had already heard. He told them about the memorial service scheduled for three p.m. at the Camellia Cemetery. Finally, he gave Clay a glowing introduction to the staff, turned the newspaper management over to him, and left the building.

Clay's remarks were brief and fitting. "I did not know Vassar Lawrence as well as you did, but I had a great respect for her journalistic ability. With your help we will continue to meet the high standards she set for this paper." Some of the ladies were brushing away tears and Clay did not want to prolong the meeting. He asked for their support and understanding during the transition and closed his remarks with, "We have a newspaper that's got to go to press. Let's get busy."

Clay turned the key to Vassar's office and opened the door. No trace of any personal items were left in the office. Her desk was bare except for two computers, a calculator and telephone. Clay put his attaché case down, slipped off his sport coat and hung it on a rack next to the door. Clay asked Martha to pull tear sheets representing a random sampling of all the reporters work and the same for advertising. Then he loosened his tie, rolled up his sleeves, and started to work on the lead article. He worked nonstop until it was finished. After he proofed it one last time, he typed the article's heading as well as the paper's headline. "*Chronicle*'s Editor Found Slain" was set in bold 67 point, Helvetica font. Clay gave the reward and the information concerning it a prominent side bar on the front page. Ash Walker had been very specific that any calls about the reward should be called in on a *Chronicle* hotline. He had left a written memo to Clay that all responses were to be reported for his review before they were forwarded to the Camellia City P.D. "I don't want anything to slip through our fingers," he had said.

Clay was interrupted twice before the paper went to press. Both were telephone calls. One was Ed Williams from the *States Times* and the other was Brian. They had heard about Vassar's death and were concerned. Ed was pleased about the editor's position but equally worried. "Clay," he said, "I believe you have walked into a bad situation. Something's not right down there, for that matter, things have never been right down there. You need to get back to Jackson—the sooner, the better." Brian said, "We need to get together and talk about this." Clay tried to reassure them, but neither believed him.

Ed would be unable to attend the memorial service. He was flying to Atlanta on an early afternoon flight, but he urged Clay to call if he needed him when he got back.

It was after the newspaper had gone to press and after Martha had finished her lunch in the *Chronicle*'s lounge that Clay asked her to come to his office. He was looking over the paper and it was still open on his desk when she came in and sat in the chair in front of him. She was holding pen and note pad.

"I would just like to visit with you for a few minutes," Clay said.

"Sure," Martha replied.

"It's been a hectic morning."

"Yes, it has."

"And a difficult one for you, I'm sure," Clay continued. "How long have you worked as Vassar's secretary?"

"A little over five years."

"That's a long time."

"It really doesn't seem that long. I enjoy my work." She was trying to smile, but Clay sensed her nervousness.

"I just want you to know that I understand what a difficult situation you are in."

Martha smiled. "And I understand your position and how difficult it must be for you. I mean a brand new job, the responsibility, not knowing the staff and everything."

They were exchanging niceties as both searched for the right words. Clay broke into a big smile and walked over to where she was sitting and sat in the chair next to her. He wanted to remove the barrier, the desk, the boss-employee invisible wall. "What I want you to know is that if you are uncomfortable working with me so suddenly after," he paused, "after Vassar's death, then I will be more than happy to transfer you to any department." Martha seemed touched by Clay's considerate statement. "No, sir, Mr. Brady. I'm fine. Everything's okay." Clay leaned forward and cupped his hands around his knee, "Great," he said, and quickly changed the subject.

"Did you pack Vassar's personal things from the office?" he asked.

"No, I didn't. Why?"

"All her things are gone, and it was done so quickly I wondered."

"I would guess Mr. Walker took care of that."

"I suppose so. Maybe he contacted her family."

Martha responded, "Maybe he did."

"Are you aware of any files or materials that she may have been planning to give me?"

"No. Nothing that I know of."

Clay quickly moved on to something else. "Tell me about the reporters. I will know about their talent or lack of it when I read their work. I'm interested in their work ethics."

Martha told him how they interacted among the other employees—one of the females seemed immature and emotional, one of the males was sarcastic, critical of management. Sara Marks and Parker Phillips were Vassar's favorites. Of the two it was Parker that Vassar relied on. He had joined the *Chronicle* right after college and was Vassar's protegé. He put in long hours, worked most weekends and had a knack for getting a story. Everyone at the *Chronicle* liked him. His one drawback was that he had trouble with some of the diehard bigots in city government.

Clay asked Martha to set up a meeting with all the department heads for the following afternoon. He also called for spread sheets, personnel files and lineage reports. Before Martha left Clay's office, she gave him her home telephone number. "Something might come up or you may have some questions. Feel free to call anytime," she said.

After going to the lounge for a cup of coffee, Clay returned to his office and filled out corporate credit card credentials, insurance forms, and an employment application to satisfy personnel. He spent the rest of his time poring over newspaper articles and the spread sheets. Martha buzzed him at 2:30, "Mr. Brady," she said, "I'm going to be leaving for the cemetery in a few minutes."

"Thanks for reminding me," Clay replied.

He got into his Cherokee and drove past the high school, the Wildcat football stadium and rows of yellow school buses before he reached the entrance to the cemetery. He drove underneath a brick archway and followed a tiny road that wound through the monuments. He passed Serio's marble and stained glass mausoleum. Ahead was a full-sized replica of a Harley Davidson cut out of granite to honor a fallen biker. Next to it, a heart-shaped tombstone bore an inscription that read, "Raise Hell While You Can." Around the bend was the burial plot of an atheist with an epitaph he must have considered appropriate, "I have no fear of punishment, no hope of reward." Clay did not pass his mother's grave. She was in another section of the cemetery. Her simple bronze marker lay beneath a gardenia bush, her favorite flower.

Clay stopped and parked behind a line of cars. He could see a large crowd already gathering around and under a green funeral home tent. Wooden folding chairs had been placed on an imitation grass carpet. Some of the chairs under the tent were occupied. Clay walked over and stood near the tent. He nodded a greeting to Parker Phillips who was standing with the other staff members along the back row. Ash Walker was surrounded by the same entourage that was at his table at the Camellia Ball. Khaki Woodson looked in Clay's direction and smiled with her eyes.

Standing behind the front row of chairs was Larkin, her hands resting on the shoulders of an elderly woman seated in front of her. The lady was dressed in black. Standing alone and away from the crowd was Earl Bower, Vassar's brother. He was a tall, gaunt man. He wore a summer straw planter's hat, a camouflage shirt with jeans and combat boots. Sitting obediently beside him was a golden Labrador retriever. Earl Bower was the most bizarre personality in the county. Day and night he walked the streets of town with his dog, picking up pieces of paper and tin foil. He would carefully mark x's on the sidewalk with chalk and mumble unintelligible phrases. Most of the town's citizens avoided and feared him. Few of them knew that he was the most decorated hero of World War II in all of Topisaw County.

Ash Walker started his eulogy a little after three. He spoke of Vassar's contributions to the community, her friendship, her professional career and her abiding faith. In closing he made reference to Vassar's murder and expressed confidence that those responsible would be brought to justice. He praised the fine manner in which the Camellia City Police Department was handling the case. He asked a minister to close with a prayer. The urn was placed and covered and the memorial service was over. Earl Bower quickly disappeared behind the tombstones.

THE WHITE CADILLAC on the street that bordered the cemetery went unnoticed as it passed. Rancey James was satisfying his curiosity. He wanted to see what kind of crowd a dead newspaper editor would draw. He turned to Toxie Hux, sitting next to him, "I don't mind telling you Toxie," he said, pointing to the crowd in the cemetery, "Vassar Lawrence didn't mean shit to me." Toxie grunted his agreement as Rancey lit up a Winston.

CLAY WALKED OVER to speak to Larkin, and she introduced him to the lady in black, "This is Rose Bower," she said. "Vassar's sister-in-law." Rose Bower was in her 60s. She spoke with a polished southern accent and carried a walking cane that added to her sophisticated appearance. Larkin tugged at Clay's coat sleeve and whispered, "Rose wants to talk to you. Will you walk her to her car?"

"Sure," Clay answered.

When they were away from the crowd, Rose opened her purse and handed Clay an envelope. "Vassar asked me to give you this if anything happened to her."

Clay quickly put the envelope inside his coat pocket. "Clay," she said, "If you ever need to talk to me I'm in the telephone directory, please feel free to call."

When they reached her car she removed the snap-on shades from her glasses, put her cane in the back seat and drove away. Clay reached inside his coat pocket and removed the envelope, opened it and read the message inside. "Clay," it read, "if you are reading this then you know that those involved in this story will stop at nothing. Forget the project, leave the newspaper and this town or you will surely be killed. I'm sorry to have involved you. Vassar Lawrence."

On the way back to the *Chronicle*, Clay dissected Vassar's note. If she had become that apprehensive, why hadn't she told him more at the Camellia Ball? Maybe she didn't think it would happen so soon. Maybe things got too hot. Maybe she changed her mind about the investigation. Perhaps that was what she would have told him on Monday if she had lived. Clay's mind raced with maybes. One thing that had never made sense to him was why Vassar had not discussed anything about the investigation with Ash Walker. He was even more puzzled now after he had met Ash. If Vassar had a super investigation to unleash, with his connections and money, he would have brought in an ace investigative reporter or two from *The New York Times*. Clay remembered how adamant she was standing on the dance floor of the Camellia Ball. "I do not want Ash to know under any circumstances," she had said.

Clay returned to the *Chronicle* and picked up where he had left off with his work. The remaining hours raced by until Martha stuck her head in his door. "It's five, Mr. Brady, do you need anything before I leave?" she asked.

Clay told her no.

"Have a good night," she said.

It was past eight o'clock when he picked up his attaché and a stack of tear sheets to read at home and called it a day.

MEANWHILE DALLAS DAWSON, the sheriff of Topisaw County, had just gotten home from his office at the county jail. He placed a plate of food in the microwave to reheat. It was his wife's card night, and she had wrapped his supper and left it on top of the stove. As he waited, he picked up the newspaper and read the bold headline. It was Clay Brady's by-line that caught his attention. That would be Carl's brother, he thought to himself, as he tore it out to put in his wallet. There was no need to read the lead article. He already knew all the details. That is a lot of reward, he thought. $50,000 could buy that fishing camp on Lake Mary he had always wanted, a new boat and motor and all the fish bait he would need for the rest of his life. What a pity someone in law enforcement could not qualify for the reward. His theory of who killed Vassar Lawrence was based on more than a hunch.

CHAPTER EIGHT

R AY JEAN HUX had been up since daylight. She had a
lot to do before she left for work at the convenience
store. There were clothes to wash, a trailer to clean and dishes to stack. This morning she was trying to be especially
quiet because her 15-year-old sister had spent the night with
her and was still asleep. Toxie would be nursing a hangover
from the night before and would be in a rotten mood. The
last thing she wanted was to wake him.

Toxie heard Ray Jean as she was leaving. He ran his hand
through his greasy hair and reached over to the night table
for his cigarettes. He found an empty pack, crumpled it, and
cursed. He got up and walked into the living room and
kitchen. At one end of the living room was a fuzzy white sofa
and arm chair, a La-Z-Boy recliner and a television set. On
one wall was a picture of Elvis and a heart-shaped clock. On
another was a mounted deer head. In every corner of the
room was a rifle or an assault weapon, and on the coffee
table was a .45 automatic.

Toxie opened the refrigerator door and, reaching for something to eat, found a cold piece of fried chicken and stuffed it
into his mouth. He turned up a quart of beer and a line of
bubbles raced to the bottom of the bottle. Wiping his greasy
fingers on his underwear, he walked to the other end of the

trailer where Ray Jean's sister was sleeping. On the way down the hall he looked outside to make certain Ray Jean had gone, locked the door and fastened the inside chain. He walked quietly to the bedroom, opened the door and looked inside. Ray Jean's sister slept soundly, her long auburn hair covered the pillow and one leg was partially covered with a sheet. She wore only a tee shirt and panties. Toxie stared at her.

When the girl's eyes opened, Toxie was lying beside her propped up on one elbow, staring. She pulled the sheet up to her neck.

"What are you doing in here?" she shrieked. With her next breath she called out for Ray Jean.

"I'm just lookin'," Toxie said without moving, "ain't no law against lookin' is it?"

The girl started to get up. Toxie grabbed her arm, "Wait a minute," he said. She resisted, trying to jerk loose, but Toxie tightened his grip.

"Turn me loose, Toxie. I'll tell Ray Jean."

Toxie's mood turned nasty. "You won't tell Ray Jean nothin'." He grabbed at the bottom of her tee shirt and jerked it over her head. Her firm, but still developing breasts, were completely exposed. She was terrified now and struggled wildly trying to free herself. Still holding her wrist tightly with one hand, he slapped her across the face with the back of his other.

"Shut up," he said, "don't you dare scream or I'll choke you to death." One hand was now firmly around her throat. "Do you understand me?" he said.

She was gasping for breath. He released his hands from her throat. She didn't move, her heart was pounding inside her chest.

"That's more like it," Toxie said. She stared at the ceiling. She could hear him talking beside her but pretended he was not there and that this was not happening. "Have you ever done it before?" Toxie asked.

She shook her head no, beginning to cry. He took the hand that he was holding and pushed it inside his shorts. Her fingers jerked away when she touched it. She made a lunge with her body in a desperate attempt to free herself. Toxie grabbed her by the hair, jerked her back down and slapped her across the face. He came down on top of her. "Please, please don't," she begged.

"You gonna like it, you little bitch. You been prissin' around me, just askin' for it and now you gonna get it."

He slobbered around her mouth, fondled her and ripped her panties off. She cried in pain as he raped and sodomized her. It seemed to have lasted forever. As he finally climaxed, Toxie bit brutally into one of her breasts and this time she screamed loudly. Toxie rolled over.

"It wasn't so bad, was it?" Toxie asked hatefully. "When your sister was your age she was begging me for it and, after you have the time to think about it, you'll want some more too."

She turned her back to him, shaking violently as she curled up in a fetal position. Toxie stormed out at her, "Go wash up and take these with you. I don't want Ray Jean to see 'em." He threw her torn panties at her. "If you tell her what happened I will fuckin' kill both of you. Do you understand?"

"Yes," the girl answered as she burst into tears again.

AT THE TIME the rape was occurring at the East Side Trailer Village, Clay was at the *Chronicle* in a meeting with Parker Phillips. Parker was born in Camellia City and had spent his early years in the government housing projects provided for single parents who qualified as indigent. His mother was a determined woman and soon found work in the school cafeteria. By the time Parker entered the first grade, she had enough income to move them into a small house close to the school. He had a desire to succeed and the ability to fulfill those dreams. He excelled academically, graduating with honors from the University. Although he had other offers when he received his degree in journalism, he jumped at the opportunity to come back home and go to work for the *Chronicle.* Vassar Lawrence, his mentor, had taught him newspaper from the bottom up. Printer's ink was definitely in his veins. He was married to Tawana Phillips who was employed at Ash Walker's Topisaw County Bank.

Parker sat across the desk from his new boss, relaxed and confident. They discussed Vassar's murder before Clay got down to business. "Parker," he began, "I've spent most of the night reading over some of your work."

"What did you think?"

"I like what I've read."

Parker smiled. "I'm open for criticism. Where do you see need for improvement?"

"I don't have any criticism, in fact, I'm very impressed with your style. But I would like to know what you think about this newspaper."

Parker replied, "Do you want my honest opinion?"

"Of course."

"I believe it's a disgrace." Parker picked up a paper on the corner of Clay's desk and handed it to him, "Look at it," he said, "this paper does not report, represent or reflect this community."

Clay listened as Parker explained, "This county's population is 49% black. The only reporting of our activities is in the police report. Occasionally, one of our outstanding athletes makes the sports page." Parker's voice had an edge of sarcasm. "You'll never read a human interest story about a black or a feature on any of us."

"I didn't realize that," Clay said.

"I'd like to write a feature on Frank Mingus. He is a resident of Camellia City—he has been featured in many books and publications, but you won't read about him in the *Chronicle*. He's even been given a prominent place in the National Civil Rights Museum in Memphis."

Clay straightened his back in the chair and thought to himself, I know full well what happens to journalism when the black agenda is given too much attention. Jackson television is a perfect example. If someone traveling through the state stopped at a motel and turned on one of the local channels during the nightly news, they would swear they were in an African country.

Parker went on, "Just yesterday I was in a meeting of concerned black leaders about another matter. They complained to me that they can't even get their 'Letters to the Editor' published."

Clay tried to hide his thoughts, but Parker sensed his true feelings. "I appreciate your input," Clay said, in a noncommittal manner. Parker cautioned, "As I see it, Clay, you can diffuse a lot of resentment by just being fair."

Clay thanked him and, concluding the conversation, urged him to stay on top of the Vassar Lawrence murder investigation.

The new editor spent the rest of his morning meeting with department heads. Early in the afternoon Martha buzzed him. "Khaki Woodson is here to see you," she said.

"Thanks," Clay said, "send her in."

He was standing in the doorway when she reached his office. Khaki was dressed in a conservative navy suit and looked very professional. She carried a canvas portfolio. "Have a seat," Clay invited. "Would you like Coke or coffee?"

"No thank you," she smiled, "I've just finished lunch."

"What brings you to the *Chronicle*?" Clay asked, easing into the chair next to her.

"Ash suggested that I talk with you. I hope you'll help with a project I'm working on."

"I'll try. What type of project?"

"As you know, there is an abandoned college here in town, Wentworth. It's very old. I'm doing a feasibility study for a group in Atlanta that is interested in turning it into something commercial."

Khaki reached into her portfolio and pulled out some material. "This will explain what we have in mind." Clay took the papers and Khaki continued, "We need support from the community."

"And that's where the *Chronicle* can help."

"Yes. Maybe a series of articles or something to generate interest."

"I don't see any reason that we couldn't do that," Clay replied. He wanted to know more about Khaki, "Are you from Atlanta?" he asked.

"No, actually I'm from Virginia."

"And how did you get to the Deep South?"

"By choice. This opportunity came up and I grabbed it."

"You even have the southern accent to go with it," Clay teased.

"I didn't know I had one," Khaki laughed.

"It's slight."

"I'd be happy to show you the college and tell you what we intend to do there."

"I would like that, but it will have to be some other time. I'm snowed under right now."

Khaki was embarrassed. "I'm sorry," she said, "I should have made an appointment."

"Not at all. I didn't mean it that way. I would like to see it with you."

"Fair enough." Khaki squirmed in her chair trying to end the conversation gracefully. "Then the *Chronicle* will support the project?"

"I'll read the material and if I have any further questions, may I call you?"

"Of course," she said, digging in her purse for a card. "This is my number. I'm not listed in the book; I've only been here a few months."

Clay turned the conversation away from business, "And what if I don't have questions but would like to call?"

"Then by all means, do." Khaki smiled again. There was a comfortable silence between the two of them. "I must be going and let you get on with your work."

"I'm glad you came by. I do have one question."

"What's that?"

"The perfume you wear. I remember it from the night I met you at the lake. What is it?"

"It's called 'Eternity' by Calvin Klein. Do you like it?"

"Oh, yes, I like it," Clay was flirting with her and she knew it.

"You have my card," she said, smiling at him as she walked toward the door.

THE REST OF THE DAY went without interruption until late afternoon. Martha buzzed Clay again. "Sheriff Dawson is here to see you."

"Sure, send him back to my office," Clay responded.

In a minute Martha buzzed him back. "The sheriff asked if you could come to the front to see him?" Clay thought that was a little unusual but agreed.

Dallas Dawson did not look like a lawman. There was nothing about him that read typical southern sheriff. He was medium build, thin and arrow straight. He wore no uniform, western hat or firearm. Instead, he was wearing a brightly colored golf shirt and casual slacks. The only symbol of his authority was a gold badge that folded over his belt. Dawson had served Topisaw County for three terms and was almost ending his fourth. Over the years he had built an astonishing network of informers. If something happened in his county, all he had to do was sit back and wait. Someone would come to him with the information. He knew the county like the back of his hand, knew the people and their daily routines. If they were suddenly out of pocket, he knew it. If someone strange came into the county, he knew that also. He resented it when people talked about the unsolved murders in Topisaw County. He would quickly add that they were not unsolved but rather unprosecuted.

Dallas Dawson reached out to shake hands as Clay approached the receptionist's desk. "Mr. Brady, Dallas Dawson."

"Just Clay," Clay said to him, smiling.

"Clay, I was wondering if we could talk a few minutes?"

"Sure," Clay replied. "Come on back."

"What about in my car?" Dawson pointed out to the parking lot.

"Fine," Clay answered. "Martha, hold my calls."

As they walked outside the *Chronicle*, Dawson spoke, "You don't look like you need looking after. You look more than able to take care of yourself. In fact, you look more fit than your brother."

"You know Carl?"

"You bet. He asked me to check on you when you got to town."

"Then Sheriff, if you know Carl, you must know he has an older brother complex."

Dawson broke into a big grin. "Yeah, maybe, but he's a damn good officer."

"How do you know him?"

"Recently we attended a hostage training course together. That's when he told me you were coming to town."

By now the two had reached the sheriff's unmarked car. Dawson looked up at the late afternoon sun and pulled a handkerchief from his back pocket. "Damn, it's hot. Too hot to sit in the car. Let's go over there," he pointed to a large shaded oak. "I saw your by-line in the *Chronicle*," Dawson pulled the reward article from his pocket, "what kind of response have you gotten to this?" he asked.

"None yet."

"That's interesting," Dawson said as he leaned against the tree and drew a line in the ground with the sole of his boot. "Tell me, Clay, what brings you to Camellia City?"

Clay pointed to the building, "The *Chronicle*."

"How do you know Ash Walker?"

"I don't, really. Vassar Lawrence hired me, not Ash Walker."

"And she's dead," Dawson said with a grimace.

"Yes, sir."

Sheriff Dallas Dawson had been called to the Lawrence crime scene out of professional courtesy. The Camellia City Police Department had jurisdiction, and when he arrived he was given the high hat as usual. There had been a long history of friction between the two departments. This time he laughed to himself. He knew who killed Vassar Lawrence.

"What do you think, Sheriff? Do you think the P.D. has any leads?"

Dawson laughed out loud and spit on the ground. "Hell, those boys couldn't find a menstruating bull in a twelve-inch snow."

Clay chuckled. It had been a long time since he had heard that southern expression. "I've heard about all the unsolved murders down here."

Dawson became serious and corrected, "Not unsolved. Unprosecuted—and there's a hell of a difference."

"The D.A.?"

"Yep. Like I've always said, you can't trust a man whose

ass is wider than his shoulders and when you see our D.A., you'll know what I'm talking about."

"You really believe that?"

"Well, that may be stretching it a bit. It's really politics. It's who you know."

Dawson's mood changed. His gray eyes squinted. "I've checked you out, Clay, partly because of your brother's interest and partly out of curiosity."

"Curiosity? About what?"

"About why you came to town, and I don't believe it was to report the news of Topisaw County. You don't have any business being connected to Ash Walker in any way."

Dawson had Clay's attention. He was very aware of the techniques of a good law enforcement officer. Clay thought if Carl trusted this man then he would also. "Vassar wanted me to do some investigating," Clay said.

Dawson shook his head, "On what?"

"I'm not sure. She was killed before she could tell me, but I believe her death was connected to the investigation."

"Why?"

"Because she was receiving death threats."

"From whom?"

"A man named Rancey James."

Dawson sucked air though his teeth, "I knew it," he said aloud.

"Now," Clay said to Dawson, "I've told you what you wanted. You tell me what you know about Vassar's death... off the record, of course."

"I know who killed her," Dawson said confidently.

"Rancey James?"

"He was part of the conspiracy, but not the killer."

"Who then?"

Dawson reached down on the ground, picked up a twig and scratched the back of his head as he collected his thoughts. "I've been after Rancey James for the past 16 years. He's been involved in just about everything that has given this county a black eye."

"And you've never been able to catch him at it?"

"I've caught him all right, a lot of times."

"What happened?"

"He's got pull, connections. A few phone calls and he slips through."

"Who's his connection?"

"You're getting ahead of me. Let me finish. I keep an eye on Rancey. He doesn't know it, but I do. About 30 days ago Rancey had a visitor from Louisiana. They met at the Wal-Mart parking lot and went off in Rancey's car. My deputy got the number off the Louisiana plates. The night of Vassar's death, that same car was back at the truck stop."

"Coincidence?"

"Hardly. After the murder I ran the plates. They came back on a Feret Du Boise. Feret Du Boise, a.k.a. Albino, is a known hit man. He has records as long as your arm—in and out of Angola."

"So what about Feret?"

"We're working on it. Believe me, we're working on it."

"So, Rancey and this Feret killed Vassar?"

"That's part of it."

"And the other part?"

"That's why I'm here. Rancey James can't blow his nose without Ash Walker's approval. He's done Ash's dirty work for years. Now all of this is off the record."

Clay nodded yes.

Dawson went on. "So, if Rancey killed Vassar, Ash knew it. If Rancey killed her, Ash Walker wanted her killed... he's the connection. That's why we're standing under this tree talking and not inside Ash Walker's building. I don't trust him. He's probably got that place bugged."

"Sheriff, tell me about Ash Walker."

"Ash Walker runs this town. He has had a strangle hold on it for years. He controls everything, the economy, the politics—even one of the churches."

"How?" Clay asked. "How did he get control? Money?"

"Yes. And lots of it. Nothing, I mean nothing, happens here without Ash's approval. If a doctor or lawyer comes to town they go to see him. If they don't they soon find themselves on the outside. You don't get ahead that way. Not in this town."

"Are you telling me that a man his age could still be that interested in control? He's way past retirement age and apparently has all the money he could ever want."

"People like Ash never retire. Power to him is like carrion to a vulture. Regardless of how much there is, there is never enough."

"How did he get that kind of power?"

"First of all he married the right girl, from the right family. She had money and Ash, to my knowledge, has never made a bad business decision. He's involved in timber, oil, real estate, construction, banks—you name it."

"And the newspaper?"

"That's peanuts. Just one of his toys, but it does provide him a way to manipulate opinions in this town."

"That is so completely different from the impression he made on me when I met him," Clay said.

"Oh, he fools everyone at first. Ash Walker is smooth and charming, comes across as a perfect gentlemen. He can tell you to go to hell and make you enjoy the trip. If you cross him he will never let you know that he is angry, but one day you will be walking down the street and your head will leave your body. You will never know what happened."

"Yeah. I know the type," Clay said.

Dawson continued. "Ash Walker represents an extreme—

the aristocracy. In the middle you have a lot of people that are decent and hard working and appreciate the town for what it is."

"I didn't know anything about Ash Walker when I left Camellia City. I knew the name, that's all."

"Believe me, Clay," the sheriff said in a serious tone, "Ash Walker is not someone to be connected with in any way and he damn sure isn't anyone to cross. My advice to you, son, is to find another job as quickly as possible and forget whatever Vassar told you. There's very little opportunity for a young man with your talent in this town. I'd move on. But that's your business," Dawson quickly added.

Clay thanked Dallas for his visit, information and advice and spent the rest of his workday thinking about what had been said. Clay did not relish the idea of working with one of Vassar's killers, but there was no way he was going to leave Camellia City just now. He was right on the cutting edge, the adrenalin was flowing and he loved it.

At five o'clock Clay left the *Chronicle*. He stopped at Larkin's and found her sitting on the pier. He pulled up a chair beside her. The sky was turning from magenta to gray and the definition of the undergrowth near the water's edge was disappearing in the darkness. They watched a boat in the distance. Its running lights rose and fell as it crossed the water heading for shore. "Tell me Larkin," he said, "were Vassar and Ash Walker lovers?" Larkin was taken by surprise. "Why do you ask that?" she said.

"I just wondered."

"Yes, they were. Mother told me they had been for years."

"What happened?"

"I don't know for sure, but I can tell you what I think. I think Ash became too interested in Khaki Woodson."

CHAPTER NINE

CLAY WAS AT THE Camellia Café eating a Spartan breakfast of dry toast and coffee when an older man wearing a felt hat and a 1970s concoction of polyester and patent leather entered the restaurant. From a table of blue collars near Clay, several voices called out, "Hey, Rancey." One of them yelled, "You can have this chair, Rancey. Been saving it for you." The name caught Clay's attention as the man pulled out a chair and sat within arm's reach of the reporter. Each person at the table played to Rancey as if he were some sort of celebrity and, when the ex-Exalted Cyclops of the Ku Klux Klan was sure he had an audience, he began a diatribe unlike anything Clay had ever heard.

"Let me tell you what happened to me yesterday," he said without being prompted. "I went down to one of those government give-away deals to get some blueberry bushes."

One of the men joined in, "Yeah, they were giving away two for every family, wasn't they, Rancey?"

Rancey nodded his head, continuing his story, "And just like those goddamned niggers, anything that's damn free, you can bet those son of bitches are gonna be there."

"You right about that, Rancey. Half of 'em won't even plant the damn bushes." Someone else had joined in.

"Hell, no, that's too much like work," another said, "they'll just let 'em die. But they have to get 'em. They just can't help theirselves."

Rancey took over again, gesturing between long drags on his Winston, "Well," he said, "I looked up and there was about a hundred of those son of bitches lined up, all wanting that free shit. I said to myself, 'I'm just gonna leave. I'll buy my own goddamn blueberry bushes.'"

"That's right, Rancey, hell, you could buy the whole damn truckload and never miss it."

Rancey held up his hand like a minister quieting a congregation, "But then I changed my mind. I stayed in that line, and when it started inching up and it gets to where there are only five people ahead of me what do you think happened?"

A chorus went up around the table, "What, Rancey? What?"

"A car pulled up and three old nigger women got out, and somebody up front hollered out, 'Hey girl, come on up here with us.' Do you believe they broke in the line right in front of my ass?" Rancey was loud and seemingly unconcerned about who might overhear his conversation.

One of the men asked, "What did you do, Rancey? When them niggers broke line and all?"

"Hell, I told the bitch, 'This ain't your goddamn living room. You can't just invite anybody you want to up here. Those son of a bitches have to go to the back of the line just like everybody else.'" The crowd at the table roared approval. "Good for you, Rancey, you tell it like it is."

"That ain't all the shit I told her. I stuck my finger in her face and I told here that if a white person tried to break in line in front of *them*, their asses would be out on Highway 51 marching about it."

"That's the goddamn truth," said one of the men, "and I'll tell you what pisses me off, Rancey. I'll be standing in line to check out at the grocery store with barely enough money in my pocket to pay for the high-priced shit, and one of them blue-gummed niggers is standing up ahead of me with a fist full of food stamps. She's eatin' free and she'll drive off in a Cadillac."

Grunts of agreement went up all around the table as another of the men said, "I know the bastards were mistreated in the past, but in 1964 they marched hollering they wanted equality. They ain't working for equality. They're working to get the advantage over us. They have a completely different set of rules and laws where they can do whatever the hell they want to do, and we're supposed to work our asses off to give it to them. And, on top of that, they're trying to make us fuckin' like it."

Rancey had the table fired up now, and he loved it. He took the conversation over again, "It's the damn Jews' fault."

"How do the Jews figure in, Rancey?" Someone at the table coaxed him along.

"Money, they're in it for the money. They started the NAACP just for the money because they damn sure don't give a shit about the niggers. They say 'we know how you niggers feel cause we were mistreated too.' Then they bought up all the major TV networks and 99% of the newspapers in this country, and they make money off keeping this shit stirred up." The crowd at the table was nodding. Rancey took a deep breath but he wasn't finished yet, "I can tell you what's gonna happen." He paused dramatically and took another drag off his Winston to give his boys time to react. "The Republicans are gonna cut back on all these give-aways, and that's when the niggers are gonna come to my house and your house and take what they want. The Democrats are pushing this gun control where when it happens, the white folks won't have any guns to defend themselves or protect their families." The crowd sat spellbound, listening to their guru. Rancey continued, "We'll all be sitting in our living rooms with our nuts in our hands. Not me, mind you.

Nobody is going to tell Rancey James what to do about his gun, but that's what this gun control thing with the Democrats is all about. A Democrat is nothin' but a nigger turned inside out."

The men at the table roared with laughter. "You got that right, Rancey."

"I just hope," Rancey was winding down now, "that I'm still alive when this race war comes, and boys, it's damn sure coming. I can't wait to shoot those little niglets running for cover."

Clay was listening in total disbelief. Something very evil was surfacing in Camellia City. After hearing this, it was easy to believe that a man filled with so much hatred could have killed Vassar Lawrence. He was in no mood to finish his breakfast and left immediately for the *Chronicle*.

In the *Chronicle* lounge Clay poured a cup of coffee to take to his desk. He stopped on the way and asked Parker Phillips, "Could you stop what you're doing and come to my office for a short meeting?"

"Of course," Parker smiled. "Good morning, Clay," he said cheerfully.

There was no response from Clay, so Parker followed him to his office and sat down to wait for the meeting to begin. Clay seemed pensive this morning and did not make polite conversation. Instead, he got right to the point. "Parker," he said, "I would like for you to become our managing editor." Parker fought to control his excitement over the offer as Clay continued, "There will be a substantial increase in your salary to go with it."

"I can sure use that," Parker said, breaking into a huge grin. "Are you sure you want me for the job? What about..."

Clay held his hand up, interrupting him before he could finish. "Yes, I'm sure. I am also telling you that you will be free to implement your ideas about stories from the black community as we discussed yesterday."

"I appreciate that, Clay. I got the feeling yesterday that you were not sympathetic to my position on that."

Clay smiled slightly, "We'll talk more about that later," he said, looking at his watch. "Right now we have to get this paper to press."

Parker returned to work happy about his new promotion but wondering about Clay's strange mood. At noon he stuck his head inside Clay's door, "What are your plans for lunch?" he asked.

"I don't have any," Clay answered.

"How long has it been since you have had a real meal, Clay? I mean soul food?"

Clay laughed and put his pencil down, "It's been a while."

"There's a place across the tracks that's got the best pork chops and greens that you have ever tasted. My treat... what about it?"

"You're on. Let's go."

The two men got into Parker's aging Nissan. When he turned on the ignition the car was filled with the sounds of jazz. Parker reached to turn down the volume, but Clay stopped him, "That's Jimmy Smith. Are you into jazz?"

"It's about the only thing I listen to. My mother had a real passion for it, you know—Miles Davis, Wes Montgomery, John Coltrane and Charles Mingus. What about you?"

"I've been hooked on it for years," Clay answered.

"If you get down to New Orleans," Parker said, "you've got to hear Steve Blailock."

"Blailock?"

"Yeah. Plays a mean guitar, has incredible fingers. He's played with the best but now has his own group."

"Where does he play?"

"Sometimes at Snug Harbor on Frenchmen Street."

"I'll keep that in mind," Clay said.

They crossed over the railroad tracks to the east side of town and rode down Summer Street. The buildings and dwellings were mostly substandard, covered with graffiti. Parker brought the Nissan to a stop at a signal light. A group of black males was gathered on a curb drinking malt liquor and talking to a short man holding a cell phone. "The one with the phone is Sugar Red, one of Camellia City's drug dealers. I went to high school with him," Parker said. Sugar Red had dreadlocks, his shirt was unbuttoned to his waist and around his neck were thick gold chains. As he spoke, a gold-capped tooth glistened in the sunlight. As Parker pulled away from the light, Sugar Red recognized the car and acknowledged Parker by making his fist into a Black Power gesture.

Bertha's was a railroad foreman's shack that had been converted into a café. A friendly black woman greeted them at the door and called Parker by name. "We would like to sit in the back, Bertha, something private," Parker said.

Clay liked the laid back feeling of the place: red checkered table cloths, skillets of cornbread, pots of greens and iced tea by the pitcherfuls. As they ate lunch, Clay told Parker about the conversation he had heard earlier that morning at the Camellia Café.

"So that is why you were willing to let me run some of my stories in the paper?"

"Yes, it is. But let me be straightforward with you, Parker. I do have a degree of racial bias. This whole race thing has always turned me off. But hearing that conversation this morning blew my mind."

Parker was not shocked by what he had heard Clay relate. "That type of extremist has always frightened me, too. But I must admit, Clay, we have the same Rancey James-type mentality in the black community."

"Yeah, I know." Clay was listening as Parker went on to describe the other extremists.

"They won't get out in a public place and express their feelings, but in the privacy of our churches, and even more so in secret meetings, they are extremely vocal. They advocate a violent solution to any problems and they, too, are armed. That's why I've never been an activist. I still believe that the power is in votes, and this next sheriff's election may prove my point," Parker explained.

When the customers began to leave, Parker pushed his plate aside. "I want to thank you for the opportunity you have given me," he said.

Clay looked up. "You're doing a great job, and you deserve it."

Parker looked around the room, making sure no one was in earshot. "I need to level with you about something."

Clay folded his napkin. "Shoot," he said.

"I know why you came to the *Chronicle*."

"Really?" Clay did not change expressions.

"Yes. I should have told you what I know before now."

"What do you know?"

Parker's mood became even more serious. "One Saturday morning before you came down to interview with Vassar, Tawana, my wife, wanted to use the car so I asked her to drop me off at the *Chronicle*. I needed to do some research in our stacks in the morgue. I didn't have my car parked outside so no one knew I was there. I heard someone arguing inside Ash Walker's office. It became very heated and I could hear every word."

Clay wanted to hear more. "Go on," he said.

"It started with a sarcastic remark Vassar made about Khaki Woodson and escalated to deposits of money that Ash had been receiving from the Defense Department. She said she knew of over a million dollars in transactions."

"What?!" Clay exclaimed.

"Wait, there's more," Parker continued. "She accused Ash of

being involved in some incident that happened in 1943 at Camp Middleton and threatened to expose him if he did not pay her $250,000."

"Are you telling me that Vassar was blackmailing Ash?"

"Pure and simple."

"Did she say what the incident was?"

"No."

"What did Ash say?"

"He said that he thought she was crazy and that if she ever brought it up again, she would regret it."

"Did he offer her any money?"

"He said he wouldn't give her a cent."

Parker pressed his fingers against his forehead trying to keep his thoughts in sequence. "I feel like I have been partly responsible for the argument—maybe even her death."

"Why? You couldn't help overhearing their argument."

"No," Parker continued, "because I told her about the rumors."

"What rumors?" Clay asked.

"It had to do with some black soldiers that were transferred to Middleton from out west and the trouble they caused in Camellia City. I became interested in the rumors and started doing a little investigating on my own."

"What did you uncover?" Clay asked.

"I found old newspapers that substantiated racial disturbances in Camellia City involving these black soldiers. There were a number of articles covering a couple of months, but then I couldn't find anything else."

"What happened? Do you know?"

Parker went on, "Rumor has it that these men disappeared—vanished overnight. One superstitious black lady told me it was voodoo. Of course no one really believes that. I asked Vassar if I could do a story on it."

"What did she say?" Clay asked.

"She said 'no.' But the odd thing is that she asked me repeatedly after that about the rumors. She wanted names of people that might know something. She said that she was going to talk to her brother about Camp Middleton. He served on that base, she said."

Clay was more than interested now. He pressed Parker for more. "So you're saying that she continued to discuss this with you after she denied you permission to do the story?"

"Precisely. But after hearing the argument she had with Ash Walker, I knew that she had found out something beyond what I had told her. And, after you came down to interview, she never mentioned it again. That's when I put two and two together. The best investigative reporter in Mississippi comes to Camellia City to be a feature editor at the *Chronicle*? No way! She hired you to get the story, didn't she?"

Clay hesitated, looked away for a moment and then made a decision, "Yes," he said, "she did."

"That's why she was killed, wasn't it?"

"It's beginning to look that way." Clay was puzzled, "Parker," he said, "she told me she hadn't discussed this investigation with anyone."

"She lied to you, Clay. She was setting you up, man. What did she tell you about the story?"

"Not much. Only that it was big, involved the military and the federal government. She was to give me the details when I came to work at the newspaper."

Parker paused, took a deep breath and looked into Clay's eyes to ask the next question, "Did Ash Walker have her killed?"

Clay did not flinch, "I certainly think so."

"So we're working for a man that could be involved in a conspiracy to commit murder," Parker repeated the unthinkable to himself.

"It's beginning to look like we are."

"Tell me, Clay. If I put you, Vassar and this story together, don't you think Ash Walker has put it together too?"

"It has crossed my mind."

"Then, what are you going to do?"

"It's not what I'm going to do, it's what *we* are going to do. We are going to get the story."

Parker smiled broadly and started firing the questions. Clay stopped him. "There's just one thing you must understand going in," he said.

"What's that?"

"You could get yourself killed."

"I don't look scared, do I?"

"No, but you have a wife to consider."

"Don't try to talk me out of it, Clay. I'm in, regardless."

"This is how I've got it figured," Clay began, "we have a month before Ash Walker returns from Europe. For that month we are going to use his newspaper to our advantage. We'll get to work immediately on Camp Middleton. You will run traps in the black community."

Parker was following closely as Clay continued, "I want all the rumors documented, everything, every word that's said. I'll work from another angle. I'll find out what's available in the government records through the Freedom of Information Act."

"Okay," Parker said eagerly.

"Three weeks from today we will break a feature story on the base, slant it toward nostalgia, but plant a hook in it that may catch us some fish. Are you tracking with me?"

"Exactly."

"We'll have to be careful. Don't use the telephone at the *Chronicle*. We must assume that the place is bugged. We'll conduct our meetings here at Bertha's."

Parker agreed. "Ash is going to be mad as hell, Clay."

"Sure, I know that. We will both be fired, but then we can

put 100% of our effort into this project. Don't worry. If this thing is half as hot as I think it is, we won't have to find jobs, they'll find us."

At that moment the two reporters merged their destinies. They celebrated their new bond with a high five over Bertha's red-checkered tablecloth.

CHAPTER TEN

LATE IN THE AFTERNOON on Thursday the phone rang. "May I speak to Clay Brady?" Khaki Woodson asked when the receptionist at the *Chronicle* answered.

"Just a minute, please."

The *Chronicle*'s new editor picked up the phone, "Clay Brady," he said.

"Clay, this is Khaki. I wanted to thank you for the feature article in yesterday's paper on Wentworth College. It was excellent."

"I'm glad you liked it," Clay responded warmly, "we'll be doing more."

"I'm also calling to see if you would be my partner for some mixed doubles in tennis Saturday. They want to play around seven at Willow Wood."

"Sure, I'd like that. I haven't played since I left Jackson, so I may be a little rusty."

"That will be our excuse if we need one. I don t think we will; Larkin tells me you're pretty good."

"Don't ever listen to Larkin. But, thanks for asking me. I've been wanting to meet some of the tennis people at the club. Would you like me to pick you up?"

Khaki hesitated. "Thank you, but, I'll just meet you there."

"Okay then. I'll see you Saturday around seven."

Clay leaned back in his chair, gripped an imaginary tennis racket from the air and followed through with a powerful forehand. "Good shot!" he said aloud, not knowing that Martha was standing in the doorway with an armful of papers watching him. "What are you doing?" she asked, laughing.

"Practicing my tennis, Martha. Practicing my tennis," Clay said, not embarrassed in the least.

"Well, this should bring you back to reality. This stack needs proofing and this correspondence needs your signature," she said, placing them on his desk.

KHAKI WOODSON lived in a condominium close to the *Chronicle*. A New Orleans couple owned it and planned to keep it vacant until their retirement, but Khaki persuaded them to lease it for a year. She had been careful in choosing a place. It had to be private—a place where she could come and go without being noticed and a place where visitors could come without being watched. She was also looking for excellent security. This small but elegant condo had all of the requirements. It was exquisitely furnished. Khaki loved beautiful things. Being the only daughter of a Newport News shipbuilder had afforded her a rich cultural background. For high school graduation her family gave her a summer in Europe. At the University of Virginia she was an accounting major, but she selected a minor in fine arts to complement it.

She was very athletic and, at an early age, became accomplished as an equestrian and tennis player at the finest summer camps in Virginia. Her favorite was sailing. Sailing was more than a hobby—it had become a passion. Some of Khaki's earliest memories of her dad were images of the two of them on the Chesapeake Bay with their sailboat heeling over, cutting through the water. The last summer before her father died, the family chartered a sailboat and sailed to the islands off the coast of Honduras.

"ARE YOU GOING to work late again tonight?" Martha asked as she put the last of the correspondence in his basket.

Clay shook his head yes.

"Would you like me to close your office door?"

"No, just leave it open."

It was almost eight p.m. when Clay put down his pen and decided to call it a day. He turned off his computer, picked up his briefcase and locked his office. He had a file that needed to be returned to the morgue before he left the building. He walked past the advertising department, through the press room and unlocked the door to the morgue. An eerie glow of light seeping under the door of Ash Walker's private office caught his attention. He watched it for a moment in the darkness of the morgue. The light moved underneath Ash's door and changed from bright to dim. Someone was inside with a flashlight. As he felt his way toward the door in the darkness, he bumped into a metal shelf and something fell to the floor with a loud crash. Instantly, the light from underneath the door disappeared. Clay pressed his ear against the door. He could hear movement inside and the distinct sound of a door being closed. He quickly turned and ran through the building. Bursting through the front doors of the *Chronicle*, he raced down the side of the building toward Ash's private garage and entrance. The garage door was locked and there were no cars parked close to the building.

After going back inside the *Chronicle*, he picked up a phone and called Ash Walker's answering service. When the service answered Clay asked, "Is Ash Walker back in Camellia City?"

"No, he's not. Ash Walker is in Europe."

Clay was not satisfied. "Can you be sure of that?"

"Why, yes," the startled operator said, "we just had an overseas conversation with him a few minutes ago. Do you need to reach him? Is this an emergency?"

"Oh, no," Clay answered, "not at all."

When Clay left the *Chronicle*, he drove back to the garage and checked it again. Everything was secure. Driving toward the lake, Clay collected his thoughts. Someone had been in Ash's office. How did they get in and why were they there? Someone left in a hurry and disappeared into the night without leaving a trace. As he approached Larkin's Landing, he saw cars parked all the way to the highway. When he reached his cabin Clay called his friend, Brian, in Jackson. After a little small talk, he invited Brian to come down to Dixie Springs on Saturday. "I really need to see you," he said. Besides, weekends on the lake were pretty rocking, and he wanted Brian to meet Larkin. "She's your type," he assured Brian, "I think you'll like her."

"Then you can definitely book me, man," Brian said. "I'll be at the airport at ten o'clock. That's in the a.m.," he quickly added. "Tell me," he teased his friend, "have you met any knock-out women down there?"

"Only one," Clay answered seriously, referring to Khaki, "but she's such a knock-out that she will stop your heart."

CHAPTER ELEVEN

BOUT TWO BLOCKS from the Camellia Café, Toxie's car died again. This time it would not start. Toxie got out, pushed it to the curb and kicked the door panel violently with his steel-toed boots. He cursed it for worthless junk.

Clay Brady had already arrived at the café and was enjoying his coffee when Toxie walked through the door.

"I need to borrow your phone, Tina," Toxie said.

She pointed to it on the counter, and Toxie was facing Clay as he dialed. "Rancey," he said, "can you pick me up at the Camellia Café? I've got car trouble."

Clay looked up sharply when Toxie said, "Rancey." Seeing Toxie Hux standing there holding the telephone brought old memories rushing back. During his senior year in high school, on a Saturday night, all the kids had congregated in a parking lot next to Walker Boulevard. Everyone was enjoying each other's company, standing outside the cars listening to music when, all of a sudden, a yellow convertible turned into the parking lot at such a high rate of speed that it almost turned over. The driver, slowing down some, now headed for the crowd. Right on his bumper was a pickup truck in hot pursuit. The car squealed to a stop and so did the truck. In an instant, a rough looking, much younger Toxie Hux ran over to the car and jerked a male high school student out of the car. In a fury of one-sided licks, Toxie had beaten the youth to his knees. Toxie was trying to pull the boy up on his feet by the hair of his head. "I'll teach you to smart off at a red light!" he screamed.

That's when Clay entered the picture. He walked out of the crowd and went over to Toxie, "He's had enough," Clay said firmly, "you've beaten him. He's no match for you."

"And who in the goddamn hell are you, a referee?"

"No. He's just had enough."

"Maybe you want some of me. Maybe you're a better match," Toxie taunted.

Clay summoned up his courage. Captain Ted Brady had not raised a coward. "Maybe so," he said, looking Toxie right in the eye.

There was a long silence. Toxie was sizing up the young football player. Thinking that the confrontation was over, Clay turned and started to walk away. All at once the side of his head exploded, and the next thing he knew he was lying on the ground. When he regained consciousness, he was looking into the pretty green eyes of Cheryl Scott as she wiped his forehead with a napkin soaked in ice. Toxie had quickly fled the scene to avoid the police. For weeks after the incident, Clay took a lot of ribbing from his buddies. Everyone knew that Toxie had knocked Clay out with a blind-sided sucker punch, but his friends called him "One-Punch Brady." Their jokes were laced with adolescent admiration that Clay had dared to stand up to the bully. After his encounter with Toxie Hux, Clay was told just how vicious and cruel his opponent could be. In a fight with a pulpwood hauler outside a bar, Toxie was so enraged that he picked the beaten man's head up and placed it face down on a concrete curb. The man's mouth was open and he was gasping for breath, the eyewitness told Clay. With one kick to the back of the head with his steel-toed boot, Toxie shattered all of the victim's front teeth. Clay had never forgotten that story, and all of those memories flooded back to his mind as he watched Toxie.

"Good, I'll be waiting," Toxie said and hung up the phone. Realizing that Clay was staring at him, he gave him a menacing look. "What in the hell are you staring at?"

"You," Clay responded, and, in a firm voice, continued, "I'm looking at you."

"You're a smart ass," Toxie said, "and you don't look bad enough to be a smart ass. Don't I know you?"

Clay did not answer but pushed his coffee over to the side, never taking his eyes off Toxie. Tina broke the tension. "I don't want any shit started in here, Toxie. I'll call the law in a heartbeat. You wait for your ride outside."

"The hell you say."

Tina reached for the phone. "Fuck you, Tina," Toxie said as he walked toward the door. Pointing his finger at Clay, he added, "I'll see you later, dude."

Toxie waited outside until the white Cadillac pulled up. As they drove off, he flipped the finger in Clay and Tina's direction.

"I'm sorry," Tina said to Clay.

"You don't owe me an apology. It's not your fault."

"He's just worthless trailer trash. Hangs around with Rancey James," Tina said, trying to explain.

"Who's Rancey James?"

"More trash."

Before Clay could ask any more questions, a customer had gotten Tina's attention. Clay finished his coffee and left for the office.

At the *Chronicle*, Clay chatted briefly with Martha before going to his office. "I have a busy morning planned," he told her, "I would appreciate it if you would hold all my calls." She agreed. He worked, uninterrupted, until after one o'clock when Parker stuck his head in the door and pointed to his watch. Clay leaned back in his chair, stretched and yawned. "Have you been to lunch?" he asked.

"No," Parker replied, rubbing his stomach, "and am I ready!"

"Bertha's?"

"Bertha's."

The two walked out of the building together and Clay pointed toward his car when they reached the parking lot. "Let's go in mine," he said.

"Sure," Parker said, starting toward his own vehicle, parked nearby, "but I want to get something first. I'll be right back."

When he slid next to Clay in the Cherokee he handed him a tape, "See how you like this," he said.

Clay pushed the tape in, and the unmistakable sound of Mississippi Delta Blues came out of the speakers. "I've got a '53 Buick, gonna paint it green with a broom." Clay laughed out loud at the lyrics. "Who is it?" he said, "I love it."

"Steve Blailock. The guy I told you about the other day."

"I thought he was mainstream jazz."

"He is, but on this album he does a little blues and Dixieland to go with it. You like Delta blues?" Parker asked.

"Raised on it. My best friend, Brian Cothern, is from the Delta. You'd like him. He's an ex-Navy fighter pilot, now making big bucks as a medical rep. Has his own plane. Great guy."

Inside Bertha's, Clay and Parker discussed business. First, Parker handed Clay an article on Frank Mingus that he wanted to run as a feature on Sunday. Clay read it and agreed. Then, to Clay's surprise, Parker showed him the field notes he had already compiled on the Camp Middleton story that the two planned to break soon.

Pretending to gather information for a nostalgic newspaper article on the war years to avoid suspicion, he had found people willing to talk. Merchants told stories of the economic windfall of those years and remembered good times and good friends. Others told sad stories of watching the trains leave the station filled with soldiers, knowing that many would never return. One lady said, "There were tears and goodbyes for brave new daughters and sons, and there were gifts of nylons and Evening in Paris perfume." One man in the county described how he came to town, shined shoes for soldiers for ten cents a pair and finally saved enough dimes to buy his first suit of clothes at J.C. Penney's.

One elderly woman recalled the urgent wartime process of creating Camp Middleton—when farms which had been in the same family for generations were suddenly snatched up by the federal government under the power of eminent domain. Residents had little choice but to accept what the government offered to pay for their land, then move all of their family's belongings and establish a life elsewhere. Homes, schools and even churches were disrupted for the sake of building the new Army base. With emotion still strong in her voice, she related, "It's so sad. It wasn't worth it. It wasn't worth it at all. Of course, when your country is at war, I guess you do whatever you think's right."

When asked specifically about the year 1943, Parker had gotten a variety of answers, "Oh, that was the year Franklin Roosevelt was President," or "Betty Grable was Hollywood." More than a few remembered that JoJo's was the hottest night spot in Camellia City. An automobile dealer remembered that $750 would buy a new Ford car. A grocery store owner recalled choice round steak was selling for 20¢ a pound. A black blues singer told him that he only paid $2.50 for a round trip ticket on the train to see the Zulu king in a Mardi Gras parade.

However, Parker came across something of far more interest. Two ladies who worked as civilian maids on the Army base told how, in the summer of 1943, things changed drastically after a group of new soldiers arrived on the base. A white lieutenant was found murdered, hanging from a piece of barbed wire. He had been castrated and his body mutilated. A few days later, a white civilian lady that worked at the PX was found murdered. She was in her second trimester of pregnancy. Her body had also been mutilated and the fetus cut from her womb. "That's when they closed the base to civilians and we lost our jobs," the maids had said.

"That's it!" Clay exclaimed when he finished reading about the murders. "That's just the hook we need. We can ask for information from our readers. Maybe something else will surface."

"What do you suggest we do next?" Parker asked.

"Try and find someone to corroborate the maids' story."

"Have you searched the existing files on Camp Middleton?"

"Yes, and I've requested a lot of technical data on the base from the Archives in Jackson. We'll put it all together and break the story as scheduled."

Parker nodded in agreement as he began to put his notes away. Clay was thinking aloud, "We need to ride over to the old Camp Middleton site as soon as possible. Do you know anyone that could show us around?"

Parker laughed, "I know it like the back of my hand. But we can't see it all. Most of that property has reverted back to its original owners, and we could not get access to it."

"That's a fairly large area we're talking about, isn't it?"

"Absolutely, Clay. It covers 53,000 acres."

"I've got an idea. Meet me at the Camellia City airport Saturday morning at ten o'clock. We'll fly over it."

Clay stared blankly into space for a moment as he thought, "I need to talk to Vassar's brother."

"Earl Bower?"

"Yeah."

"That's one weird dude, man."

"Maybe I should use Bertha's phone, give Rose Bower a call and set it up."

"Mrs. Bower can't set it up," Parker said, "they're divorced. The last I heard he was living over Damico's Grocery."

"Then I'll go there after work today and see if I can find him."

Clay left the *Chronicle* at six p.m. and drove downtown to Damico's. The Italian grocery store had been a landmark in Camellia City for years. Primo, wearing a white apron, was the third generation to own the establishment. He had planned for his son Tony to carry on the tradition. When he saw Clay, the big Italian reached out his arms to greet him with a hug.

"Clay, it's been a long time," he said.

They talked for a while about Tony and the accident, and then Primo changed the subject abruptly, "Come on back," he said, "the first 'welcome home' beer is on the house. What's your flavor?"

Primo took him to the back of the store. Behind a partition was a row of old-fashioned ice boxes full of beer and next to them, an oyster bar. Four men sat at a table playing Dominoes. A naked light bulb was attached to a long cord that hung from the ceiling and, in a corner in the back of the store, there was a staircase that led to some living quarters. A golden Labrador retriever slept peacefully at the bottom of the stairs.

"You remember how it works," Primo explained, "The beer is in the boxes. If you want some oysters, ask Frankie. He will shuck them for you." Primo was pointing to a teenage Italian boy grinning behind the counter. "You keep up with what you get and pay me on the way out. It's that simple... nothing fancy here."

"I can handle that," Clay said, following Primo back up to the front of the store. "Primo," he said, as he peeled at the label on his beer, "I came by to see Earl Bower. I understand he lives upstairs."

Primo stopped, picked up a cloth and started wiping the counter. He scratched a spot with his thumbnail. "Today's not a good day," he said.

"Why?" Clay asked.

"He has good days and bad days. Today's been a bad one. He has problems, you know."

"Yes, so I've heard."

Primo shrugged his shoulders. "You might want to come back tomorrow."

Clay did not persist. "I'll tell you what. Let me give you my card." He scratched out the *Chronicle* number and penned in his home telephone number instead. Handing it to Primo he said, "When you feel the time is right, give this to him and ask him to call me."

In the dingy room above the Italian grocery, Earl Bower was hearing the voices again and cursing the hallucinations that brought them. The figment was always the same—he was going down into the dark, deep shaft in the earth. At the end of the shaft was a subterranean tunnel and a crystal chamber filled with light. Then his eyes would open and he would hear the muffled voices that spoke of death and agony. Walking over to the closet, he removed an olive drab ammunition box. The voices, trapped inside, must be released before they would grow silent. Frantically he consulted the lunar tables, formulas and cryptic messages that he alone monitored from a cosmic mind tap. Finally, in desperation, he walked down the narrow hall seeking the companionship of his dog. "Bugle," an unsettling, raspy voice called out from somewhere up the stairwell, "Bugle, come here, boy." The Lab's ears perked up, and he slowly stretched before trotting up the stairs toward the voice and into the darkness.

CHAPTER TWELVE

A T PRECISELY 10:00 A.M. Saturday morning, Brian's plane touched down at the Camellia City airport, and Clay, Parker and Larkin were waiting for him. After taxiing up to where they were standing, the noisy propeller spun to a stop.

Brian stepped from the cockpit sporting Ray Bans and a lightweight flight jacket. His hair, prematurely gray, was cut short and blew slightly in the breeze as he walked toward them. Brian was Navy aviator from the tip of his toes to the top of his head. After playing football with Clay at Ole Miss, he went directly to Pensacola, Florida following graduation. He received his wings there and was assigned to the aircraft carrier *USS Carl Vinson* during Operation Desert Storm. Proudly he flew his F-14 Tomcat on 130 sorties over Iraq. Not wanting to be kicked upstairs behind a desk in Navy administration, he chose to return to the private sector after his six-year military obligation ended.

Since college days at Ole Miss, Brian Cothern had been Clay's closest ally, best friend and confidant. Larkin nudged Clay in the ribs, "What a hunk," she said, under her breath. Brian lifted his hands in a gesture. "Where's the party?" he asked.

"I thought you were the party," Larkin answered, grinning.

Clay introduced Brian as they walked around the Mooney admiring its sleek lines. "Would y'all like to go up for a spin?" Brian asked.

"Sure," Larkin was quick to respond. She slipped in next to Brian, and moments later they were breaking through the clouds over Topisaw County. About three miles south of Camellia City they flew over acres of farmland that were crisscrossed with a network of asphalt roads.

"What's that?" Clay asked Parker.

"That's where Camp Middleton used to be."

Larkin had become intrigued with the airplane's instruments and Brian was answering her questions. Parker continued, "Late in 1941 the Army laid plans for the base, chose this site and sent letters to all the property owners telling them they would have to sell. They disrupted hundreds of farmers and their communities around here."

"I'll bet a lot of people didn't like that," Clay commented.

"Some did, some didn't. The Army told the landowners that they would have first choice of buying the land back when the base closed."

Parker pointed to the river below which twisted and turned through the landscape of south Mississippi. Brian nosed the plane down closer to the ground to give them a better view. Acres of thick cypress trees appeared on the horizon. As the plane drew closer, the marshes where they grew became distinct.

"That's the swamp," Parker explained, "and somewhere in the middle of it is the Louisiana state line."

"Was that also a part of the base?" Clay was pressed against the window to get a better view.

"The Mississippi side was."

A sprawling, rusting group of buildings and railroad tracks on the banks of the river caught Clay's attention. "What's that?"

"A salt company. A salt dome runs underneath the swamp and the river."

"It looks deserted."

"Yeah. Been deserted since World War II," Parker said.

"Who owns it?"

"Ash Walker—and the 1,000 acres that surround it."

Brian circled the camp again. This time Parker pointed out what remained of concrete bunkers, reservoirs, and firing ranges. "Down there is the old camp amphitheater. Joe Louis once boxed there."

"How do you know so much about Camp Middleton, Parker?"

"Stories. All the old timers have stories. I just listened to them."

Brian was headed in the direction of the airport. "You guys want to see anything else?"

Larkin answered, "Yes, Dixie Springs."

In a few minutes the four of them could see the water of the lake reflecting in the sun. "It seems so small from up here," Larkin said. "Look, there's the Landing, my house, and that tiny place with the tin roof is Clay's cabin." By now she was pulling on Brian's arm with excitement. "What do you think?"

"I think a drunk front is moving in and is going to become stationary right over your house."

Larkin laughed. "You mean a cold front, don't you? Land this plane and we will try to get there before it settles in."

When the plane landed, Larkin invited Parker and his wife to join in the festivities at the lake. Parker explained that Tawana was having to work Saturdays at the bank. "She's a real workaholic," he said, "I've never seen anyone as dedicated to her job. Please ask us again sometime."

Friends of Larkin's were already gathering by the time they returned from the airport. By noon everyone was enjoying the sun, eating boiled crawfish, and a few boarded the party boat to tour the lake. Larkin did not let Brian out of her sight. They were the last to jump on the boat before it left the pier. Clay steered the craft to open water, pushed a Bob Seger tape into the stereo and slowly pulled back on the throttle. They cruised past weekend cabins and luxury houses that lined the steep banks of the lake and eased past piers and shaded coves that looked cool and inviting. When they reached the deep water near the dam, Clay shut off the engine and threw the anchor overboard. Larkin pointed to a concrete platform near the dam. "That's the control valve," she explained to Brian, "the water underneath it is cold and deep. I'll race you there if you're game."

"You're on." Brian was loosening his sandals and in seconds the two plunged in and were swimming toward the platform.

"I believe that Larkin has finally met her match," someone said to Clay as he reached inside the ice chest for something cold to drink. The long pontoon barge rose and fell gently in the water. Clay settled back to enjoy a weather-perfect Saturday afternoon when something caught his eye across the lake. He spotted a familiar-looking blonde figure in the distance. He strained to see better, but the figure disappeared into the shrubbery surrounding the estate. He continued to watch but didn't see it again. There was no way to be certain, but it looked like Khaki Woodson. When Larkin and Brian returned from their swim, Clay asked Larkin, "Does Dr. Thomas still own that property?" He pointed in the direction he had been looking.

"Not any more," Larkin replied, "Ash Walker owns it now. Why?"

"No reason," Clay answered, "I just wondered."

Larkin's tiki torches flickered in the dusk of late afternoon. Clay walked toward the cabin to dress for his tennis match with Khaki. Brian was so taken with Larkin and with life on the lake that he decided to spend a couple of days before leaving on a business trip to Houston. He and Larkin were taking the barge out for another cruise to watch the sunset. There was a message on Clay's answering machine when he reached the cabin. It was Khaki. "I'm sorry, Clay, something has come up. I'm going to have to cancel our tennis match. Call when you get a chance." Clay played the message back again. All afternoon Brian had kidded him about the elusive Khaki Woodson. He reached for the phone and then put it back down. I'm not going to call her now, he thought. The ball is in my court—at least for a while.

On Sunday Clay talked privately with Brian. "This is the reason I wanted you to come down," he said as he methodically began telling him everything: why he joined the *Chronicle*, Vassar's murder, what he had been told by Sheriff Dawson and Parker Phillips. He ended with Ash Walker and Camp Middleton. Brian's response was immediate, "What do you need?" he asked.

"I need you to get some information on Camp Middleton for me."

"What kind of information?"

"Anything you can find. If I request it, a red flag might go up, but with your military connections no one will suspect anything."

"I'll be in Washington next month. Say I find something, how do I get the information to you?"

"Page me. I'll go to a safe phone and call you back."

"If the Army and Defense Department are involved," Brian said, "then the Defense Intelligence Agency is probably in on it, too. If whatever you're looking for involves their dirty linen, it may be impossible to find. I'm sure it will be highly classified." Brian hesitated, "I just happen to know a certain female, a cryptologist, at Fort Meade, Maryland. She can get access to anything and she owes me an I.O.U." Then looking very serious, he said. "but that would be strictly between us... you and me."

"Certainly," Clay agreed.

"I'll see what I can do."

CHAPTER THIRTEEN

EARLY MONDAY MORNING Clay poured himself a glass of orange juice, shaved his sun-burned face and took a long, hot shower. The sofa was empty—Brian had not slept there. On the way to the Camellia Café, he planned his day. He had two articles and an editorial to write.

Dallas Dawson was the first person he saw when he reached the café. The sheriff was sitting behind a stack of pancakes and a cup of coffee.

"What's happening, Clay? Pour yourself a cup and join me."

They talked for a while before Clay told him about the argument between Vassar and Ash that Parker had overheard. "It adds up, doesn't it?" Dawson said. "What do you think she had on him?"

"I don't know, but I plan to find out."

Dawson dabbed his last piece of pancake in syrup and was about to say something else to Clay when a man walked over to the table and interrupted their conversation.

"I need to talk to you, Sheriff," he said bluntly.

"Have a seat and join us," Dawson said politely.

"Naw, I'll just stand. What I have to say won't take long. I want to know what y'all are gonna do about this nigger situation."

"What situation?" Dawson asked.

"These break-ins, robberies and harassments that merchants like myself have to contend with." The man's face was starting to grow scarlet, "There's not a business on Presley Boulevard that hasn't been burglarized in the last two months. Some have walk-in robberies in the broad open daylight. I've had two myself."

"Did you report them?" the sheriff asked.

"Hell, yeah. My wife and I run our business and she's scared to death. Yesterday a doped up, aids-infected buck nigger came into my place of business and demanded to use the phone. I was in the back working, and she told him the phone was for business use only. He called my wife a white mother fucker! I heard it and I came unglued, man." The man's face was red and the veins were popping out on his neck from rage as he continued, "I ran to the front, grabbed him by the neck and by the balls and threw the bastard out in the street. He started to come up and I put a Smith and Wesson in his face. One more word and I'd have blown him to hell."

"I'm sorry to hear that. You should have called us," the sheriff said.

"Called you? What good would that do? There's never a deputy or policeman around when you need them. They're too busy drinking coffee and chasing pussy."

Dallas Dawson was accustomed to criticism. The red-faced man was not finished. "Every day I see Sugar Red over on Summer Street wearing ten pounds of gold chains. He has two beepers and a cell phone to his mouth. Everybody knows he's a dope dealer, and what do y'all do about it? Nothin'!"

"What you say is correct, sir," Dawson said, "about Sugar Red, but we're more interested in who's supplying him. We're doing all we can with the funds we have to run our department."

"Right," the man said sarcastically, "but I can tell you this. Y'all will shit when we decide to take the law into our own hands." The man threw up his hands and walked away.

Tina interrupted. "Telephone, Sheriff," she called out. The sheriff shook his head in disgust and walked over to the counter to answer the phone.

"I've got to go," he said when he came back, "accident on the interstate. I'm going to take a couple of weeks off starting tomorrow. If something comes up, you can find me at Buck Snort. Got to build a dog pen before hunting season." Dawson gulped down his last swallow of coffee, "do you know where the deer camp is?"

"Yes, I do."

"You take care, son," Dawson said as he picked up his cap and left.

When Clay reached the *Chronicle*, the employees were talking about Parker's feature article on Frank Mingus that had appeared in Sunday's paper. A full-page spread on the civil rights activist was even more startling because of a stunning old photograph of Mingus protecting Dr. Martin Luther King during one of the marches in Alabama. The article did not exaggerate Mingus' role in the movement but simply reported the facts of his involvement with world leaders.

Clay had barely reached his office before the repercussions from the article started. The mayor of Camellia City was the first to call.

"Mr. Brady," Fats Norton said, "I understand that you're one of our boys."

"I beg your pardon?"

"You were raised in Camellia City, weren't you?"

"That's correct."

"Well, we're glad you're back home and, as you may not know, I'm the mayor but I sell insurance, too. If you need any, I can sure use the business," Fats chuckled.

"I'll keep that in mind," Clay said.

"The reason I'm calling is my concern over the feature article in yesterday's paper."

"On Frank Mingus?"

"Yes."

"What's your concern?"

"Well, my concern, Mr. Brady, is that you would not be more sensitive to our situation here."

"What situation?"

"Our Negro situation. We try very hard to keep a firm hand on things."

"I'm not sure I understand what you are trying to say."

Fats' tone became more sarcastic, "I don't have to draw a southern boy a picture, do I?"

"What's your complaint, Mr. Norton?"

"I don't like seeing a nigger's face plastered all over a paper that I have respected for years—that's my complaint. You're too young to remember, but a lot of us remember what happened to our university."

"Ole Miss."

"That's right, and to our town in the sixties. I don't want you stirring up a manure pile."

"What kind of article would you like to see?"

Fats was silent, then blurted out, "I think one on me might be appropriate. I'm the mayor, you know. I've never gotten a full-page article in the paper."

"I thought you might suggest that," Clay replied.

"Let me put it this way, Brady," Fats' voice grew nastier, "we're not going to have that type of journalism in this town—no way. I'll discuss this with Ash Walker." He slammed the phone down in Clay's ear.

All morning, calls came in as a result of the article. Calls opposing the story greatly outweighed the number of those that supported it but, by noon, the circulation department had reported a dozen new subscriptions from the black community because of the feature.

The real explosion came in the afternoon. Clay heard the loud, vulgar voice before he came out of his office to see who was causing the uproar. It was Rancey James, and by the time he reached the reception desk he was waving his newspaper and cursing at everyone in sight. He threw the rolled up newspaper across the reception desk and demanded that his subscription be cancelled.

Clay stepped up, "What's the problem?" he asked.

"That goddamn nigger article. That's what the problem is. I want to see the son of a bitch that wrote it."

"If you have something to say, you can say it to me—I'm the editor and I approved it."

Rancey shook his finger in Clay's face, "You ain't shit—Ash Walker runs this paper and, when he gets back to town, he's gonna bust your ass for turning the *Chronicle* into a nigger tabloid."

Clay turned to the receptionist, "Cancel his subscription." He looked at Rancey, "You've had your say. Now, are you going to leave or am I going to call the police?"

CHAPTER FOURTEEN

T HE CAMP MIDDLETON STORY broke on schedule the following Sunday. A full section relived the war years, the construction of the base and the economic prosperity of the day. References to rumors of the sudden disappearance of troops were carefully laced throughout the text, and questions were subtly planted to elicit responses from readers who might come forward with information. The story carried both Clay and Parker's by-line and, in a sidebar, they requested that readers with information about Camp Middleton contact them.

The Lear Jet with Ash Walker aboard touched down at the Camellia City airport only a few hours after the newspaper hit the street. His Sunday afternoon was spent quietly at home going through a mountain of mail and messages. When he got to Arthur Fisher's message, he drove to his office at the *Chronicle* to return the call in private. Arthur was at home when he called.

"I have found the leak at the bank," Arthur said immediately.

"Who is it?" Ash asked.

"Tawana Phillips. Does her name ring a bell?"

"No, it doesn't."

"Her husband is a reporter at the *Chronicle*."

Ash thought for a moment, "Phillips, Parker Phillips. His

wife?"

"Yes. That's why she talked so freely to Vassar. She didn't think she had done anything wrong. She said Vassar told her she was taking care of some business for you and needed the information."

"So that's how she found out?"

"Yes. What do you want me to do, Ash? She's a minority and terminating her could have repercussions."

"As soon as we hang up, call your attorney. Tell him she broke confidentiality, then fire her. I want her out of the bank first thing tomorrow morning."

Ash Walker did not know his conversation was being monitored and taped. A tiny transmitter, smaller than a pencil eraser, had been placed inside his telephone receiver while he was in Europe. Before he left the office, Ash checked his answering machine. There were no messages from Lee Bradford. Good, he thought. Maybe now that the leak has been found this whole matter would be resolved.

It was after dinner when Ash started pursuing the stack of newspapers on his desk. When he saw the article on Frank Mingus he was furious and had just finished reading it when calls came in from Fats Norton and Rancey. It was sometime later that he found the Camp Middleton article and read it over and over, trying to decide what to do.

Ash Walker was faced with a dilemma. Above all he did not want Lee Bradford to know that the problem had resurfaced. He knew that the article on Camp Middleton was much more than a coincidence. There had to be a link between Vassar and Clay. He never would have believed that Clay would be so bold right on the heels of Vassar's murder. The article itself was not too obvious to the average reader, but he caught the hook and, if others did, it could open up a real stinking can of worms. Ash weighed his options. He could not let Clay know he was reacting to the Middleton article—that would be a dead giveaway. Removing him from the paper would take some real finesse but would be much simpler than terminating the young reporter's life without Bradford getting wind of it. Before he slept he came up with a solution.

MONDAY MORNING Clay arrived at the *Chronicle* and stopped in the lounge for a few minutes to talk with Parker. He picked up his mail from Martha and went to his office. There was a warm note from his brother, Carl, inviting him to visit in New Orleans. Across the bottom of the page Carl had written, "Hope you like your new job." Clay read it twice, folded it and put it in his attaché.

Around 9:30 a.m. at the *Chronicle*'s switchboard, the receptionist was putting a sobbing Tawana Phillips through to Parker.

"You got what?" Parker asked in total disbelief.

"I got fired," Tawana repeated, "just a few minutes ago."

"Where are you?" Parker asked.

"At a pay phone." Tawana was becoming hysterical.

"Tawana, Tawana, calm down. I'm sure there has been a mistake. They couldn't just fire you."

"Yes, they did," Tawana continued. "They had my check cut and everything. Mr. Fisher told me he was disappointed in me."

"Disappointed in what?" Parker was becoming angry.

"Disappointed because I broke confidentiality."

"Broke confidentiality?"

"Yes," Tawana sobbed into the phone.

"What confidentiality? What do you mean?"

"He said I disclosed some information about one of Mr. Walker's accounts." Parker held the phone out in complete disbelief.

"Tell me exactly what happened, Tawana," he said in a calm but firm manner.

"A few months ago I gave Ms. Lawrence some information about one of Mr. Walker's accounts. I thought it was all right with her being your boss and everything."

"Tawana, why didn't you tell me about it?"

"I didn't think I did anything wrong."

"Listen to me, I can't come to you now. Just do as I say. Promise me."

"I promise."

"Go to your mother's and tell her what has happened. I'll come over at noon. It's not the end of the world. Everything will be okay, I promise." Parker was careful to hide the worry in his voice.

BEFORE NOON ASH Walker walked into Clay's office. "How's it going, Clay?" he said in a friendly tone.

"Great," Clay answered.

"Could I interrupt you for a few minutes?"

"Sure," Clay said as he shook Ash's hand. "How was Europe?"

"Wet. It rained almost every day." Ash told Clay about the highlights of his vacation, including a detailed account of the night spots in Amsterdam. "Amsterdam," he said, "makes a man feel like he's 21 all over again. But you're too young to appreciate that quite yet, Clay," he added.

It was hard to believe that the man in front of him could be the same person that was involved in a conspiracy to commit murder. His manner was caring, almost fatherly. He asked Clay how he liked living at Dixie Springs and if he had had an opportunity to enjoy any tennis at Willow Wood. When the conversation got to the *Chronicle*, Ash said, "You have made a lot of changes in our paper in such a short period of time." He rose from his chair and walked to the office door, "Do you mind if I close this?" he said.

"Not at all," Clay responded.

"I'm going to ask you to do something for me—a favor," Ash said as he began to preface his statement. "I'm fully aware that when you and I last talked that I promised not to interfere with matters of personnel, but something has come up."

"What?" Clay asked guardedly.

"I guess you could say it's a personal matter. It involves Parker Phillips. He's been made managing editor, I understand."

"Yes. And is doing an outstanding job. He's putting in a lot of long hard hours."

"I want you to fire him." Ash said it as casually as you would ask someone the time of day.

"You want me to fire Parker?" Clay asked.

"Yes, immediately."

"Why?"

"I'm not a racist," Ash said hypocritically, "but it's that Frank Mingus article. We can't have that. Parker Phillips is a malignant troublemaker—a troublemaker that will have to be removed."

Clay stood up and walked to the window to collect his thoughts. Finally, he turned to Ash, shaking his head, "I can't do that."

"You can't or you won't?"

"Both. I'm the one that approved the article. Not only is it quality journalism, but this paper must show some degree of fairness to the black community."

Ash showed no disappointment—everything was playing out just as he planned. "I was afraid that you would say that," he said.

"I'm sorry, it's a matter of principle."

Ash rose from his chair. "That's unfortunate, Clay. Very unfortunate." Rapping his knuckles against the desk, he turned and left Clay standing in the middle of his office.

Parker listened in silence when Clay told him about what Ash had asked him to do. Then he related to Clay the conversation he had just had with Tawana and told him she had been fired.

"I'll just resign," Parker said. "I don't want to put you in a bad position."

"No way," Clay replied, "we knew that we would both lose our jobs, but we are not going to make it that easy for him. If he wants to fire us then he'll just have to do it."

"You're right. I'm going to just sit tight."

The rest of the day went without incident.

THE NEXT MORNING Michael Tipton was waiting outside the *Chronicle* for someone to open the door. He was the senior partner of Tipton, Tipton and Associates and the attorney that handled Ash Walker's affairs. When Martha arrived for work she knew something important was about to happen. Michael Tipton did not make courtesy calls. "Good morning," she said cordially.

"I'm here to see Clay Brady."

Martha looked over at Clay's office, then in the direction of the parking lot. "He's driving up now," she said.

Clay opened the *Chronicle*'s doors, whistling, nodded to Martha and walked briskly past the balding attorney standing next to her. Martha followed him to his office. "Clay, Michael Tipton, Mr. Walker's attorney, is here to see you." For the first time in weeks deep furrows returned to her forehead.

"Send him in."

Michael Tipton, wearing a seersucker suit carrying a stuffed briefcase, entered Clay's office. Tipton's face was flush and bloated from years of too many martinis. He introduced himself and took a seat in front of Clay's desk. "Mr. Brady," he said, "I'm afraid that I'm not here this morning on a very pleasant mission."

"Oh?" Clay responded.

"No, as a matter of fact, I've been sent to terminate your employment."

"You mean you have come to fire me?"

"We had hoped for a letter of resignation, you know, to save both parties embarrassment."

"No way."

"As you wish." Tipton reached into his briefcase. "I have a check here." He handed it to Clay. "The amount pays off your contract in full. You can see Mr. Walker is a generous man."

Clay did not comment.

"Mr. Walker wants you to vacate this office immediately."

"That won't be any problem," Clay responded.

The lawyer closed his briefcase and stood up. "If I were you Mr. Brady, I would take that check, pack my things, and leave Camellia City as soon as possible."

Clay glared at the attorney, "Is that a threat?"

"No, just good advice." Tipton turned and left Clay's office and knocked on Parker Phillips' office door. Before Clay could clean out his desk, Parker burst into his office waving a check. "Well, he did it. I've been fired," he said. Clay looked up, "Me too, and I'll bet he wants you out immediately."

"Yeah."

He packed, said goodbye to Martha and gave her the keys. In less than an hour he was walking out of the *Chronicle* for the last time. Clay got into his Cherokee and headed for Buck Snort Hunting Club about ten miles from town. He bumped along a rough farm-to-market road until he saw the sign at a gravel road that led to the camp. He took a left and eased underneath a canopy of oaks and pines. Patterns of sunlight filtering through the trees spotted the narrow road ahead of him. Minutes later he pulled up to the camp house and stopped beside Dawson's four-wheel drive. The house was an old two story, constructed of unpainted heart of pine.

Beat-up rockers and an old sofa sat on the front porch that ran the length of the house. Chalk white antlers were nailed to the porch's post, and dirt dauber nests were stuck to the tin roof.

When Clay got out of his Cherokee, he could hear Dawson calling out to him, "I'm back here behind the house. Come on back." Clay found him at the dog pen. The sheriff was driving the last staple into a post. "What do you think?" he asked Clay as he backed up to survey his morning project.

Clay pulled on the wire, "Looks good." Three hounds pressed against the fence and licked at Clay's fingers. "Fine looking animals," Clay said.

"Thanks. That one's my favorite." Dawson was pointing to a black-and-tan. "He is cold-nosed and long-running."

"Cold-nosed?"

"Yeah. Can pick up cold trails."

"Oh, I see," Clay said smiling.

"Do you hunt, Clay?" Dawson asked.

"Killed an elk once, but I haven't been in a long time."

Dawson put down his hammer, picked up a water jug, and started walking toward the camp house. "Find yourself a chair," he said when they reached the front porch, "and tell me what brings you out."

Clay told him about being fired. "Does your brother know yet?" the sheriff asked.

"Not yet. I'll call him later."

Dawson slowly unscrewed the lid from his water jug and turned it up to his mouth. Trickles of water ran down the corners of his mouth and dripped on his blue denim shirt. He wiped his chin with the back of his hand and continued talking. "So, Clay, what are your plans?"

"I'm going to find out what Vassar Lawrence discovered that got her killed."

Dawson shook his head. "Maybe we can help each other."

"How's that?"

"You want the story and I want Vassar Lawrence's killers, all of them. Whatever you find out should be an airtight motive. You tell me what you find out, and I'll watch your back."

"That sounds fair enough," Clay said.

"You have a firearm?" Dawson asked.

"Yes."

"Then keep it with you. I'm afraid this isn't going to be easy," Dawson said.

"You mean the investigation?"

"Ash Walker has friends in very high places."

"Like his friend the senator?"

"Yeah. Ash and the senator have a neat little drug business going on down here. Rancey and a redneck by the name of Toxie Hux oversee that operation. I tipped off the state narc boys about it. They investigated and told me that it was a no-win deal and that we would never be able to prosecute Walker. They told me not to pursue the matter."

"What did you do?"

"Nothing. But the D.A. contacted the FBI and asked for their help. He told them he wanted to know why Ash Walker was untouchable."

"What did they say?"

"Very little. Told him they would check into it, but that was almost a year ago, and he doesn't know anymore than he did. When he calls they give him the run-around."

"What about a capital murder charge?"

Dawson looked down at the ground, then up at Clay. "The son of a bitch won't beat that, not if I can help it." Dawson cocked his head to one side and put his finger to his lips. He lowered his voice. "Something's up." There was an eerie silence around them, not a bird chirping, not a squirrel barking. The shadow from a hawk soaring above crossed the yard and then, like a lightning bolt, a ball of brown and white feathers streaked to the ground. There was a loud thump and the squeal of a baby rabbit. In the opening in front of the camp house, the hawk, with the rabbit clutched in its talons, rose and disappeared over the tree tops. "Life in the wild is uncertain, isn't it?" Clay commented.

Dawson stared into the distance. "Life is uncertain period." The two men sat in silence for a little while before Clay spoke. "Sheriff," he said, "tell me, did you read the Frank Mingus article?"

"I did."

"What did you think?"

"I think it was well deserved and overdue."

Clay was surprised. "Really?" he asked.

"Really."

"What about the article on Camp Middleton?"

"Yep. I read it, too. I was just a chap back then, but it brought back some memories—good article."

Clay smiled and settled back on the sofa. "Sheriff Dawson, I was raised in Topisaw County, but the truth is, I know very little about its history. Tell me how you see this race/hate-type mentality that I'm encountering everywhere."

Dallas Dawson propped his legs up on a chair, "Boy," he said, "this county's history is as violent as the tornadoes that rip through here."

"I know that," Clay said, "but how did it start?"

"In the 1920s there was a blood-sucking Texas Tick that came through here and contaminated all the cattle. Farmers lost their milk and beef production. The federal government mandated a program to build concrete vats that would hold an arsenic solution for dipping livestock."

"Arsenic? Didn't that kill the cattle?"

"No, but it wasn't popular with the farmers. The government sent inspectors and Range Riders to execute the plan, and they poached on private property making sure every one of those four-legged animals was dipped."

"What happened to those that would not comply?"

"Hell, they were fined. Some of them were beaten if they were too stubborn."

"Did everyone fall in line?"

"No. They came up with a solution. They hated the federal government and distrusted every one of those 'gol-darned' programs. One hot summer night, 17 of the vats were blown to bits. That sent the inspectors and Range Riders packing, fearing for their lives."

"Blown up with dynamite?"

"Right. And the answer to government interference around here was born. This dynamite solution was passed down from generation to generation. It worked."

Clay was listening intently. The sheriff took another long draw from his water bottle and continued, "During the Depression a stream of hookworm-infested farm boys left the fields to come to town in search of work in the railroad shops. For the first time they would have to compete with black men for jobs."

"I'll bet they didn't like that." Clay said.

"No, they didn't. Losing out to the blacks over jobs as scarce as those built resentment. But these boys not only resented the black men but any kind of change in the status quo."

"What we called 'redneck mentality,'" Clay said. "I knew that in the sixties all hell broke loose, but then after that the Klan started breaking up. I thought that was something positive."

"No, it really wasn't. Its members just went underground. Now they are in secret cells all over the county. One of their divisions meets regularly out at the old fire tower. They don't think I know that..." Dawson paused, "but I do. All in all,"

Dawson concluded, "we're probably sitting on a time bomb in this county. Anything could happen at any time. My advice to you would be to leave and never look back."

Clay laughed out loud. "That's the second time I've heard that advice today."

Clay thanked the sheriff for his time, "I'd better let you get back to your dog pen," he said as he looked at his watch. He shook the lawman's hand and left for Dixie Springs.

On his way to the cabin, Clay stopped at Larkin's house and found Khaki's Volvo wagon parked in the driveway. Khaki was on the phone in the kitchen and, when she saw him, ended her conversation abruptly. "I've been up to your cabin looking for you. You really should lock your door. I went inside and I think I recognized your decorator." Clay laughed as Khaki continued, "Yes, the stained glass and plants definitely had Larkin's touch." Clay leaned on the counter next to her and listened as her conversation became more serious. "I just came from a Wentworth College fundraiser meeting with Ash Walker and your name came up. He said you are no longer with the *Chronicle*."

"That's right," Clay was matter-of-fact.

"That's why I came up here. I wanted to see you and talk to you." Khaki seemed genuinely concerned, "What happened?"

"I guess you could say that Ash Walker and I have different ideas about management."

Khaki's question became more probing, "Vassar Lawrence actually hired you, didn't she?"

"Yes, she did."

"And the two of you shared the same ideas?"

"She was killed. I never had the chance to find out."

"Do you have any theories about that? About her murder?"

"No," Clay answered, "Do you?"

Khaki looked away quickly, "No," she said, "and I don't suppose we ever will."

"I wouldn't bet on that," Clay said. A smiling Larkin burst through the front door. "I just took your friend to the airport. You didn't know he was here last night, did you?"

"Brian was here last night?"

"Came in late and had to leave real early. Something came up with an account, but he'll be back."

"You sound pretty sure of yourself," Clay teased.

"Honey, I'd bet my life on it. What are you two doing here so early?"

Clay told her about the job, and the three of them chatted for a while. Finally, Khaki said she had to go back to close her office. There was something about Khaki Woodson that concerned him. Underneath her seductive beauty was a veneer of professional coolness that he could not figure out. Was she caring and concerned or just curious?

She touched his arm warmly, "What are your plans? Does this mean you will be leaving Camellia City?"

"I haven't made any definite plans, but I won't be leaving anytime soon." Clay was studying her for a reaction. There was nothing to read. "Stay in touch," she said.

"Okay," he said, "thanks for coming up."

When Khaki reached her office, she picked up her phone and dialed a familiar number. "I've planted the bug in the cabin, and Clay Brady has no plans to leave Camellia City anytime soon."

CHAPTER FIFTEEN

T HE NEXT NIGHT Clay was alone when he received an anonymous call at his cabin.

"You the Brady from the newspaper?" the caller asked.

"Yes, I am."

"You the one looking for information on Camp Middleton?"

"Yes," Clay said, "let me get a pen."

"No," the caller said and quickly added, "not over the phone."

"Where can I meet you then?"

"You know where the fire tower is at Felder's Ridge?"

"Yes, I do."

"Meet me there, but come alone. You understand?"

"Yes," Clay said and looked at his watch. "It's 9:15 now. What time do you want me to be there?"

"Ten. But come alone."

Clay heard a click on the other end and then a dial tone.

Felder's Ridge was a good 30-minute drive from Dixie Springs, and Clay lost little time as he sped down the country roads. When he reached Felder's Ridge, he turned right on a one lane gravel road that came to a dead end at the 100-foot steel structure.

The Cherokee rolled to a stop. Clay looked for a car or

truck but saw neither. He turned off the engine and head-lights and checked the clock on his dashboard. It was 9:55. As he sat and waited, he opened the glove compartment and took out his fully-loaded nine millimeter automatic and stuck it underneath his belt in the small of his back. At 10:15 he reached for his flashlight, got out of the Cherokee and walked toward the fire tower. He thought he would climb up a few flights of the tower steps to see if he could see any car lights headed in his direction. As he walked, he panned the treeline with the beam of his flashlight. "Hello," he called out in the still, dark night.

No answer.

He called out again—still no answer. Less than 100 yards away, Toxie Hux sat in a pine thicket listening and watching.

Clay flashed his light in the direction of the tower—and that is when he saw the silhouette of a figure sitting half way up the first flight of steps.

"It's me, Brady," he announced as he walked toward the person. Clay was much closer now and flashed his light directly on the seated figure. Instantly Clay froze in his tracks. A motionless black man sat tied to the steps in a pool of blood. Clay instinctively reached for his pistol and walked cautiously closer. Eyes as lifeless as peeled grapes stared back at him. The bloody dreadlocks partially covered the knife wound to his throat. The gold chains were no longer around his neck, but Sugar Red's gold front tooth glistened in the light of the flashlight. Clay reached for his hand—there was no pulse. Turning off the flashlight, Clay bolted for the Cherokee. In less than a minute he was speeding down the gravel road, leaving the dead dope dealer behind.

Toxie had been watching it all. He had a double handful of gold chains to pawn and had killed two birds with one stone, he thought to himself. Sugar Red would never hold out on Rancey again, and Clay Brady would be leaving Topisaw

County come sunup—he would bet his boots on that.

CHAPTER SIXTEEN

IN BERTHA'S BACK ROOM, Parker listened intently as Clay told him about finding Sugar Red at the fire tower.

"Did you tell the authorities?"

"Yes," Clay answered, "I called and reported it, but I did not identify myself. There would have been too many questions."

"Right. Who do you think killed him?"

"I don't know, but I do know somebody wanted to send me a message. I strongly suspect Rancey James or Toxie..."

Parker interrupted, "If you get any more anonymous phone calls to rendezvous, call me. It's too dangerous for you to go alone."

Clay agreed. Their conversation turned to Camp Middleton and their investigation.

When he and Parker finished their afternoon session at Bertha's, Clay stopped by a pay phone and called Carl in New Orleans. Carl answered on the first ring, "Homicide. Lieutenant Brady." The sound and warmth of Carl's voice brought back memories of a hundred other phone calls Clay had made over the years. "Carl, this is Clay."

"What's up, Brother?" Carl asked.

"I got canned."

"You got fired from the *Chronicle*?"

"Yep."

"Hell, son, that was a short career. What did you do?"

"I thought we might get together. I need to talk to you, but I don't want to do it over the phone."

"Something's up?"

"Yeah."

"I figured that. You want me to come up?"

"No. I can come down there, but I'd rather not come to the Department."

Carl thought a moment. "What about the fountain next to the Riverwalk? How does that sound?"

"That's good. What about 3:00 Friday?"

"That will work. Are you all right?" Carl asked.

"Yeah."

"You sure?"

"Positive."

"Then I'll see you Friday. But if you need me before then, call."

Clay hung up.

When he got to his cabin he checked his messages. Khaki had called just to say hello. Clay stretched out on the sofa and punched in her number. Khaki sounded pleased to hear his voice. He said, "I wanted to know if you would like to try some ribs down at Skinney's tomorrow night?"

Khaki sounded enthusiastic, "You don't know how much I would like to, but I'm leaving in the morning for New Orleans. I will be there looking at property for the rest of the week."

"What if I told you that I have to be there on business Friday afternoon?"

"Then I would say you'd better call me. I'm staying at the Hilton on Poydras. We should be finished early Friday afternoon."

After she said goodbye to Clay, Khaki made another call. "Clay Brady is going to New Orleans Friday. He'll be driving a black Cherokee with Mississippi plates, PXV-089."

A LIGHT RAIN was falling Friday afternoon as Clay drove down Interstate 55 on his way to the Big Easy. At a rest area near the Louisiana state line, a casually dressed man wearing a New York Yankees baseball cap waited patiently for Clay's Cherokee to pass. When he saw it go by, he eased the gray Crown Victoria out of the rest area and on to the interstate without being noticed.

As Clay neared Independence, the low-flung clouds ahead of him were beginning to break into patches of blue. At Manchac he crossed the bridge over Lake Maurepas. On one side of the highway and below him was Middendorf's, a popular seafood restaurant. On the other side was the Tickfaw River. Ahead, as far as he could see, was an alligator-infested swamp.

Traffic was heavy as he neared the city. An accident had one lane of traffic completely blocked, and momentarily the man in the Ford lost the Cherokee at Williams Boulevard. Clay looked at his watch when he turned on Poydras. He was right on time. Under the canopy of the New Orleans Hilton, an attendant stepped from the curb to take his car. Clay slung the overnight bag over his shoulder and went inside to register. After leaving his bag in his room, he left the hotel and walked the short distance to the Riverwalk.

The Riverwalk was a leftover from a past world's fair —a long string of buildings on the banks of the Mississippi River that had been turned into a large shopping mall. Its unusual architectural design and outside fountain made it a favorite resting spot for tourists. Carl was sitting on a concrete bench near the fountain when Clay walked up. Carl Brady was ten years older than Clay and, at 43, was beginning to show signs of pressure and stress from 16 years with "New Orleans' Finest." His once-sharp facial features had become less defined, and the physique that he had enjoyed as a rookie had slowly eroded and stopped just short of obese. His sport coat needed pressing, his white shirt was frayed, and the tie that hung from his neck was too thin. The detective, however, had a heart as big as the Superdome.

The two brothers exchanged a warm greeting and sat down on the bench. Carl dug into his coat pocket and pulled out a bag of peanuts. "Now, Brother, tell me what's on your mind."

"How much time do you have?" Clay asked.

"As much as you need."

Clay started from the beginning. When he told him about Vassar's murder and Dallas Dawson's suspicion about the Albino, Feret Du Boise, Carl interrupted.

"Did you say Feret Du Boise?"

"Yes."

"I know that subject well," Carl said. "When I worked Vice I busted him on more than one occasion. As far as I know he's right here in New Orleans. I'll do a little checking and see what I can find out." Carl pulled a note pad from his pocket and jotted himself a reminder.

Clay picked up where he left off, and by the time he finished, a pile of peanut hulls covered the ground by his feet. Carl cracked open the last peanut from his bag and was about to speak when something across the fountain caught his eye. The detective stood up and nudged his brother's arm, "Let's get a cup of coffee. We can finish our conversation inside." Before they walked away, the man in the baseball cap raised his camera with the telephoto lens and snapped the picture he wanted. Both men were in the viewfinder and the badge that folded over Carl's belt was clearly visible.

Inside the Riverwalk, Carl stopped by the Sharper Image window and pointed to a new gadget on display. Over Clay's shoulder he could see the man with the camera standing a few storefronts away. The brothers walked to the escalators that took them to the second floor. At the first snack bar Carl ordered two coffees. "You still drink it black?"

Clay nodded. As he put it to his mouth he grimaced, "My gosh, it's strong."

"You're in Louisiana now, man. This is what we call a cup of coffee."

Clay followed Carl through some glass doors leading outside to a balcony overlooking the river. Below them a steamboat was loading tourists for an excursion. Carl stood against the balcony rails and resumed his conversation where he left off at the fountain. "So, Sheriff Dawson told you about Rancey and Ash Walker, and you and Phillips decide to go for the story?"

"Right."

"Tell me, Clay, what could have happened so earthshaking on a military base?"

"Good question."

"And, no offense, but who in the hell would care what happened 50 years ago? You're the reporter, but we're talking the 90s, man. You know, Waco, the Federal Building in Oklahoma...it would take a big story."

"I believe Vassar would have known that, Carl."

"Vassar might have been yanking your chain to get to Walker."

Carl grew serious. His concentration was broken by someone moving behind the glass doors. "I'll tell you what I think. I think you are in a world of shit."

"How so?"

"For a number of reasons. First, you know how I feel about anything that might be connected to the military. You know, Dad would have had a birthday last week. Did you remember?"

"Yes, I did."

"Second, you're running around all over south Mississippi, with a black man, asking a bunch of rednecks the same questions that got Vassar Lawrence killed. And third, there's this Woodson blonde that you haven't even mentioned a word about. If she's fucking Ash Walker, then that alone could get you killed." Carl could tell by the way Clay looked that he had struck a nerve. "And, finally, someone is already on your tail. He's inside, Yankees cap and camera, do you see him?"

Clay looked inside, "Yes, now I do."

The man with the camera, suspecting that he had been spotted, disappeared into the crowd. Carl threw his coffee cup in the trash and put an arm around Clay's shoulder. "All I'm saying is that if you believe that this story is worth it, and I'm sure you do, then you're going to have to go for it—but be careful. Dawson says that Rancey is mean enough and Walker is smart enough to get you killed. And don't underestimate Ash Walker, old men have less to lose. If the government is involved, they can bring in some heat that would make those two old men look like choir boys."

"I know."

"So, now that I've had my say, how can I help you?"

"I don't need anything yet. I just wanted to lay it out. Tell me, apparently you've been talking to Sheriff Dawson. Did he tell you about Khaki Woodson?"

"Yes, he did. He has some suspicions about her and is afraid she could cause you some trouble. Are you heading straight back to Mississippi?"

"No. I thought I might kick around the city, and go back tomorrow morning."

"If you need a place to stay we have a spare room, and you know you're always welcome. Laura's cooking lasagna tonight."

"Thanks, but I've already checked into the Hilton down

the street. But tell Laura I'll take a rain check on that lasagna."

As they walked out of the mall, they said goodbye and Carl warned him once again to be careful. "Watch your back," he said. Carl did not return to the station after leaving Clay at the Riverwalk. Instead, he told his partner that they had a personal matter to work. He explained that Clay was an investigative reporter on assignment and that he had picked up a tail in New Orleans. "I'm going to make sure he doesn't get hurt in my city," he said. Carl and his partner watched Clay's every move and when he returned to the Hilton, they were close by.

The telephone was ringing in Khaki's hotel room when she opened the door. It was Clay calling from the lobby. In less than 30 minutes she had showered and changed clothes, picked up her leather shoulder bag and was headed for the elevator. She found Clay scanning the pages of *The Times Picayune* and eased up behind him, gently tapping him on the shoulder. "That didn't take long, did it?" she asked.

"It was worth the wait—you look wonderful. I thought we might ride out to Lake Ponchartrain, watch the sunset and have dinner. How does that sound to you?"

"It sounds great!"

When Clay and Khaki emerged from the Hilton, Carl's partner whistled under his breath, "Your brother sure has good taste in women." Carl studied the blonde smiling up at his brother and played a hunch. He picked up his cellular phone and called the Hilton front desk, "Khaki Woodson, please," he said when they answered. Immediately, they were ringing her room. "Just what I suspected," Carl exclaimed when he hung up. Quickly, he instructed his partner to go inside the hotel and pull any information he could find on Khaki's guest registration. "I'm going to follow them. Get a uniform to pick you up and we'll rendezvous later."

The Hong Kong Chinese restaurant shares the beach of

Lake Ponchartrain with an exclusive New Orleans yacht club. When Khaki saw the sailboat masts, she forgot her appetite. "Clay, let's look at the boats first," she said excitedly as they got out of the Cherokee. She was dragging Clay down the pier. A breeze from the south rattled the sailboat's halyards against metal riggings as she walked by. There were sailboats of every size and description, but she had spotted her favorite. *The Lottery* was an auxiliary sloop with 38 feet of beautiful lines. She was snow white with black and moved elegantly in her slip as the swells rose and fell. As they drew closer to her, they could see a distinguished looking man and woman dressed in ice cream colored clothes sitting underneath a canvas awning in the boat's cockpit. The man was wearing a captain's hat. Khaki was telling Clay all about sailboats and sailing. The man in the captain's hat could hear her clearly. He was impressed at her apparent knowledge of sailing and was taken by her effusive compliments. As they moved down the narrow walkway to get a closer look at the boat, the captain spoke to them politely. "As you can see, the sun is well over the yardarm; come aboard and join us for a cocktail."

Khaki looked eagerly to Clay and hoped he would say yes. "Sure," Clay answered, and Khaki reached up for the older man's hand. As Clay climbed aboard, the captain introduced himself. "I'm Paul Blanchard and this is my wife, Frances." Clay and Khaki in turn introduced themselves.

"Join me in the galley, Khaki, and we'll make the drinks," Frances said, after the men had given her their drink preferences.

Khaki put the finishing touches on a tray of hors d'oeuvres that Frances took out of the cooler, and they returned topside to join the men. Captain Blanchard was saying to Clay, "My boat is new, but I'm not." Clay guessed that their well-tanned host was in his late 60s.

"The Captain is retired Navy, Khaki," Clay explained, as he brought the women into the conversation.

"And a veteran of years of sailing for pleasure," said the attractive, vivacious Frances, as she glanced lovingly at her husband.

"I thought this boat must be owned by one of the new casinos," Khaki said, "with a name like *The Lottery*."

"Oh, no, we're just hoping to get some very select charters from the new gaming industry," the silver-haired sailor responded.

They had almost finished their drinks when the conversation turned from sailing to "who do you know?" Paul Blanchard was surprised to learn that Clay's brother was the same Carl Brady that he had known for years. "Our seats are right next to Carl and Laura's at the Superdome."

"I guess you've consoled each other many times, watching the Saints lose," Clay said.

"Too many times," Blanchard agreed.

"What a small world," Frances said, as she stood up to prepare a second round of drinks.

"We'll have to be going," Clay said, declining the drink offer. "I have made reservations at the Hong Kong, and they promised me the most romantic table in the house to impress this lady. I don't want them to give it to someone else." He winked at Khaki.

They invited their hosts to join them for dinner, but the Blanchards explained that they were expecting friends for dinner on the boat. "You guys are welcome aboard 'The Lottery' anytime," Captain Blanchard said.

"And please tell Carl and Laura we said hello," added Frances.

The Hong Kong was dark—its only light were the candles on the table and the lights from the marina. Its rattan furniture and oriental decor gave it a feeling of intimacy. Clay had asked for a table near a window. When the waitress came, he ordered drinks. Khaki loved the place. "Is the food equal to the atmosphere?" she asked.

"Absolutely," Clay smiled at her.

"Clay," she said softly, "thank you for bringing me here." She rubbed the side of his fingers sensuously with her own. She liked his rugged good looks and the sexy way he looked at her. When his hand curled around hers, she felt an instant response. In a restaurant packed with people, there seemed to be only the two of them. When it became too dark to watch the boats at the marina, Clay ordered dinner. They had decided on shrimp and lobster. Khaki looked beautifully mysterious in the flickering candlelight. He was crazy about her.

Carl was waiting outside the Hong Kong when his partner caught up with him. "What did you find on her?" Carl asked.

The partner handed him a slip of paper, "Not much," he said, "credit card and Mississippi driver's license number, home address, that's about it." Carl thanked him and told him to go on home for the night. He was going to solo the stake-out from here. Carl picked up the mike on his radio, "12 to Central."

"This is Central. Go ahead."

"I need anything I can find on a Khaki Woodson, Mississippi driver's license 425-76-8076."

"12, do you have this subject in custody?"

"Negative. I'm in the blind."

"10-4."

Clay and Khaki talked over dinner about everything from music to politics. Khaki asked him all about his past, where he had lived, the college he attended, playing football and his newspaper career. She asked a lot of questions about his investigative reporting for the *States Times* and specific questions about Vassar Lawrence's death. She had many questions about his short stay at the *Chronicle*, but Ash Walker's name was never mentioned.

Clay was not as comfortable answering questions as he was asking them, so he skillfully began to regain the conversation and turn it around. Khaki was open enough about her past, almost too open. Her answers seemed canned. After dinner, over coffee, he asked her how she became interested in sailing. She told him about her dad, his love for boats and the Chesapeake Bay. She had made an unforgettable trip with her father to Cayos Cachinos, the island off the coast of La Cieba, Honduras. She described how untouched it was, with water so clear you could see forever, reefs teeming with beautiful fish, palm trees, sparkling sand and parrots. It was an island that could only be reached by boat or seaplane. "Very few people even know that the tiny resort on the island exists," she said. "If a person ever wanted to drop out and never be found, that's the place to go," she concluded.

The waitress brought Clay's check and a fortune cookie for Khaki. She broke it open and pulled out the paper with the fortune that read, "Make a wish." She handed it to Clay and closed her eyes.

"What did you wish?" he asked.

"Can't tell," she said. "It's a secret."

On the way back to the city, Clay told Khaki that there was a place in the French Quarter that he wanted them to check out.

"And I'll bet they play a little jazz there," she teased.

"I sure hope so. A friend of mine told me it is the place to go."

Clay turned off Esplanade onto Frenchmen Street, drove one block past the Praline Connection and parked in a lot across from Snug Harbor Jazz Bistro. Snug Harbor has the reputation of being New Orleans' premier jazz club. A hostess led them through a restaurant with black slate floors and walls of old brick and cypress. Large photographs of jazz greats decorated the interior. The two-story music room in the back had a seating capacity of only 90 people. The hostess directed Clay and Khaki to a table on the upper floor overlooking the stage. Stars twinkled through a glass skylight directly above them. The room's atmosphere was as cool as the jazz they would hear for the next three hours. Parker had been right, Clay thought, this is definitely where it's happening in the Big Easy. It was after they had heard two sets that Clay and Khaki left the Bistro and, as they rode back to the hotel, both were silent. Finally, Khaki asked the question that had to be asked. "Clay, are you involved with anyone?"

"No," he answered, "Are you?"

"Not really," she said.

He wanted to know what "not really" meant but chose not to pursue it. Go with the moment, he thought to himself. Here he was with the most beautiful woman he had ever seen, in one of the most romantic cities in the world. It was after midnight and the last thing on his mind was asking more questions.

In the unmarked car parked a discreet distance from the Hilton's entrance, Carl's two-way radio broke the silence.

"Central to 12."

"Go ahead, Central."

"I have the information you requested. Do you want it now?"

"10-4."

"Subject has a valid Mississippi driver's license, no tickets, no warrants."

"Anything else?"

"I'm still checking."

"10-4. Make me a copy if anything else turns up and put it in my basket."

"WHAT FLOOR?" Clay asked when they walked inside the

Hilton elevator. Khaki held up three fingers. He looked at her—she was looking at him. He pressed 15 and pulled Khaki to him. "You didn't press my floor," she whispered in his ear. "I know," he replied, and then he kissed her—a long exploring kiss that lasted long after the elevator door opened. In his room overlooking the city where, for centuries, dreams and loves had been lost, Clay and Khaki found each other.

Clay was awakened the next morning by a maid knocking on his door. He reached over for Khaki, but she was not beside him. Streams of warm sunlight from the partially opened blinds filled the room. He called her name. No answer. The only thing that remained from the night before was the smell of her perfume on the pillow beside him. He searched for his shorts, found them and looked at his watch. It was almost eight a.m.

In the bathroom he found the note she left him sticking out of his shaving kit. "You were sleeping so peacefully, I couldn't bear to wake you. I'll tell you how special last night was when I see you. Give me a call when you get back."

Clay took a long hot shower, dressed and checked out of the hotel. He couldn't get her out of his mind. He found a jewelry store in the Riverwalk and looked there for the special gift for her. It had to be perfect, just the right size, something petite in gold. He wanted a sailboat. He found it in a black velvet display box, purchased it and had it gift wrapped.

On his way back to Camellia City, he stopped at Manchac for coffee. While he enjoyed his coffee and read the morning paper, a busy Khaki Woodson was inside his cabin at Lake Dixie Springs going through all his files, his letters, even his laptop computer. She was certain that not even Larkin had seen her drive by and was positive no one had seen her picking the lock. Her search was interrupted by the telephone ringing. The answering machine activated after a few rings, and Carl Brady left his message—"Brother, give me a call when you get in. I have some information on your blonde that may interest you." Khaki thought to herself, "Not just yet, Carl, not just yet." She pressed the erase button and continued her search.

When Clay returned to Camellia City, he tried to call Khaki but failed to reach her at her office or at home. He ran a few errands, went by the grocery store and drove to the lake. Khaki's Volvo was parked outside Larkin's as he pulled in. They stood in the kitchen looking at each other like two sophomores on their first date. Larkin quietly watched, amused at their change in behavior. "I almost forgot," Clay said, "I have something for you." He went out to the Cherokee and came back with the present.

"Well," Larkin said, "have I missed something with you guys or what?"

Khaki tore into the tiny package, opened the box and pulled out the gold chain and sailboat charm. "Oh, Clay, it's beautiful!" She kissed him again and turned around so that he could fasten the clasp around her neck. She stood smiling in his arms until Larkin broke the mood. "Are you two going to tell me what happened in New Orleans or not?"

Both Clay and Khaki shook their heads and answered, "No way."

"When is Brian coming?" Clay asked Larkin.

"I think he will be flying in tomorrow," she answered.

"Good. Maybe we can get in a little tennis. How does that sound to you, Khaki?"

Khaki looked pensive. "It sounds good, but I'm afraid I can't. I've got to go back out of town on business."

Clay was disappointed. "But you've just gotten back."

"I know, but I have to leave for a couple of days. It's not like I wouldn't want to play. It sounds like fun, really."

"I understand."

"Are you sure?"

"I'm sure."

The three of them made margaritas and walked out on the deck together. A short time later, Khaki said that she had to go back to the office and finish up some paperwork. Clay said, "I was hoping you could come by the cabin for a while."

"Not this time, I can't. I've got a lot to do before tomorrow. I've just got to go," Khaki said apologetically, "I'll see you as soon as I get back."

CHAPTER SEVENTEEN

THE CAMP MIDDLETON MYSTERY began to unravel Sunday morning. Clay was drinking coffee and watching some bass feeding around his pier when his beeper went off. The calling number left a District of Columbia area code. He grabbed his car keys and raced down to the nearest pay phone outside the Landing. When he returned the call, a female answered from a pay phone in Washington. Clay could barely hear her for the street noise on her end of the line. "I am a friend of Brian's. I have some information on Camp Middleton in my computer," she said, "send me your public key and I will encrypt the information to your e-mail. There's more, but all of this information is classified and may take a while." She hung up.

As Clay was hanging up the phone, Larkin's red Miata pulled off the highway and came to a stop next to him. A grinning Brian was driving. "What's up, buddy?" he called to Clay over the engine noise. "Is something wrong with your phone?"

"No," Clay said, "I was getting some important information." He gave Brian a thumbs up signal.

Larkin's expression was one Clay had never seen on her before. "What's wrong?" he asked, "are you two fighting?"

"Of course not," Larkin rebuffed.

"Go ahead and tell him," Brian said.

"Tell me what?" Clay was curious.

Brian coaxed again, "Go ahead."

Larkin spilled it. "I hate to tell you this, but I just saw your girlfriend when I was picking up Brian at the airport."

"Really?"

"She was getting in Ash Walker's Lear Jet, and he was with her."

Clay felt it. It was as if someone hit him in the stomach with a baseball bat.

Larkin angrily continued, "The way she was with you yesterday—and now this morning she's leaving for a la-la with Ash Walker. She's a friend of mine, but she was just using you."

Clay held up his hand, "Don't say anymore. I get the picture, believe me, I get the picture."

For the first time, Larkin saw him speechless. Brian tried to ease the situation, break the tension, "Come on down to Larkin's. It's party time. We'll burn some meat, pop a few tops and let the good times roll."

Clay smiled, masking his feelings, "Sounds like what I need, but I have to do some work first. You guys go ahead and I'll catch up to you later."

When he reached his cabin, he called up the decoding utility on his laptop computer and the e-mail opened. The word "CLASSIFIED" came up on the screen in bold caps. Clay scrolled down the page. The first document from Brian's contact was on a NAACP Legal Defense Fund letterhead and was from their office on Fifth Avenue in New York. The letter was dated June 5, 1943. It was addressed to the Honorable Ted Stringer, Acting Civilian Aide to the Secretary of War in Washington, D.C. It was a cover letter stating that the NAACP lawyers had taken the attached deposition from Corporal George Johnson concerning treatment of black soldiers at

Camp Middleton in Camellia City, Mississippi.

Corporal Johnson, under oath, stated in his deposition that the military police and civilian authorities in Camellia City acted in concert with each other to administer cruel treatment to the 344th Infantry from the time the regiment arrived in Mississippi. Corporal Johnson gave examples of beatings, a shooting by civilian law officers and cruel punishments for such infractions as walking on the "white only" side of the street in Camellia City. Military police as well as civilian authorities refused to allow the colored soldiers to mix with local colored population, saying that the "Northern niggers would spoil the local colored people." Corporal Johnson left Camp Middleton and Camellia City absent without leave on June 3, 1943 at 12 o'clock, fleeing in fear of his life. The deposition was sworn to and notarized in Birmingham, Alabama.

Clay moved on to the second document. It was a strong letter of protest to the War Department from a black staff sergeant at Camp Middleton dated June 7, 1943. Again, it related that military police and civilian authorities were taking it upon themselves to whip the 344th Infantry into submission and to "subjugate" them. This letter asked, "Could the War Department be collaborating with the civilian authorities of the South in subjugating this regiment which has caused such a disturbance in the past few months, by knowingly sending them to a place where racial conflict is inevitable due to the stubbornness of both factors? If such is the case, then we, the soldiers of color, might just as well lay down our arms, for the fight in which we are so willingly sacrificing our lives is already lost."

Clay then read another letter from a black soldier who had been stationed at Camp Middleton. This soldier asked the profound question, "Why should I go overseas to fight for freedoms that I don't even have here in my own country?"

Clay read through several sworn testimonies of eyewitnesses to crimes against black soldiers. One, the brutal murder of a soldier just off the base by a civilian sheriff, was particularly descriptive. "Five colored soldiers in the town of Camellia City were stopped by military police who ordered one of them to button up his shirt sleeve. The soldier informed the MP that the button had been detached and he had been unable to replace it. Two MPs leaped from their jeep, brandishing black jacks, and one of them proceeded to attack the soldier who had no button on his shirt sleeve. The remaining soldiers persuaded the other MP to let the men fight it out and let the best man win. But the MP, obviously getting the worst of the battle, noticed the sheriff of the town, Mr. Gregory, coming up with his two deputies and called out, 'Sheriff, shoot this nigger!' The soldier then straightened up and said, 'No, you won't shoot me.' Whereupon Sheriff Gregory drew his revolver saying, 'The hell I won't!' and, firing point blank at the soldier, struck him in the chest. The sheriff then turned to the MP and asked, 'Any more niggers you want killed?'"

The letter went on to tell of other disastrous encounters between the Negro soldiers and military police.

The last and most earnest plea to the War Department was dated in early June of 1943. It, too, was classified. Corporal Thomas Lowery wrote for help begging, "Please, from my heart, do something for the fellows and myself who are so unfortunate as to be in this State of Blood—Negro blood— that is constantly flowing in the streets." Corporal Lowery's desperation was bone chilling, and Clay read quickly this account of white MPs armed to the teeth beating defenseless men. "Yesterday, Sunday, a soldier of the 344th was shot and killed by white MPs. We aren't even safe in the Post area. From the white section of camp came four armored scout cars, each with about ten MPs. Tonight, just an hour ago, one of my fellow soldier friends came back from an intended overnight pass. He had been beaten about the head by the white MPs." Corporal Lowery begged for help fearing for his life, declaring that all firing pins had been removed from the rifles and ammunition had been confiscated, leaving them defenseless.

Clay re-read the information and called Parker to come to the cabin immediately. When Parker read the letters, he was surprised that they had not been able to find any hint of these problems in their research.

"Why didn't these incidents make the newspaper?" he asked Clay.

"That's a good question. They must have issued a gag order, that's all I can figure. Parker, remember the information from the military maids about the murders after the 'new troops arrived?' Do you suppose the 'new troops' could have been the 344th?"

"I don't know."

Parker picked up the staff sergeant's letter and underlined the part where he accused the War Department of collaborating with civilian authorities of the South in subjugating the regiment by sending them to a place where racial conflict was inevitable. He wrote in the margin next to that paragraph, "Check this out."

Clay was disappointed in himself for not thinking about racial tension as being an angle in the story. "What kind of investigative reporters are we, Parker, not to have asked any questions about race? Still, I am surprised that we would find racial unrest on an Army base, and during wartime." The telephone interrupted their communication. Clay did not answer. Khaki left a message on his answering machine, but he had decided he would not return her call.

Parker was a student of black history and quickly gave Clay a briefing on the role of the black soldiers in World War II and some of the trouble they encountered. "You realize that black and white troops were segregated in World War II, and many Army bases reported racial problems?"

Clay was about to suggest that they research that subject more extensively when the telephone rang, again interrupting their conversation.

Clay said, "This gives us the situation from the black perspective, but I would like to know both sides. Why was the military mistreating black soldiers?"

"I don't suppose documents exist that tell that side of the story, Clay," Parker said.

It was impossible for the two reporters to know what was actually happening on the base at Camp Middleton on the 8th of June in 1943 at 17:00 hours. Ash Walker kept those secrets locked away in the Evangeline File.

CAPTAIN ASH WALKER was ordered to report to headquarters immediately upon his arrival at Camp Middleton. He walked past two MPs that guarded the door to General Peters' office and stepped inside. After snapping to attention, Peters introduced him to the other officer in the room, "Captain Walker, this is Inspector General Matthews." The two men shook hands and Peters motioned to a chair in front of his desk. They inquired briefly about how he left things at Camp Maxey and turned quickly to the business at hand.

General Peters picked up a pipe from the ashtray on his desk and started filling it with fresh tobacco. "Captain Walker," he said, "before we begin I want you to understand that few men in the history of the Army have been given orders with such macabre ramifications. Your young age would be of concern but, upon evaluating your past performance, your ability to problem solve, and with your psychological profile, we are certain that you will be able to carry out these orders to the satisfaction of the U.S. Army."

"Thank you, sir, for your confidence."

General Peters lit his pipe. "We have a real crisis here at Middleton." He handed the Captain a folder marked "TOP SECRET." "This base is being threatened by a mutinous new infantry of colored soldiers. The fact that they were sent here to Mississippi and the Deep South was not by chance. I'm referring to the 344th. Their infamous past is all documented in the file you are holding. You will also discover that an element within the 344th is responsible for two gruesome murders on this base. We do not know how many of them were involved nor have we been able to ascertain who the troublemakers are. The 344th is rapidly getting out of control.

"This mutinous anti-authority attitude is very contagious. You know, even more than I, what has been taking place on all our military bases since April 1, 1941 when the first Negro inductees entered the service. Riots, clashes with the military police and incidents of violence against civilians are reported everywhere. Anti-American groups are fanning the racial unrest. If these soldiers that are so hellbent on mutiny should succeed, it would become a problem of astronomical proportions. Negro soldiers that are exemplary military men at present may become influenced, and white soldiers may see the strength of union and join in. You can easily see the gravity of the situation. Our war effort could be defeated from within. That's why you have been assigned to this base."

The General leaned forward and looked straight into Captain Walker's eyes as he made his next point, "If out-and-out mutiny occurs with Negro soldiers serving in the Armed Forces, it goddamn sure isn't going to be on my base. Your orders, Captain, are to control the present situation which is now way out of hand. If it cannot be controlled, then it must be eliminated."

A small cloud of smoke seeped from around the General's pipe. "Your first priority is to prepare a report on what has

already transpired on this base concerning this matter. It will
be sent to Washington over the Inspector General's signature. Washington is already breathing down our necks on
this. The War Department has knowledge of letters that have
been sent by members of the 344th to sympathetic organizations, newspapers and even to the Deputy Chief of Staff.
Captain Walker, I want you to put the best possible face on
that report. The General, here, can give you more details on
what we need.

"One other thing," he said in conclusion, "you have free
rein to handle this matter as you see fit. Any personnel from
this base or any other base can be at your disposal." General
Peters leaned back in his chair and made one more effort to
emphasize the importance of the mission, "Captain," he said,
"if you handle this matter satisfactorily you will be able to
write your own ticket. However, if you should fail, then I'll
warn you now, shit always rolls downhill. Do you understand?"

"Yes sir."

"Set up a meeting with Major General Matthews, and
report back to me at 15:00 hours tomorrow. That will give
you time to review the file you're holding. Any questions?"

"No, sir."

"You're dismissed."

CAPTAIN ASH WALKER sat alone in the Officer's Club at
Camp Middleton. He lit up an English oval cigarette to enjoy
with his martini and began to reflect on his short military
career. At the time of his graduation from high school in
Camellia City, the possibility of war was widely speculated.
He had selected Texas A&M as his college and distinguished
himself there scholastically and in the Army ROTC.
Graduating with honors, he immediately went into the Army
as a second lieutenant. Lieutenant Walker requested assign-

ment to the Criminal Investigation Division, and the request was granted. His first assignment at Camp Maxey in Paris, Texas was to deal with bootleggers and black marketeering. His expertise in handling criminal matters was quickly recognized, and he rose in rank. With the promotion to captain, he was assigned to investigate racial problems that were surfacing on U.S. Army bases.

Maybe he was young but he had paid his dues, he thought to himself as he bit into an olive. This new assignment offered opportunity, and he thought of one of his favorite passages from *Julius Caesar*:

> *There is a tide in the affairs of men,*
> *Which, taken at the flood, leads on to fortune;*
> *Omitted, all the voyage of their life*
> *Is bound in shallows and in miseries.*

THE FLOOD of tide was definitely upon him, but at the moment he had no idea of the fortune it would bring.

CHAPTER EIGHTEEN

CLAY AND PARKER'S DAY began at the drive-thru window at McDonald's.

"Two coffees to go," Clay said.

"And one sausage biscuit," Parker added.

When they got their order they drove to the outskirts of town, to the site of what had once been Camp Middleton. Arriving, they explored the asphalt roads that networked and dead-ended in broom sage and briars, finding concrete bunkers, ammunition dumps and the remains of foundations where the tar paper barracks once stood. Rising from the undergrowth was the tall masonry chimney of an incinerator. Digging in the dirt around it, they found charcoal and bits and pieces of debris burned long ago. Just off the maze of roads on a level area was an old baseball field. Clay and Parker got out of the Cherokee and walked over to home plate. Walking the bases in silence, Parker finally spoke, "Clay, if you listen closely, you can almost hear them cheering."

The reporters spent hours riding and looking, trying to get a feel of the area. They did not, however, go over to the west boundary of the camp where the railroad track, the swamp and the river ran together because of the "No Trespassing" signs. On the way back to Camellia City, they discussed how the northern soldiers must have felt when they arrived at

Camp Middleton. "It must have been quite a shock," Clay said, "the heat, ticks, spiders, water moccasins, alligators, gravel roads, logging trucks and redneck drawls. It must have been about as hospitable as a fresh grave in a wet cemetery." When they returned to town, Parker left to do some research at the library and to follow up on some leads the military maids had given him.

It was mid-afternoon when Clay checked his e-mail and found something from Brian's contact. This time when he brought it up, he realized that she had hit pay dirt. It, too, was classified.

CONFIDENTIAL MEMORANDUM
DEPUTY CHIEF OF STAFF
UNITED STATES ARMY
WASHINGTON, D.C.

FROM: Major General Taylor L. Matthews, Inspector General
DATE: June 14, 1943
SUBJECT: 344th Infantry, Camp Middleton, Mississippi

Pursuant to your instructions I have had Captain Ash Walker, head of the Criminal Investigation Division of Camp Middleton, Mississippi, investigate the reports of racial tension and riots in the all colored 344th Infantry at Camp Middleton. What follows is his official report.

1. While stationed in Tucson, Arizona, before being transferred to Mississippi, the 344th Infantry engaged in numerous breaches of military discipline which resulted in outbreaks of violence. These events resulted in death and injury to both civilians and enlisted men. Following these eruptions a new and up-to-date camp with all possible con-

veniences and recreational facilities was built for the regiment. The sentiment is that they profited much by their disturbances. Corrective action, both in Tucson and at Camp Middleton, have been totally ineffective. This regiment resorts to mob action to show disapproval of conditions which are accepted by other troops. My investigation shows the 344th to be a dangerous and thoroughly undisciplined outfit.

2. Following a Thanksgiving mutiny in Tucson, the regimental commander took steps to eliminate from the regiment the ringleaders that were instrumental in the mutiny. About 16 men were court martialed and sent to prison for life. Over 50 others were transferred into other regiments. Recent occurrences here at Camp Middleton establish that this was not effective. I am of the opinion that the worst possible solution would be to transfer this organization to another station because this is very possibly the motive behind some of these disturbances. Breaking the regiment into small groups for transfer will only result in the ringleaders going unpunished for mutinous conduct. It would further encourage them to create unrest and promote mutinous conduct in the colored units to which they would be assigned.

3. The 344th Infantry arrived at Camp Middleton on Wednesday, 26 May and Friday, 28 May from its former station in Tucson. A number of sources establish the fact that there was general bragging on the part of the men to the effect that they were going to take over Camp Middleton, the town of Camellia City, and the state of Mississippi. These statements were so general and so persistent as to cause serious alarm on the part of the civilian population in the nearby community. (It appears that these remarks were also very disturbing to the colored troops already in camp).

4. On Thursday, 27 May, one day after the first contingent arrived, an event took place which indicated that these boasts were not idle threats. A group of men from the 344th visited the colored service club and were boisterous and refused to obey the rules of conduct in effect, namely removal of caps, wearing complete uniforms, avoiding indecent language and the introduction of beer into the club. It took about an hour for the hostess and the non-commissioned officers in charge to clear the club of these men after the prescribed closing time on this particular night.

5. On Friday night, 28 May, the camp exchange was temporarily closed by the exchange officer because of the profane, disrespectful, and threatening conduct of these men. Following the closing, a group of several hundred men from the 344th broke into the camp exchange, rifled the stock, and caused damage to furnishings and fixtures.

6. On Saturday night, 29 May, a number of men from the 344th visited the town of Camellia City and marched around the town in formation using indecent and profane language in the presence of all encountered. This group, approximately 74 men, was arrested by the civil police, consisting of the town marshal and a number of deputized citizens armed with shotguns. The soldiers were released to the military police.

7. On Sunday afternoon, 30 May, a member of the 344th was stopped outside the camp by a military policeman because the soldier was improperly uniformed and had no pass. Following a brief argument, the private assaulted the military policeman and was attempting to take his pistol when the county sheriff arrived on the scene. The sheriff reports that

upon his arrival the military policeman was on his back in the jeep with the colored soldier on top of him. The soldier, noticing the arrival of the sheriff, jumped out of the jeep and made a lunge for him. Upon refusing to halt when ordered to do so, the soldier was shot and killed by the sheriff. Information of this incident was immediately transmitted to the commanding officer of the 344th.

8. The Commander and his officers reported that, fearing a riot, they ordered the removal of rifle pins from all rifles and an officer guard on all supply rooms in the regiment. A group of men in Company C stormed the supply room and obtained rifles and ammunition. A crowd of several hundred members of the regiment assembled near the regimental exchange and a riot squad from the military police attempted to maintain order. They were forced to fire into this group in an effort to stand them off. Local citizens are demanding that the regiment be transferred out of Camellia City. They have armed themselves to protect their lives and property and insist on the 344th's immediate transfer to another station.

In my opinion the only way ringleaders may be known is for the regiment as a whole to be placed in such a disciplinary state that it will make known the ringleaders and trouble-makers within the unit. General Peters has proposed drastic and yet untried action that should result in bringing home to the sounder thinking members of the unit that the ringleaders must be disclosed and that all mutinous conduct must be suppressed by them. Further, it will bring home to other colored organizations where unrest is prevalent and mutinous conduct is smoldering that the Army is prepared to take vigorous, disciplinary action to suppress such conduct. The recent marked increase in disturbances where colored personnel are involved indicates that such notification would not only be timely but appropriate.

A decision as to the appropriate action to be taken in this case must be made with the understanding that the citizens of Camellia City and adjacent communities will vigorously protest through their congressmen the non-removal of this regiment from Camp Middleton. As previously stated, they are highly disturbed by the present situation and feel the need to defend their lives and property by openly carrying arms. Notwithstanding that protest may be made, I concur with the following action recommended by General Peters and carried out under his orders. Our strategy will be to:

1. Isolate this regiment by removing them to a remote area and confining them there.
2. Training programs will be required for this organization which will keep the men exceedingly busy, a program which may require additional officers who will be provided if necessary.
3. Members of the 344th will not be permitted to visit the town of Camellia City or other communities in the vicinity until the regiment is restored to normal status.

We are hopeful that the above action will eliminate the current unrest but we are prepared, in the event that it should fail, to execute an alternate plan.

CLAY LEFT the computer on and walked out on the pier to let the report soak in. The sun was casting shadows from the trees into the water on the lake, and Larkin's ducks were making their way to their nests. This had to be the story Vassar was looking for, maybe only the tip of the iceberg, but at least a part of it. One thing was evident—Ash Walker was a major player in whatever happened. There was obviously another side to the events that happened at Camp Middleton in 1943.

CHAPTER NINETEEN

E ARLY THE NEXT MORNING Clay was sitting in the back room at Bertha's waiting for Parker. He was eager to share the information on Camp Middleton.

When Parker arrived, Clay gave him the computer material and Parker read it carefully, re-reading some parts twice, before he put it down and looked up. "Yesterday when I read the letters from those Negro soldiers, there was no doubt they were fearing for their lives. Their desperate tone might have been a little dramatic, but they were scared to death. Now, after reading this, God, I can see why! With white citizens and the military police armed against them, no wonder they were fearful."

Clay spoke up. "I don't see this as only a race thing. If this report is to be believed, it is the defiance of authority pure and simple that is the issue here. If those soldiers had been white, it would have been the same thing."

"Do you think it was wise to send these black troublemakers to the very heart of Dixie?" Parker asked.

"No. Not unless the Army needed a scapegoat."

"Right. And who, in 1943, would question a few unruly black soldiers killed in a racist southern town? Maybe they were even hoping the townspeople would help them out a little bit, kill a couple of black soldiers and send a message to the rest."

"That's possible."

Parker went on, "Can we believe this report of Ash Walker's is factual?"

"I don't know."

"How many soldiers were killed by the riot squad when they were forced, as Walker put it, to fire into this group? There's no mention of how many were left dead or injured."

Clay listened carefully, then spoke, "You've raised some good questions. I still maintain that if there were black soldiers threatening mutiny, the Army would have to deal with them in any manner necessary to restore order."

Parker shook his head. "That's just Southern white mentality, man. I'll never understand it."

"That's just bullshit, Parker. I'm not a racist and you know it."

"Maybe. But you still don't get it. I want you to promise me that if something should happen to me, you'll do me a favor."

"What is it?" Clay asked.

"I want you to go to Memphis to the Civil Rights Museum—the one in the old Lorraine Motel."

"Why?"

"Because a light just might turn on in your head."

"That stuff is just propaganda, Parker."

"Just promise me," Parker insisted.

"Okay, I promise. But nothing is going to happen to you— or to me, for that matter." Parker picked up a handwritten lunch menu and broke the tension, "Let's talk about something we can agree on."

"Now you're talking. Who's gonna buy lunch?"

Over lunch the men decided that they had to find someone who was actually on the base in 1943. That's when Clay remembered Earl Bower. "I've got an idea," he said, "I'll let you know how it turns out."

ROSE BOWER'S HOUSE was a small two-story Victorian structure trimmed in lots of gingerbread woodwork. It was in a
transitional, once affluent, section of town. Its outside paint
was peeling off, and there was a tear in the rusty screen door.
The outdated doorbell rang when Clay pressed it.

Rose Bower came to the door wearing a chenille robe and
house shoes. Her head was wrapped in a bright-colored scarf
and she was holding a book with her fingers inserted
between its pages to mark her place. "Rose," Clay began
apologetically, "I should have called first, but I've been wanting to talk to you since Vassar's funeral. Is it a bad time?"

"Not at all," Rose said politely, "Come on in."

She started down the long hall from the foyer into the
back of the house. Small gold-framed pictures of family members hanging high on the walls were the only decoration.
They walked past a living room and dining room where crocheted doilies were draped over the back of the sofa and arm
chairs. There were collections of bric-a-brac and dusty glass-
ware in every room. Paper shades over the windows were
drawn to the bottom, and a smell of mildew suggested that
the rooms had not been used for a long time. Her small den
was well illuminated, sparsely furnished and cluttered with
stacks of books. "Reading is my passion," she said, "as you can
see." She moved some magazines from a chair and offered
him a seat. "What brings you over?" she asked after they had
exchanged a few niceties.

"I've tried unsuccessfully to see your ex-husband. I need
to talk to him."

"Have you tried Damico's?"

"Yes. He does live upstairs, but I haven't been able to see
him. I left word for him to call me, but so far he hasn't."

"He won't, Clay. He's very suspicious, especially about

strangers."

Clay chose his words carefully. "Rose, I was hoping that you might help me. Maybe you could get in touch with him and tell him it's most important that I talk with him. That is, if you're comfortable with that."

"If I do, Clay, he will want to know why. Otherwise I'm sure that he won't agree to it."

"Tell him I want to ask him something about his sister. It may help to solve her murder."

"Earl really loved Vassar." She paused, "How is everything going at the paper?"

"I'm no longer with them."

"Oh, I see. Are you still living in Larkin's cabin?"

"Yes, I am."

She returned to Clay's request. "I can't promise Earl will call, but I do promise that I will try. Give me your number."

Clay gave it to her and she wrote it down. "You'll have to forgive my manners. What about a cup of coffee? I was just making a fresh pot when you came."

Rose came from the kitchen with the coffee and sat across from her guest. A cat emerged from a stack of books and sprang to her lap. "Would you mind," Clay said, "if we talk a little about Mr. Bower?"

"Not at all. What do you want to know?"

"Anything. Just tell me about him."

Rose settled back in her chair, set her cup down on the table beside her and stroked the back of the cat curled in her lap. "Earl and I were sweethearts before you were born," she began. "We started dating in the tenth grade. He was a handsome devil, always taller than the rest of the boys his age. His folks were hard workers. His dad was an auto mechanic. Anyway, even though they were from the wrong side of town, it didn't matter. Earl was popular because of sports. He was a real good football player." Rose smiled, "He was the envy of all the boys and the heartthrob of all the girls." She picked up her coffee cup, took a swallow and continued, "I know this much. I was head over heels in love with him. We ran off and got married as soon as he graduated. He had a football scholarship to play for LSU so we got a small apartment just off campus. Looking back, those were the happiest years of my life." Rose looked out the window for a moment, "But the good times were short-lived. War broke out, and Earl dropped out of college and was drafted. He left for Camp Maxey in Paris, Texas to do his basic training and came back here to Camp Middleton for some training before he was shipped overseas."

Clay interrupted, "What year was that, Rose?"

"That would have been around 1943. But he wasn't here long. He was shipped overseas." Rose stood up from her chair and walked over to a desk where she opened a drawer and pulled out some papers. "This is a letter that I received not long ago from one of his old Army buddies. He said Earl was supposed to go to Washington to receive the Silver Star. I wonder if he ever did."

"When did his mental problems start?" Clay said.

Rose's recollections became more painful, "When he first returned from the war he seemed normal. He could talk of the prison camp and remember the good things like learning to make turnip soup and the importance of equally sharing whatever came their way. He seemed to enjoy civilian life. Then, without warning, the spells started. He was in and out of the V.A. hospitals."

"Which ones?" Clay asked.

"The first one was in Gulfport, then New Orleans. It was a nightmare. Nothing about Earl was the same when he came home from the war. His feeling about me and about his friends had changed. Before the war Ash Walker was one of his closest friends, but afterwards Earl detested him. It was the same about the military. Even his interests and hobbies changed. Everything except fishing." A smile returned to her face, "Gosh, that man loves to fish. His behavior became so extreme that he was institutionalized. When he was released, he came home and told me he couldn't take it anymore. He just walked out of the door and left. Later we were divorced. Now he is just a tall, thin recluse that walks the streets of Camellia City with a dog as his only companion. How pathetic," Rose concluded, "what a waste."

Clay thanked her for what she had shared and on the way to the door he asked, "Rose, you never remarried?"

"No," she said, "somehow another special someone just never came along for me."

CHAPTER TWENTY

WEDNESDAY MORNING found Parker Phillips driving out to a remote area of Topisaw County after being told that a man named Proby Lewis wanted to see him.

Proby Lewis was watching a talk show on television when he heard a knock on the door. "Go see who that is, Sister," he said. A middle-aged woman rose from her chair and walked through a modest farm house to the front door. She returned with a nice looking 30-year-old man that introduced himself as Parker Phillips. "Daddy, it's the newspaper man," she called out as she ushered him into the living room.

Parker studied the frail man still sitting in his chair. He looked older than his 70s, the veins on his thin hands were strutted, and the black skin that covered them looked thin and stretched. He was wearing a pair of cotton pajamas and a blue bathrobe, and a homemade quilt covered his legs. A tiny plastic tube ran from an oxygen canister and stopped at a fork beneath his nose. On a small table next to his chair was a pack of Red Man chewing tobacco and a coffee can for spitting.

Proby spoke in a hoarse whisper. "Have a seat," he said. He studied Parker for a few minutes and then spoke again, "I thought you would be a white man." Parker grinned, "No, sir, I'm not."

"Are you the only black man that works for the paper?"

"I'm the only black reporter, but I'm no longer with them."

"I'm sorry to hear that. Did you do a good job for them?"

"I did my best."

Parker changed the subject and pointed to the TV. "What do you think of those talk shows?" he asked Proby Lewis.

"You don't want to know what I think." Proby looked over at his daughter. "Sister, turn that thing off and let me and this young man talk by ourselves for a while." Sister walked over to the TV, turned it off, and left the room.

"Tell me your name again, son."

"Parker Phillips."

"Well, Parker, the reason I called you is I heard you were asking a lot of folks questions about Camp Middleton."

"Yes sir, I am."

"What are you trying to find out?"

"I have reason to believe that something important happened on the base in 1943."

"What have you found out so far?"

"Not much."

"Do you know what can happen to somebody that asks too many questions in Topisaw County?"

"Yes, I do."

Proby shifted slightly in his chair. "And that don't scare you?"

"No, sir, it doesn't."

"Then you are either a mighty brave man...or a fool."

"I'm not a fool, sir."

Proby looked down at his hands, "I've been scared for 52 years, would still be scared if they hadn't told me I've got cancer. Nowadays they tell it just like it is. They say I don't have a whole lot of time left, and I made up my mind that I'm not gonna be scared another day. That's why I called you. I've waited a long time to tell this story—longer than you've been alive."

"That's why I came, Mr. Lewis. I want to hear what you have to say."

Proby began. "It's about Camp Middleton. It was in the fall of 1943. I can't tell you the exact month, but it was fall because the persimmons were ripe. I remember it as clear as if it happened yesterday. I came up during the Depression. Times were real hard. If Daddy hadn't had this farm, we would have starved to death. When the war broke out, things around here got better. They started building Camp Middleton, and I got a job with a construction company driving a truck. I hauled gravel from Greensburg, Louisiana to the base. I got to know every back road." Parker was taking careful notes. "In Greensburg I met a Mr. Fontenot. He was a Frenchman that had a real racket going. In those days it was against the law to sell any alcohol in Topisaw County, but Louisiana was wide open. Mr. Fontenot was a bootlegger, and when Camp Middleton opened up he offered me a job with good money and I took it." Proby paused to rest.

"I worked at night. My job was to meet a boat once a week on the river, load up a truck with liquor and hide it out in the swamp next to the railroad tracks near the west gate of the base. At midnight an Army truck would ease out of the west gate, cross over the tracks and turn down beside them in the woods where I was hiding. Then we would switch the liquor from my truck to his. It was always the same driver. He was always alone and never late. We did this once a week for, I guess, two years without a hitch. He never asked my name and I never asked his. All I know is that he was an officer." Another pause for Proby to breathe the oxygen.

"On a fall night in 1943, I was waiting beside the railroad track. It was a full moon so bright that you could almost read a newspaper. I remember so well because I could see ripe persimmons on the ground close to where I was standing. At midnight the truck pulled up like always to where I was hiding. We were unloading when we heard a train coming. A train had never come by at that time of night while we were making our switch. We stopped what we were doing and walked over to a clearing. I guess we must have been 25 yards from the train when it passed. It was an engine pulling three flatbed railroad cars. On the cars were bodies—dead bodies—hundreds of bodies stacked like cord wood. Blood was everywhere, even dripping off the sides of the cars."

Parker interrupted, "Did you say hundreds of bodies?"

"Yes, hundreds of dead soldiers, and they were all black," Proby continued. "The officer standing with me was white, and I remember his exact words when he saw them. He said, 'Holy Shit! It's those goddamn niggers!!' The train was moving real slow down the tracks and I saw it as clear as day. Almost could have reached out and touched it. At first we just stood there... then the officer turned to me, pulled out his side arm and put that .45 right in my face. He said, 'We didn't see anything, you got that?' I said, 'Yes sir, I didn't see nothing.' Then he said, 'If you value your life you won't ever peep a word about this.' I said, 'No, sir, I sure won't.' I was so scared, I was shaking like a leaf."

Parker asked, "What did you do next?"

"I finished loading that truck, left the swamp, drove to Mr. Fontenot's place, parked the truck and left the key in it. I never saw the truck, Fontenot, Camp Middleton or the officer ever again. I came back here to my daddy's place and told him I was ready to farm. I never told him what I saw that night—him or anybody else until now. You're the first person I've ever told." Proby paused again to rest. His breathing was labored.

Parker asked him a lot of questions. He repeated the same story. "Were the soldiers in some sort of accident? Maybe an explosion?" he asked Proby.

"I don't know. All I know is that they were as bloody as slaughtered hogs."

"Where was the train taking them?"

"I don't know. The tracks came out of the base and ran down the side of the swamp to the river."

"Mr. Lewis," Parker finally said, "do you know of anyone else that was on the base at that time?"

"You mean civilians that worked on the base or men stationed there as soldiers?"

"Either one."

Proby thought for a minute. "I believe Mr. Bower, a war hero in Camellia City, was out there, but his mind's not real good and I don't think he would talk to anybody anyway."

CLAY AND PARKER met as planned in Bertha's back room at 4 p.m. Looking very pleased with himself, Parker eagerly told him what he had uncovered. When he finished relating all the details of the Proby Lewis story, Clay asked, "Do you believe him?"

"Absolutely."

"Do you think he will go on record with his story?"

Parker had been waiting for him to ask that question. He fished in his coat pocket and came out with a video cassette. Clay stared incredulously, "You have that interview on tape?"

"You bet."

"Outstanding, Parker, outstanding. Would he agree to do a deposition?"

"He said he would, but he said we had better hurry. He's in real bad shape and he may not last long."

"Where do we go from here?" Parker asked, as he handed Clay the cassette.

"I'm still working on this Earl Bower angle."

Clay and Parker left Bertha's, and Parker took the long way home, totally preoccupied with what Proby Lewis had told him. He was so lost in the moment that he was unaware of the white Cadillac that followed at a discreet distance behind him.

CHAPTER TWENTY-ONE

WHEN CLAY REACHED his cabin, his telephone was ringing. When he answered, an unfamiliar voice spoke in a raspy whisper. "This is Earl Bower. Rose said you wanted to talk to me."

Clay was surprised that Rose had been able to get a response from him so quickly. "Yes, I do," he replied.

"What do you want?"

"Could I come to Damico's?"

"No." Earl was firm. "I'm going to walk my dog around Wentworth College. Do you know where that is?"

"I know where it is."

Earl continued, "There's a bell tower in the center of the quad. The sidewalks meet there. You'll find it."

"I'll be there in 30 minutes," Clay said enthusiastically.

"Don't make me wait. I hate to wait," Earl said tersely.

In less than 20 minutes he was walking on the abandoned campus to meet Earl Bower. A block away a man in a parked car pressed the transmit button on his two-way radio.

"Victor to Dawson."

"Dawson, go ahead."

"Subjects entering Wentworth campus."

"Wentworth College?"

"10-4, I'll be out of my vehicle."

"10-4."

There's something unsettling about empty school buildings at night, and Wentworth being deserted was even more foreboding. Even with a full moon overhead, it was difficult to see the sidewalk. Lights that once illuminated the area had long been broken by vandals. Neglected hedges lapped over the sidewalks. A cat on a nocturnal chase came out of nowhere and bolted across his path. An easterly wind rattled the windows in the old dormitories, and unlocked doors shifted and squeaked on their hinges.

Clay found the bell tower, and Earl was not there. He sat down on a masonry bench and waited. A hand came out of the hedges behind him and grasped his shoulder. Clay jumped.

"You're trespassing, you know," a shrill voice said, and Earl Bower emerged from the bushes holding a Labrador on a leash. Bugle sniffed Clay as he stood up. Earl Bower was tall, almost a head taller than Clay, his body thin—almost emaciated. Bugle barked and pulled against the leash.

Then Clay introduced himself and shook Earl's hand.

"Well," Earl said, still standing, "you got me out here. Now what do you want?" There was an edge in his voice.

"I won't take much of your time, Mr. Bower, I would like to ask you a few questions. Don't you want to sit down?"

"No. You sit if you want I'm standing." He was not looking at Clay. His head was moving back and forth searching out into the darkness. Clay got right to the point, "I think I know who is responsible for your sister's murder."

"Who?"

"I have reason to believe that Ash Walker killed her."

Earl's head turned to Clay, "What reason do you have to believe that?"

"Let me rephrase that. I believe that Ash Walker had her killed."

Earl sat down on the bench. "Why would he do it?"

"She was trying to blackmail him."

"I don't believe it."

"It's a fact."

"With what?"

Clay and Parker with all their effort had only been able to come up with the military maids and Proby Lewis. He was certain that Vassar's information had to have come from Earl Bower. In a millionth of a second he decided to go for it, "With the information she got from you."

Clay waited with closed eyes for the answer. If he was wrong or if Earl denied it this interview was over. The silence seemed to last forever.

"What I told her about Camp Middleton got her killed?"

Clay could feel the adrenaline rush to his head. The verbal trap that Earl Bower had just stepped into slammed shut. "Yes, sir, I believe it did."

Earl sat on the bench holding his head with his long hands, "What do you want from me?"

Clay rose to his feet, "I need for you to tell me what you told Vassar."

"She didn't tell you?"

"She talked to me, but I need to hear it from you."

Earl looked up at Clay, "What you are asking will get you killed. You don't have any idea what you are up against."

"I'm prepared to take that chance."

"I'll say this much, you're cocky. I'm surprised you showed up tonight. Most people are afraid of me. What specifically do you want to know?"

"I want to know what happened when the 344th Infantry came to Camp Middleton."

In a whisper Earl began. "I didn't get to the base until late August, 1943. Ash brought me in from Camp Maxey. He was with the CID and they could do most anything they wanted.

When I arrived in Middleton, I found out all hell had broken loose."

"Were you with the CID?" Clay asked.

"No, I was regular infantry. Ash said he needed someone he could trust to assist him directly in a top secret mission. The all black soldiers of the 344th had gotten totally out of control. They were murdering civilians and enlisted personnel. All measures of discipline had been tried to correct the situation and bring them back in line."

"So you and Ash were really close in those days?"

"Hell, yes. I saved his life swimming when we were kids."

"And what happened to that friendship?"

"That was something personal that happened after the war."

"So you were told about the top secret mission...," Clay was prodding now.

"Right. He told me that we had to eliminate the problem, that an entire base was on the verge of mutiny." Earl's concentration was interrupted. His Lab's ears had perked up.

"So what did you do?" Clay asked.

"We took care of the problem. That's all there was to it."

"So that's the end of the story?" That's it?"

Clay leaned closer to Earl's face. "Mr. Bower, my life and yours may well depend on how quickly Ash Walker is behind bars. I know about the bodies on the train, so don't jerk me around."

Earl leapt to his feet, "I didn't tell Vassar about any bodies. How did you find that out?"

"I have an eyewitness."

"Impossible."

"Then how would I know?"

Earl was still trying to figure it... "Ash Walker and I are the only two eyewitnesses left." Bower was visibly agitated, but he sat down again. Clay spoke softly and with kindness. "Mr.

Bower," he said, "my father never came home from Vietnam. He may be dead or maybe not. I'm fully aware of what the military is capable of doing. I believe that you've been carrying something terrible inside yourself for a long, long time. Don't you think it's time to let it out?"

Earl shook his head. "If I do, we're dead men."

"Maybe not."

In the middle of the abandoned college, the walls of silence that had separated Earl Bower from reality for 50 years began to crumble. He began, "What happened at Middleton in '43 could have happened on any Army base in the United States. It was not a southern thing, and I still don't think we had a choice."

"I understand," Clay said.

"Ash Walker had tried everything to solve the problem after he was given the assignment: discipline, isolation, restrictions of every kind, even severe corporal punishment—nothing worked. A lot of pressure was being put on him from the top. He was told basically to solve the problem or else. Just before I got there he had come up with a plan. He brought in a crackerjack team of twelve black soldiers, all CID. They were able to infiltrate the 344th and identify all the troublemakers and ringleaders without arousing suspicion." Earl Bower began to wring his hands as he talked. "It all came down in the late fall. There was a full moon that night." Bower looked up from the bench and pointed through the trees, "Like that one," he said. In an instant his voice completely changed. It was like someone else spoke from inside him. "Do you ever hear voices, Clay?"

"No."

"Well, I do. Often." Earl pointed to the starlit sky. "There are cities and people smarter than us up there."

"No, I didn't know," Oh God, Clay thought, please don't let him space out now. "So, Mr. Bower, it's a night in late fall with a full moon. Then what happened?"

Earl Bower's voice returned, "Around eight o'clock that night, the 344th Infantry Regiment was marched out to the parade field. Three battalions, a total of 3,000 men. On the parade field, almost 1,200 men out of the 3,000 were told to fall out and load into waiting trucks. They were told that their night infiltration training scores were not up to par and that they were being taken immediately to repeat the exercises. These nearly 1,200 men were the ones that the CID had identified. The trucks carried them miles away to a remote part of the swamp down by the river. At a designated place, ditches had been dug and coils upon coils of barbed wire stretched across the top and around the perimeter of the entire area. Five 1919 A-1 water-cooled .30 calibre machine guns were placed in strategic position. The men were ordered to get into the ditches. Ash then called in a select group, also CID, who took their places behind the machine guns, and two men with .45 Thompson submachine guns closed off each end of the ditch. The order to fire was given. It was as easy as shooting fish in a barrel. What seemed like an eternity was over in a matter of minutes."

Clay interrupted. "Do you mean that almost 1,200 soldiers were shot?"

"Yes, and at 500 rounds per minute it didn't take long, especially with the Thompson subs down there finishing up the job."

"Why didn't they return fire?"

"Because the firing pins had been removed from their weapons. They were defenseless."

"Mr. Bower, do you know what you are saying? This is not an incident of one simple fragging. This is wholesale murder."

"That's what happened, and I have spared you the gruesome details. I'll leave that to your imagination."

"What part did you play?"

"I didn't do any shooting. I stood there with Ash Walker. After they were dead he gave me four mattress covers and told me to remove the personal items from the bodies. So I collected dog tags, wallets, pictures, religious medals and whatever they had."

"What happened next?"

"The CID loaded the dead soldiers, along with their weapons, onto railroad cars. A train hauled them away."

"Hauled them where?"

"I don't know that. Only Ash Walker knows that."

Earl continued, "After everything was finished, the members of the CID and I met Ash behind one of the troop carriers. He gave us each $1,000 in cash. Ten brand new hundred dollar bills. That was a lot of money in those days. Ash said, 'Gentlemen, this night never happened. I repeat, never happened.'"

"What did you do with the personal effects?"

"Sometime after midnight I took them to one of his warehouses in Camellia City, just as he instructed me to do."

"And what happened to the CID?"

"They were off the base by morning."

"What about the rest of the 344th?"

"Their orders had already been cut. They were shipped out that same night for the Aleutian Islands."

"When did you leave the base?"

"Two days later. Ash gave me a two-day pass to stay with Rose."

A million questions came to mind, but Clay had to ask at least one, "What happened to your friendship with Ash Walker?"

Earl's face became contorted in the moonlight, and his mouth twisted. He made an electrical sparking sound with his tongue and leaned up to Clay's face, "Ash Walker fried my brain," he said. The Labrador began to bark. "There's something out there. I've gotta get out of here. Be careful, Brady, they are everywhere."

"Who?" Clay asked.

"The death gods."

"What you have told me," Clay said, "is hard to believe."

"What I've told you is true, but then again it's like they say... I'm crazy, you know."

In the blink of an eye Earl Bower and his dog had disappeared into the night.

EARLIER, RANCEY JAMES and Toxie Hux had seen Earl Bower enter the Wentworth campus. They had also spotted Clay's Cherokee near its entrance. While Clay was talking to Earl they were circling the block. When Clay unlocked the door to his Cherokee, a car eased up beside him. He turned to see the face of Toxie Hux glaring at him through the window of the Cadillac. Toxie's hand was raised with his finger pointed like a gun. Clay could read his lips. "Bang!" he said before the Cadillac went slowly up the street.

CHAPTER TWENTY-TWO

T AWANA THOUGHT OF PARKER as she pushed her grocery cart down the aisle of the supermarket. She had never seen him as happy as he had been earlier at breakfast. He told her all about the investigation and what he had learned from Proby Lewis. Working with Clay was more like fun than work, he had said.

Parker had been more attentive since she had lost her job at the bank. This morning he had been especially thoughtful of her. As always when he left for work he kissed her goodbye, but today he came back and told her how much he loved her and promised her that after this investigation was over, they would start their family. "Why don't you ride out in the country with me today?" he suggested. "It looks like it's going to be a pretty day. Come on with me. While I get the car serviced you can go to the store, pick up some steaks for tonight and I'll pick you up at eleven. By the way," he said, "pick up an extra steak for Clay. I'm going to invite him over."

At eleven sharp Parker pulled into the driveway and blew the horn. The June sun was already high in the sky. It was going to be hot. As they rode through the countryside they listened to the radio. Tawana sang along with Whitney Houston, and Parker teased her about her voice. It was after they had passed the Topisaw Creek that Parker noticed the car behind him. Momentarily he lost sight of it as he went over a hill. Then it appeared again in his rear view mirror. Parker watched it with increased interest as it grew closer and recognized it as Rancey James' Cadillac. When he came to a country store he pulled in. "How about a Coke?" he asked Tawana. The two men in the Cadillac continued down the road.

After they left the store, they had only gone about a mile when Parker saw the white car backed up in a side road off the highway. When Parker passed, the Cadillac pulled out behind them. There was no doubt about it. They were being followed.

"What's wrong?" Tawana asked after Parker sped up.

"There's a car behind us," Parker confessed. "It's been following us."

Tawana turned off the radio. "Don't look back," Parker warned.

"Who is it?" Tawana asked.

"Two white men."

"Do you recognize them?"

"One of them."

"What do they want?"

Parker did not answer the question. "Hold on," he said, "I'm going to take that gravel road coming up on the right."

When he reached it he turned suddenly on to it, and the Cadillac overshot the turn. It quickly backed up. The chase was on.

Parker shifted down and gunned the engine. His car responded, throwing up gravel. Rocks pelted the Cadillac's windshield. Trees on each side of the road zipped by. "I'm scared," Tawana was saying. Parker pushed the car even faster. The Cadillac was right on his bumper. "There's a farm house about five miles ahead," Parker said. "I'm going to try to make

it there." Almost instantly Parker's car was hit from behind.
Tawana was screaming. Another crash from behind. Parker
lost control of his vehicle for a second, then regained it. "Get
the cell phone," Parker yelled to Tawana, "dial 911." Tawana
reached down on the floor where the phone had fallen and
quickly dialed the number. BLAM! Another blow from the
Cadillac. 911 answered. "Tell them we're on County 236
headed south of 44. We're being chased by two men in a
white Cadillac." Tawana repeated exactly what Parker said.

The Cadillac was beside them now. It slammed into the
side of Parker's car and Parker left the road. There was a loud
grinding sound as gravel scraped against metal. Tawana was
thrown against the dashboard, and the phone went dead.
Parker's car came to a stop in the ditch.

Rancey James threw his .38 revolver over to Toxie, and
Toxie was out of the car by the time Rancey had rolled to a
stop.

"Get out of the goddamn car!" he demanded of Parker.

Parker saw the gun and opened the door. "What's the problem?" he asked, trying to be as calm as possible.

"Problem?" Toxie repeated, "We ain't got no fucking problem. You're the one with the problem."

"Why were you chasing us?"

By this time Rancey was out of the car and took over the
conversation. "I want to know why you're going around asking so many questions."

"What did you say?" Parker asked.

"You're not deaf. I want to know who in the hell you think
you are, messing in somebody else's business."

"I don't know what you're talking about."

Rancey's face grew scarlet, "The hell you don't, you son of
a bitch. You're the one that wrote that article on Frank
Mingus."

Parker knew they were going to kill him. "Go to hell."

"What did you say?"

"I said you can go to hell."

Toxie slammed the side of the .38 against Parker's face. Parker fell back against the car. Sticking his head inside the car, Toxie yelled to Tawana, "Get your black ass out and be quick about it." Tawana was screaming. Toxie pulled the hammer back on the pistol and cocked it. "And shut the fuck up."

Tawana came around the car and stood next to Parker.

Toxie walked over to Tawana, put his fingers around the corners of her mouth and pulled them together. "Look at this mouth," he said lustfully.

Parker moved toward him. "She hasn't done anything," Parker pleaded.

Toxie laughed and mocked, "Now ain't that just like a nigger, Rancey, to try and give orders?" He moved right into Parker's face. "We'll do whatever the hell we want to do."

Parker spit in his face.

Toxie wheeled around to Rancey awaiting direction. Rancey didn't hesitate. "Shoot them now. Both of them."

At point blank range Toxie fired into Parker's chest. He fell. Tawana broke to run. Toxie aimed the pistol at the back of her head and pulled the trigger. She fell instantly.

"Let's get the hell out of here," Rancey said, "before somebody comes."

ONE OF DALLAS DAWSON'S deputies took the 911 call from dispatch. He was given the circumstances and location. The dispatcher told him that the emergency call was interrupted and that the caller seemed desperate. With blue lights and wig wags flashing, the deputy was speeding to County 236 to check out the call. He flew by the country store and started braking when he saw the 236 marker ahead of him. He turned on the gravel road and pressed the accelerator down. A few miles later he approached the scene. The car doors were still open. When he got close enough to read the license plate, he called dispatch for a check. When he saw the bodies in the ditch, he slammed on the brakes and was out of the car. The dispatcher on his radio was replying, "That vehicle is registered to Parker Phillips. It should be a 1994 Nissan, red in color."

The deputy interrupted the dispatcher, "I'm three miles south of 44 on 236. I have one black male and one black female that appear to have been shot. Send an ambulance and the coroner."

Dallas Dawson had stopped by his house for lunch with his wife when he heard the transmission. He bolted up from the table. "I was afraid something like this was going to happen." He told his wife, "I don't know when I'll be back. Don't worry."

Clay had been working at his computer on his field notes from the Earl Bower meeting. He had tried several times to reach Parker to tell him to come over. He wanted to tell him about Bower before their meeting at Bertha's at 4:00. Clay picked up the phone to try calling Parker again and still there was no answer. As he continued to work at his computer, his thoughts turned to Khaki. She had been on his mind constantly since New Orleans. Regardless of how hard he tried, he could not write it off as a bad experience. He wondered where she was, what she was doing, and what she was thinking.

Clay was just finishing his notes when someone knocked at his door. He opened it and a young Topisaw County deputy was standing there. "May I come in?" the officer asked.

"Sure," Clay said, closing the door.

"Mr. Brady, I have some bad news. Parker Phillips and his wife have been shot on one of our country roads."

"Shot?!" Clay exclaimed.

"Yes, sir."

"Are they all right?"

"No, I'm sorry. They are both dead."

Clay sank down on the sofa. "Who shot them?" he finally asked.

"Sheriff Dawson said to tell you, they called in that they were being followed by a white Cadillac. He's certain it involves Rancey James. He also gave me orders not to let you out of my sight. He's afraid that your life may also be in danger."

Clay sat speechless, still stunned by the deputy's news.

"I'm sorry, Mr. Brady, I haven't introduced myself. I'm Officer Thompson." Clay looked up at the officer still standing over him and read the silver name tag over his pocket. It read Victor Thompson.

"Tell me, Victor, where is Sheriff Dawson now?"

"He's on his way to the state crime lab in Jackson with the bodies. He doesn't want anybody local to be involved in the autopsy or any other forensics tests. The sheriff is determined that there will be no slip-ups in this case."

ASH WALKER sat in his office at the *Chronicle* listening as Rancey James gave him the details of what happened out in the county.

"If ever a nigger had it coming, this one did," Rancey said, "and his wife, she just happened to be in the wrong place at the wrong time." Trying to head off a rebuke, he quickly added, "This one's on the house, a two-for-one special, and it ain't gonna cost you a cent."

"Did anyone see you?" Ash asked.

"No."

"Are you sure?"

"Yeah, I'm sure."

"You didn't do the shooting?"

"No, Toxie did."

"With his gun?"

"No, with mine."

"Then you will need to dispose of it."

"Okay."

"You are sure you didn't drop or leave anything at the scene?"

"No, we wasn't there long enough."

"Where was Parker going?"

"I don't know. He just started to run. We were just going to scare the hell out of him and find out why he has been asking questions about Camp Middleton for you."

"How do you know he's been asking questions about Camp Middleton?"

"Cause I've had two niggers call and tell me he was, and that ain't all. Clay Brady's been doing the same thing."

Ash leaned back in his chair. "Yes, I know."

Rancey began to relax a little. He was happy that Ash hadn't gone off the wall about the killings.

"Brady saw Earl Bower," Rancey said.

"When?"

"A couple of nights ago."

"Where?"

"Wentworth College."

"Very interesting. Do you know why he wanted to talk to him?"

"Well, Ash, it wasn't about the weather. But don't worry—he couldn't get any sense out of Earl anyway."

"I'm not so sure."

Ash thought for a minute and considered some options. In March there was Vassar's death, now in the middle of June, Parker, both with *Chronicle* connections. Now, if Clay Brady showed up dead, an idiot would become suspicious. Ash calculated, however, that if Parker and Clay were asking about

Middleton, he had no choice.

Ash thought out loud. "Brady's got to disappear without a trace. I guess we'll need the Albino. What did he get for the last job?"

Rancey was surprised that Ash did not remember—or was this a test? "15,000."

"Maybe you should give him a call, Rancey."

"Ash, I hate that little bastard. You never know what he's thinking; besides, I'm not so sure if he ain't queer."

"What does that have to do with anything?"

"Well, have you ever known one you could trust?"

Ash laughed. "Sometimes you really amaze me, Rancey, you really amaze me."

Ash's comment went over Rancey's head, and he continued his pitch, "Me and Toxie can handle it for you. Have I ever let you down before?"

"Never."

"And we'll do it for 10,000."

"He can't turn up anywhere around here. He's got to disappear."

"You do want us to kill him?"

"Absolutely. You come up with a plan and come back tomorrow. I'll decide by then. And don't forget to get rid of that gun."

"I'll do it," Rancey said as he stood up to leave.

Ash knew that if Rancey could come up with a workable plan that he would try it. Time was of the essence. The last thing that he wanted to do was to have to call Lt. Col. Bradford and tell him that the Middleton matter had come up again.

Rancey drove slowly down a deserted road looking for a place to throw the pistol. He rolled the window of his car down and pulled his .38 revolver out. He looked at the old Smith and Wesson; it had become a part of him like a pocket knife or watch. He looked down at it again. "This is a good pistol," he thought. To hell with Ash Walker. What he did with his pistol was his business. He rolled the window up, stuffed the revolver back in his pocket and drove back to Camellia City.

DR. HENRY WATERMAN, a pathologist for the university hospital, had already performed several autopsies before the bodies of Parker and Tawana arrived. He was taking a break enjoying a cup of coffee and a cigar. He joked with the nurses. The pathologist had a vulgar sense of humor, was in his mid-40s, bald, fat and wore garish clothes under his medical coat. As he chewed on his cigar waiting for a small group of interns from the office of the public defender, he checked the wall clock in the lounge. When he was told that they had arrived, he returned to the morgue to greet them. Dr. Waterman relished a captive audience. The two victims covered with sheets in his morgue offered an unusual opportunity for him to perform for the skittish interns waiting to see their first autopsy.

He entered the room and stood between the two bodies still covered on the tables beside him. He instructed the four students and the representative from the crime lab to slip on the masks that had been provided. "You'll find the smell very offensive," he said, "but as we proceed you will become unaware of it."

Waterman turned to his assistant, "I believe a little James Brown might be appropriate," he said.

The assistant, as instructed, went over to a rack of cassettes, found the tape and pushed it in the stereo. Waterman, as he had done hundreds of times before, jerked the sheet off the corpse that lay rigid on the table. He watched as the interns reacted to the sight of their first cadaver. Their eyes had widened above their masks. Waterman got down to business, giving statistical and observable information about what he was doing. He pointed out the entry wound above the heart, turned the body over and showed that there was no sign of an exit. He took one long puff off his cigar before he began the rest of the procedure. The interns watched as he cut open the body and carefully removed and weighed each organ. He gave elaborate details as he went along. Next, he dug into the muscles of the back and removed a distorted .38 copper slug. He dropped it into a stainless steel U-shaped basin and handed it to the crime lab representative.

Taking a scalpel, he cut the skin from the back of Parker's head and pulled the scalp forward. A hi-tech saw removed the saucer-like cap from the rest of the skull. The pathologist removed the brain and placed it on a scale beside him. As he waited for his assistant to weigh it, James Brown was belting out the lyrics to "I Feel Good" on the stereo. The assistant pulled a section from a stack of newspapers and pinched it together forming a ball to fill the brain cavity. Waterman held it up examining it. "How fitting," he said. "The sports section. I never knew a black that didn't like sports." Then stuffing the paper inside the cavity, he continued, "He can read it on his way back to Camellia City."

CLAY WAS WELCOMED to the Sweet Home Missionary Baptist Church by several deacons who were expecting him and had been told of his relationship to Parker. From the foyer of the church, Clay could see the two caskets opened at the front and the families of Parker and Tawana on the first two pews. An older lady, dressed in white, offered to take him down to pay his respects and view the bodies. Emotional displays of grief were evident throughout the already crowded church as neighbors gathered for this sad tribute to two of their most faithful members. Parker's mother had become hysterical at the casket and had thrown herself over her son's body. Lady ushers, all dressed in white, were ministering to her as Clay made his way forward. He had been asked to speak as one of three presenters who would eulogize Parker. There would be a neighbor, a church member, and Clay, who was to talk about Parker as a co-worker and friend.

Clay took his place on the podium with the other presenters and several pastors who would each have a special part on the program. The organist began to play the hymns and spirituals so rich in black culture, and the music carried them to even higher levels of grief. Parker and Tawana's caskets were closed and the service began.

From behind him the choir stood and began to sing, "Precious Lord, take my hand." He and the other presenters were given three minutes on the program. The pastors, however, each gave an evangelical sermon laced with scriptural warnings designed to remind the mourners to "get right with God." They also spoke of the righteous wrath of God who condemns the senseless murders of these two young people. Cries of agony echoed in the church as the pastors pled with a loving God to deliver His people from hatred and bigotry.

Clay, still seated on the podium, could see the waves of emotion that would carry the families and friends onto another plane of suffering. In the back of the church he saw the tearful face of Khaki Woodson.

CHAPTER TWENTY-THREE

K HAKI HAD MADE UP her mind that she was going to tell Clay the truth, regardless of the consequences. Since New Orleans she had thought of nothing else but Clay. Seeing him at the funeral was so hard; she had felt his hurt. She understood why he was upset with her. If the tables had been turned, she would have felt the same way. She thought about him all day during her meeting in Jackson and almost called him. On her way home tonight, she decided, she would stop by his cabin and explain.

Clay had lost his motivation on the Middleton story. Parker's death had hit him harder than he realized. Brian and Larkin had been life savers. They came over early to his pier and picked him up on the party barge. "We're going to the control valve and get some sun," they said, "and you're going with us." They spent all day on the barge soaking up sun, and for the first time in months Clay began to relax. The water and the beauty of the lake seemed to soak up his emotions like a sponge. Late in the afternoon Brian approached his friend. "Clay," he said, "I'm worried about you. Not just this thing with Parker, but everything. You're not yourself. I'm not going to meddle in your affairs, but I'm making plans to stay here for a while just in case you need me. It's my off-season, you're my buddy and that's the way it's going to be."

Clay broke the tension and for the first time all day, smiled. "You're worse than Carl, you big dummy. I can still take care of myself." He flexed his muscles and threw a playful punch in Brian's direction.

Brian was laughing, "You'd better watch out or I'll have to whip you like a sharecropper whips his dog."

"You guys are right. I do need to talk. I'm angry. Very angry."

"Why, Clay?" Larkin reached for his hand to console him.

"I guess I'm angry at myself. I feel responsible for Parker's death. I should never have involved him. And then there is this thing with Khaki. I knew she was tied to Ash Walker. I was really stupid." Clay looked at Brian. "We've got to tell Larkin."

"You're right," Brian said.

Clay told her everything. When he finished she said, "I knew something was up, from the day Rose Bower told me she needed to see you. More than once I've asked Brian what was really going on. He would always say you would tell me when you were ready."

It was late afternoon when Clay's phone rang on the boat. It was Carl. "I can't get you to return my calls on your home phone so I thought I would call this number."

"What are you talking about?" Clay asked.

"You didn't get my message?"

"No, what message?"

"Never mind," Carl said. "Feret Du Boise is in New Orleans, as I thought. He's involved with a stripper, and they are heavy into drugs, according to my pals in Vice. I'm watching him."

"Good," Clay said.

"But there is something else. The real reason I left the message on your answering machine was to tell you that you are not the only one interested in Ash Walker. The FBI sent an agent down a couple of months ago at the request of the Topisaw County district attorney."

"Who is he? Do you have a name?"

"It's not a he, Brother, it's a she. She's agent Khaki Woodson."

Clay relayed Carl's message to Brian and Larkin. "What a difference a day makes," Brian touted as Clay said goodbye to his brother.

As he showered back at the cabin, he let it all sink in. That explained everything. He would find her if it took all night. Stepping out of the shower he heard a car drive up outside.

He slipped on a pair of walking shorts and opened the door. Khaki was standing in the doorway. Her long, blonde hair hung loosely and the night breeze blew the strands around her face. She was wearing a short summer dress that exposed her long, brown legs. He could see the outline of her body through the fabric. Her sensuality took Clay's breath, and he reached for her before she could begin to explain.

"I already know," he said, as he stroked the hair away from her eyes that were moist with tears, "Carl told me everything. Don't say a word." He pulled her to him, reluctant to take his eyes away from her face, but wanting to hold her. Clay's shoulders were still wet from the shower, and his skin glistened in the soft light of the cabin. Khaki buried her face in his neck, and her mouth made its way slowly to his. Clay gently pulled the straps from her shoulders and her dress fell to the floor at their feet. Her hand found his waist and she slowly groped for the opening of his shorts. He slipped down the lace panties and lifted her as she locked her legs around his waist. She was warm and wet against him, and he was already inside her before they reached the sofa. She pulled him down on top of her and they moved together in the rapture of passion.

CHAPTER TWENTY-FOUR

WHEN KHAKI TAPPED HIM on the shoulder the next morning, Clay looked up to see her standing next to his bed with coffee and toast. "What time is it?" he asked, stretching and yawning as he tried to wake up.

"Almost nine," Khaki answered.

"What about work?"

"I've called in. I'm taking a couple of days off." Clay smiled and reached for her. Khaki sat down on the bed with him. "We've got a lot to share," she said. "Let's see if you can do that as well as you can make love."

Clay started from the beginning and told it all, from Vassar's first phone call to Parker's funeral and ended it with his suspicions about her relationship with Ash Walker.

"That's ironical," she said when he finished. "I thought you were a DIA plant until our trip to New Orleans. I can see why you thought Ash and I were together. It wasn't that he didn't try, but it never happened. I detest the man. I came to Camellia City at the request of the district attorney to find out why Ash Walker was seemingly untouchable. My job, of course, was merely a cover and a quick ticket into Ash's circle. In one week I had picked the lock on his office and planted a bug in his telephone. I've also planted one in yours, I might add." Clay smiled. "That's pretty good work."

"Well," Khaki replied, "I like to think they taught us something at Quantico." She continued, "I overheard a conversation between Ash and Lieutenant Colonel Lee Bradford. Colonel Bradford is the head of the Defense Intelligence Agency in Washington. At the time of Vassar's murder, Ash talked with Bradford again. That's when you came into the picture. Bradford asked Ash questions about you, how much you knew, and what you had been hired to do."

"Then you should have known that I was not with the DIA."

"Not necessarily," Khaki explained. "It would not be unlike Bradford to plant someone down here just to keep an eye on Ash Walker. I'm telling you, Clay, the DIA is known for its paranoia."

Clay interrupted again, "How did you hear their conversation?"

"I have a link to my apartment and a receiver that monitors and records 24 hours a day."

"So that's why you never invited me over. You didn't want me to see your toys."

"Right."

"Go ahead," he said as he pulled her to him and kissed her, "I promise I won't interrupt again."

"I knew that Rancey James and a hit man called the Albino killed Vassar, and I heard references to Camp Middleton. When Ash left for Europe I had a field day. I was in his office every night going through files. I would take the information I needed to my apartment, copy it the next day and return it that night. Yes," she said, anticipating his next question, "that was me in his office the night you came to the morgue. There's damaging evidence in the files we can nail him on: embezzlement, fraud or tax evasion—but these would be minor compared to what we've discovered. The first week he was gone I copied the hard drive from his computer. I knew the information on it was encrypted, so I sent it to our specialist in Washington. They translated it and returned a transcript along with the hard drive. What I read in that transcript didn't make sense. Now that you've told me about the massacre, however, it all fits."

"What did you find out?"

"In Ash Walker's computer our specialist found a directory. One of these files was named Evangeline. It was in the Evangeline File that I found this information. In the sixties, at the height of the civil rights movement with racial tension at an all-time high, Ash Walker contracted with the Defense Department to forever silence a secret. It involved an undisclosed number of soldiers that had eyewitnessed and participated in something that would have immeasurable consequences if it were uncovered."

"You mean the massacre of the 344th?"

"Yes. I'm sure of that now. Ash Walker, for a sum of $2,000,000, took care of having these men stalked and murdered."

"These would have been the CID soldiers," Clay said.

"Yes. And only Ash Walker knew how many participants existed."

"Right."

"There's one thing I can't figure," Khaki said.

"What's that?"

"Earl Bower. If Earl Bower was a participant in the massacre or at least an eyewitness, why is he still alive?"

Clay explained that they were childhood friends and that Earl had saved Ash's life. "So, Ash felt he owed him?" Khaki said.

"Yes, I think so, but he was aided by the fact that Bower went off the deep end."

"Destroying his credibility."

"Exactly. But Bower also told me that Ash Walker fried his

brain. I'm certain he was referring to electric shock therapy. I'll bet you anything Ash Walker had him committed."

"You may be right. I believe that Ash masterminded a plan with two parts: the first was to massacre the soldiers and hide them; the second was to keep the number of eyewitnesses a secret. This information alone could give him blackmail material as well as wealth and protection for the rest of his life."

"That works for me," Clay said. "So where is the information you have?"

"In a mini storage in Camellia City."

"And what will the FBI do with the Evangeline File?"

"Nothing. It's government dirty laundry and they will leave it buried. They couldn't afford to expose it. Do you realize the ramifications here? A massacre of more than a thousand black soldiers killed by a branch of the Armed Forces of the United States? The Savings and Loan bail-out would be a drop in the bucket compared to the lawsuits that would ensue, not to mention the political fall-out."

"Tell me, Khaki, how high does this go? Does the President know?"

"No. The file stated that only one president found out."

"Who?"

"Kennedy. A mole in the DIA leaked it to Robert Kennedy at the beginning of the civil rights movement, and he told his brother."

"You don't suppose," Clay conjectured," that that's why..."

Khaki finished his sentence, "...they were killed? I have no idea. I certainly couldn't make that inference." Khaki looked at him. "When you put both pieces together, you have your story."

"Not quite," he said, "there's still one thing missing."

Khaki was already ahead of him. "You don't have the corpus delicti."

"The problem is, they are somewhere on land that is now privately owned."

While Khaki was taking a shower, Clay called Dallas Dawson to set up a meeting at Buck Snort.

ON THE PORCH of Buck Snort, Sheriff Dawson was very surprised that the District Attorney had brought the FBI to Topisaw County. He was even more surprised to learn that Khaki had the tape and transcript that substantiated Ash Walker's involvement in the Vassar Lawrence murder. Dawson told Clay about the progress being made in Parker's case. "There is no doubt in my mind that Rancey James and Toxie Hux are responsible for it," he said. He went on to explain that he was just waiting for the ballistics tests to come back from the state crime lab before getting a search warrant.

The sheriff asked Clay how his investigation was going, and Clay told him about his progress. "Clay," he said, "I'll be glad when you wrap this thing up. If you attract the attention of the DIA, things will really heat up."

"That's a definite possibility and something that concerns me too," Khaki said.

As they prepared to leave the camp, Sheriff Dawson looked up in the sky. "It sure is a scorcher, isn't it? Maybe we'll get an afternoon rain and cool things off a bit."

On the way back to the cabin, Clay took Khaki by her apartment and followed her inside. She showed him the surveillance equipment and checked the recordings. There were no calls. She picked up some personal things and a new bathing suit and put them in her overnight bag. "Let's go," she said, "I'm ready." When they reached the cabin, Khaki opened her shoulder bag and dug beneath her government-issue ten millimeter Smith and Wesson. She pulled out a handful of photographs and handed them to Clay. "I think you'll find these interesting," she said. Clay glanced through them. He saw himself and Carl captured on film standing near the Riverwalk fountain and on the balcony overlooking the Mississippi River. "So," he said, "the guy with the baseball cap and camera..."

"One of our agents in Louisiana," Khaki added.

"And was someone taking pictures of the 15th floor of the Hilton that night?"

Khaki broke into a big smile. "I certainly hope not."

After making sandwiches and icing down drinks for a boat ride, Khaki left the room to change clothes. "I'll come on down to the boat," she called. Clay put on a pair of shorts and Ray Bans and picked up the lunch and drinks.

As they rode to the deep end of the lake, Clay talked about Parker's murder. Then, out of the blue, he said to Khaki, "Do you think I'm prejudiced?"

"Prejudiced?" she asked, "about what?"

"About race."

"I don't know, but I certainly hope not. Why do you ask?"

"Because I think maybe Parker thought that I was. He asked me just before he was killed if I would do something for him. It was almost as though he had a premonition."

"What did he want you to do?"

"He asked me to go to the National Civil Rights Museum in Memphis."

"That was an odd request."

"Yes. I thought so too."

"Are you going?"

"Yes. I am. I think I will drive up early tomorrow morning." Khaki reached for his hand. She knew how much Parker's death had affected him. "Do you want some company?" she asked.

"Would you go with me?"

Khaki put her arms around him, "Try and leave without

me."

At the deep end of the lake, Clay tied the barge to the control valve's concrete platform. He put on some music and stretched out in the sun. Khaki stood above him. She unfastened her faded cutoffs and shirt and was naked except for the hint of an ice-colored bikini. Her body was well-tanned and, as she loosened the band from her hair, she became aware of Clay's eyes on her. She felt helpless as the heat surged through her in response to his gaze. Making one step to the side of the boat, she plunged into the water. Clay was right behind her. When Khaki came up, Clay caught her in his arms. She wrapped her arms tightly around his body and felt his muscles tense as he held her firmly in the water. She went limp and allowed him to guide her to the ladder on the boat. She could feel her heart pounding against his chest as he held on with one hand and unfastened her top to free her breasts with the other. Together, they sank into the clear spring-fed water of the lake to make love.

CHAPTER TWENTY-FIVE

T HE NATIONAL CIVIL RIGHTS MUSEUM is built around the Lorraine Motel, the historic site where Dr. Martin Luther King was assassinated in 1968.

As Clay and Khaki stepped inside and signed the guest register, he had no idea how the next few hours would affect his life. Clay was one of the two-thirds of Americans that had no firsthand knowledge of the events that marked the civil rights movement of the 1950s and 60s. He was only five years old at the time of King's assassination.

They moved through the eerie exhibits that highlighted the struggle and, as he looked at the photographs, Clay found the life-sized image of Frank Mingus. "That's the guy Parker wrote about," he pointed out to Khaki. "He is from Camellia City."

Clay paid close attention to the video and audio presentations and studied the artifacts that vividly depicted each event. He sat at an actual lunch counter among the gray sculptures of blacks, surrounded by rednecks. These figures were so masterfully reproduced he almost expected them to speak.

Khaki followed him through the burned-out shell of a Greyhound bus representing the Freedom Riders. He heard the recorded voice of President Kennedy as he tried to deal with the civil unrest at Ole Miss. But it was the last exhibit that shattered his emotions like a missile—the Memphis garbage workers' strike. Sculptures of the garbage workers portrayed them shoveling garbage into a yellow Memphis garbage truck while armed National Guardsmen looked on. Juxtaposed against the fixed bayonets of the soldiers, the helpless workers wore only a cardboard placard around their necks that read, "I AM A MAN." At that moment it all came together for Clay, and tears streamed down his cheeks. "This is it," he said to Khaki. "This is what I came for, and Parker knew it."

Khaki smiled, "Clay," she said, "This happened almost 30 years ago."

"No," Clay said. "It's happening now. That's Parker Phillips and the Camellia City mentality that is portrayed right here."

It was a long time before Clay left this exhibit. As they walked into the sunlight of the museum's parking lot, he felt as if he had experienced a Damascus Road awakening. Even that night in the lobby of the Peabody Hotel, he sat in long periods of silence and thought. Repeatedly, as they drove back to Camellia City the following day, he reflected on the impact of the gray sculptures and their simple claim to dignity.

Khaki hoped that this could serve as a closure to the death of his friend.

CHAPTER TWENTY-SIX

CLAY AND KHAKI slept late the next morning. They had breakfast on the deck and, over their coffee, they talked at length about what their next move would be.

Khaki went to the mini storage and brought the Evangeline File back for him to integrate into his notes. They discussed the paper trail filled with stealth and murder.

Before noon the telephone rang, and it was the unmistakable voice of Earl Bower.

"Brady," he said, "Rancey James has been over here at Damico's asking me a lot of questions about you."

"What did you say?"

"I didn't say anything. I have something important that I want to give you."

"I'll come over."

"No, wait until dark."

"Okay. What time?"

"Nine sharp. Come by the alley in the back of the building and stop at the rear entrance. Don't get out of your car. I'll be in the doorway waiting for you. Then we can go somewhere and talk. Don't make me wait."

"I won't."

"What kind of car do you drive?"

"A black Jeep Cherokee."

There was an edge in Bower's voice. "I'll be looking for you."

"What do you think?" Khaki asked when Clay told her who was on the phone.

"I don't know, but I'm sure going to be there at nine."

They went out on the barge and enjoyed the rest of the morning on the lake watching the fisherman coming in from early morning excursions. Finally Clay said, "Let's go to Skinney's for some ribs. I'm starving."

Turning off the interstate at the Chatawa exit, he took a side road into the southernmost part of Topisaw County. "I'm going to take the long way," he said. Winding up and down hills, they passed oak trees wrapped in Spanish moss and ivy. There were red clay banks with sandstones jutting out of them and patches of kudzu that carpeted the ground. Crossing the railroad tracks, they saw an elderly man filling empty milk bottles with artesian well water.

Clay stopped at a cemetery across from an antebellum Catholic convent. The cemetery was enclosed by a rusty wrought iron fence laced with honeysuckle and white flowers. Shade from giant magnolia trees cast shadows across the grave markers. Khaki walked beside Clay as he opened the gate and went inside. He was especially quiet, and Khaki said nothing to interrupt the solitude that he seemed to need. It was satisfying just to enjoy the serenity of the place together. At the marker of Sister Mary Raphael's grave, Clay pulled Khaki to him and said, "Parker's death has made me realize how precious life is and how uncertain it can be. Now that I've found you, I'm even more aware of it." Khaki looked up into his eyes. "What I'm trying to say, Khaki, is that I'm in love with you."

"I know," she said. "I'm in love with you, too. It's funny how quickly things can change. I thought only a few months ago that all that mattered to me was the FBI and my next assignment. Now that I have met you, all that has changed. I want to be with you," she said seductively, "and to feel you inside me is all the excitement I ever want."

The afternoon storm that Dallas Dawson had wished for came out of the southwest, and big drops of rain began to fall. They ran to the Cherokee and headed for Skinney's. Skinney's was a restaurant just across the Louisiana line, famous for the best barbecue between Memphis and New Orleans. It was owned by an Ole Miss standout and Mississippi football legend, Ralph "Catfish" Smith. The restaurant was filled with photographs of his football career and one poster of Lance Alworth, a high school teammate, snagging a pass for the San Diego Chargers. It was the perfect place to wait out a summer rain with a slab of ribs and a pitcher of beer.

When they returned to the lake, Khaki had some paper work that had to be sent to Washington. "I'll be working late," she said, "but call me when you get back from your meeting with Earl Bower. I'm anxious to know what he wants to give you. That reminds me," she said. She walked over to the telephone and in a moment returned and handed Clay the tiny bug she had planted in his phone. "I've checked carefully," she said, "Your phone is safe, at least for now. Watch yourself," she said before she drove away.

There were only a couple of cars at Damico's when Clay passed at five minutes until nine. One was Rancey James' Cadillac. He made the block and, seeing that it was no longer there, turned up the dark alley. Clay stopped at the rear entrance and the Cherokee door opened. He was only a dark silhouette. Clay eased underneath a street light and turned to speak to Bower. He saw a gun barrel pointing right between his eyes and behind it was the face of Toxie Hux.

"I told you I'd see you again didn't I, dude? Pull over there and park. What the fuck you been talking to Bower about?"

Toxie continued. Clay still didn't answer. "What would a smart ass like you and a crazy son bitch like him have to talk about?"

"Where is Earl?" Clay asked.

"Oh, so now you're asking the goddamn questions. Do you know what happens to people around here that ask too many questions?"

"I've heard."

"And to whites that suck up to niggers? Tell me, Mr. Big Shot, how did you like that nigger at the fire tower, and tell me, were you and that nigger reporter just friends or was he sharing that bitch's ass he was married to with you?"

Clay's mouth was dry and his heart racing, "You'd better kill me," he said, speaking through clenched teeth.

"I'm going to kill you all right," Toxie snarled, "but not tonight. I'm going to make you sweat. You saw how easy it is to get to you, and I can damn sure do it again." Clay glared at him. Rancey James' Cadillac pulled up beside the Cherokee, and Toxie reached for the door handle and opened it. Still pointing the gun in Clay's direction, he said, "The next time I see you I'm going to beat the shit out of you, and then I'm going to blow your fucking brains out." Toxie Hux was out of the Cherokee, "Take me to the 'Confederate,'" he told Rancey as he got into the Cadillac. Rancey slammed the accelerator to the floor and pulled out of the parking lot. Clay sat motionless in an overwhelming sea of rage and fear.

In the Cadillac Toxie was bragging, "Rancey," he said, "I scared him shitless. When can I open him up?"

"Not until Ash gives the go-ahead. And then we can't do it in this county. You already know that. Give me back my pistol, Toxie."

After regaining his composure, Clay went inside Damico's. Primo was about to close. "I'm looking for Earl Bower," Clay said, "have you seen him?"

"No. Not since noon. He left with his dog and a cardboard box under his arm. If he came back, I didn't see him."

"Do you mind if I go upstairs and have a look?"

"Help yourself, but go out the back way, I'm trying to close."

"Thanks," Clay said. "I'll do that."

Upstairs every room was empty except one. Inside it was a cot and a thin sheetless mattress. Next to it was an apple box with a lamp on it. The walls were empty except for a calendar with the lunar tables noted in red. On the window sill was a plastic statue of the Virgin Mary. He had left a note beneath the statue scrawled in pencil that read, "MOTHER OF GOD?" In the closet Clay found a couple of brightly colored Hawaiian shirts, empty boxes of dog food and a pair of worn-out tennis shoes. On the floor of the closet were countless strips of paper with meaningless numbers, letters and formulas scribbled on them. Clay called Earl's name and no one answered. Was Earl Bower out walking his dog at Wentworth campus, or had both man and dog vanished?

Clay left Damico's and drove straight down Highway 51 until he reached the Confederate Bar. He turned in. He had never stopped at the bar before... it had the reputation of being the toughest bar in Topisaw County. The Confederate's customers were primarily off-shore oil field workers, loggers and ex-cons that had spent some time in the state's penitentiary. Clay walked through the front door and immediately spotted Toxie about halfway down the bar with a beer to his mouth. Over the noise of the jukebox, Clay yelled, "Toxie Hux, I am here to whip your ass." Toxie turned around as Clay approached him and responded, "Tell me that again out back."

Clay's mouth became dry as they made their way to the back door. A hush fell over the customers and a grandstand of roughnecks followed, enjoying the excitement. Before

they reached the outside, Toxie spun around quickly, trying
to land a sucker punch. Clay dodged it and grabbed Toxie by
the neck and threw him out of the door. Toxie was back on
his feet and, with the fury of a bull, charged into Clay. The
first two licks that Toxie volleyed landed and brought blood,
then Clay connected a lightning fast jab to Toxie's nose.
Blood spewed. There was a barrage of flying fists and Toxie
was inflicting damage. A right hook crashed underneath
Clay's jaw, and he staggered backwards. Toxie stood in front
of him, planning to come in for the kill. Clay instinctively
measured his opponent and delivered a devastating number
of blows to Toxie's face and, with a boiler maker, knocked
Toxie to the ground. The crowd gathered around in amazement. Toxie struggled to his knees, wiping his eyes, trying to
clear away the blood. "He's had enough," someone in the
crowd yelled, as others began to wander back into the bar.
"I've never seen anybody whip Toxie, but you sure as hell
did. Let me buy you a drink."

Clay stood for a moment in complete exhaustion, trying to
experience the feeling of the vanquished, but it was short-
lived. As he turned to walk away, someone yelled, "He's got a
knife!" Clay wheeled around and saw Toxie, on his feet now,
holding a knife. In one quick moment, Clay kicked and
Toxie's groin exploded with pain. He doubled over and
Clay's knee slammed into his chin. The knife flew from
Toxie's hand and he fell backward to the ground. This time
Clay jumped on top of him, grabbed him by his greasy hair
and hit him again. "Tell me," he yelled, "who killed Parker?
Did you or Rancey? Tell me, or I'll beat you to death." Toxie
was spitting blood now. "Ash Walker," he said. Clay rose to his
feet and staggered through the bar and made it to his car out-
side. He took off his shirt and wiped the blood from his face.
One eye was almost closed from swelling. He picked up his
phone and called Ash Walker's answering service, "I need to

talk with Ash Walker, it's an emergency," he said.

"Mr. Walker is at Willow Wood Country Club," the service informed him, "he said to hold his calls."

Clay slammed the receiver down and headed for Willow Wood. At the club, Clay had no trouble finding Ash Walker's Mercedes. He parked beside it and waited. He checked his automatic to make sure it was loaded. For a second he considered shooting Ash Walker on sight, but even in his rage he knew that was not the way he wanted it. He threw the gun back into the glove compartment and locked it.

After what seemed like a long wait, Ash came out of the club's front door. He was alone. Clay, still shirtless, waited until he reached his car. "I want to talk to you, Ash Walker." Clay was now only steps away. "You killed Vassar Lawrence and you killed Parker and Tawana. I know it and you are damn sure not going to get away with it."

Ash listened calmly and did not move or show any sign of fear. "You are an arrogant young fool" he said. Then his expression changed and he got right into Clay's face. "Clay Brady," he said, slowly and clearly, "you're a dead man."

Ash Walker calmly got into his Mercedes and drove away.

CHAPTER TWENTY-SEVEN

THE COCKPIT GLOWED RED as the Mooney cruised through the darkness at 150 knots. It took approximately 30 minutes for Brian's eyes to adjust for night vision.

A lot had transpired in the past two weeks. An outline had already been sent to his literary agent, Adrian Keene, in New York and they had discussed the best way to break the story. Both agreed that it should have the effect of a nuclear blast, and they would need *The New York Times* and a primetime television magazine for that.

There were still no clues as to where the more than 1,000 men might be buried, but Clay knew he could not put off this meeting with Carl any longer—not after Ash Walker's threat. He would give Carl his power of attorney tonight. Khaki was certain that if the DIA were not already on the scene, they would be soon. Clay also knew from past experiences with investigations that, when a story finally came together, the loose ends would either tie up quickly or the entire investigation would collapse like a house of cards. There was still nothing on the whereabouts of Earl Bower. Clay had checked with Damico almost daily, and no one had heard from him.

Clay's concentration was interrupted by the crackling of the overhead speaker, "Mooney 79868, contact New Orleans

Approach on 120-6." It was Houston Center passing them off to New Orleans Approach as they neared their destination.

"New Orleans Approach. This is Mooney 79868." Brian's voice was strong and confident. His 5,000 hours as pilot in command were apparent as he requested permission to enter the controlled airspace.

"Mooney 79868, this is Approach, go ahead." The controller's voice was pleasant and unhurried. The traffic was light.

Clay knew this might be the only opportunity he would have to come up with an escape plan. Carl had suggested a meeting at Vera's, a seafood restaurant on the north shore of Lake Ponchartrain. According to Carl, they served the best boiled crabs in Louisiana. "It will be the perfect place to meet," Carl had said. "I'll meet you at the Slidell airport." Clay was confident that with Carl's connections and Brian's expertise in planning and timing, they would have a workable plan by the time they flew out of Slidell.

The air at 6,500 feet was clear and cool. The stars looked like diamonds thrown against a black velvet cloth. The Mooney cut through the night. Clay thought of Khaki. They had become inseparable. Her investigation of Ash Walker was beginning to wrap up, and the chances of reassignment and relocation appeared imminent. Clay watched Brian gently push the telex talk switch on the yoke.

"Approach, this is 868. I am inbound landing in Slidell." They could see the lights of the Big Easy in the distance. Brian's voice broke the silence again, "Approach, this is 868. I've got Slidell in sight."

Clay could feel the deceleration as the Mooney slowed to gear down speed. The plane banked left through a smooth 90 degree turn and was aligned perfectly on a one mile final approach to Runway 17. "Gear is down and locked, prop in, mixture is full rich, flaps 15 degrees." Brian reeled off the landing checklist as he trimmed the Mooney for approach speed. The plane began to sink toward the amber lights of the runway. In a matter of seconds they crossed over the green threshold lights and settled gently on the runway.

As they taxied to a stop, the lights of the plane found Carl leaning against his car at the end of the runway. "How was the flight?" he asked as the two men got out of the plane and approached him.

"Smooth as silk," Clay answered. Carl and Brian had met on several occasions and, when he got to Carl, Brian received a bear hug like the ones the detective reserved for his brother. On the way to Vera's, Carl shared some news of the Feret Du Boise investigation. "Our Vice boys picked up Du Boise's stripper girlfriend this morning," he said. "This time she's in real trouble."

"Drugs?" Brian asked.

"Yes. And we're talking more than a charge of possession, we're talking about doing some real time."

"Do you think she will help you with Du Boise?" Clay asked.

"That's a very strong possibility." Carl moved rapidly through the business section of Slidell. When he reached the lake front, he took a left. The road ran parallel to the lake's edge. Carl's headlights played off the pilings of fishing camps and houses that rose out of the water. "I hope you guys are hungry," he said as they pulled into Vera's parking lot. Brian followed Carl and Clay into the restaurant. He was carrying a flight bag filled with maps and charts.

Carl selected a secluded table. "I like this place," Clay said, "and the way it's built over the water." Carl pointed to the east window, "About 20 miles on the highway over there is where Jayne Mansfield was decapitated. But you boys would be too young to appreciate her."

After consuming a mountain of boiled crabs, he and Brian

got down to business. All they wanted from Clay was his destination. Brian spread out the material from inside his flight bag on the table. Carl said, "Now, what we have to accomplish here is an escape plan for one when the sugar turns to shit in Topisaw County, right?"

"No," Clay answered quietly. "A plan for two."

Carl and Brian looked at each other. "Does Khaki know she's going too?" Brian asked.

"Not yet."

Clay watched in amazement as the two men worked in tandem— Carl coming up with a game plan and Brian showing how it could be executed. After two pitchers of beer, a pot of coffee for Brian and another order of crabs, Carl and Brian presented what they considered to be a perfect plan to Clay.

"And, if anything goes wrong with this one," Brian quickly added, "I'll just fly you the hell out in my Mooney."

"That would be too risky," Carl warned. "Keesler Air Force Base is less than 50 miles away. The DIA would have access to anything they needed on the base."

Before they left the restaurant, Brian told Clay that he was bringing a float plane to Dixie Springs and would dock it at the cabin.

"You may have to get out of there tomorrow, who knows?"

CHAPTER TWENTY-EIGHT

"WHERE IS HE?" Rancey bellowed.

"Who?" Larkin asked.

"That goddamned reporter that lives in your cabin."

"I haven't seen him, and I want you out of here."

Rancey James was causing a disturbance in the dining room of Larkin's Landing. Rancey and Toxie had planned to settle the score with Clay, and this time it was going to be for keeps. Toxie was waiting outside in the car. Larkin ushered Rancey to the door. Looking him dead in the eye, she said in a soft tone, "Can you hear me?"

"Yeah. I can hear you. Hell, I'm not deaf."

"Good," Larkin said. "Then I won't have to say it but once." Then, without a moment's hesitation, she said, "You are absolutely the most despicable, low down piece of white trash I've ever seen. I want you out of my place of business now."

Rancey was totally taken aback. Brian stepped up, "You heard what she said, and if you don't leave this instant, I'm going to physically throw you out." Rancey quickly considered Brian's size and demeanor and walked to the door. Turning around, he pointed his finger at Larkin, "You'll be sorry," he said snarling, "I can promise you that." Brian took a step toward him and Rancey cowardly turned and walked out the door.

When Rancey opened the car door, Toxie was holding an open quart of beer still wrapped in a twisted brown bag.

"Are you sober enough to do a little job for me tonight?" Rancey asked. "You can pick yourself up a couple of hundred bucks."

As they rode around town, Rancey raved and cursed violently. He'd never been thrown out of a place, he said, and who did that bitch think she was anyway? Toxie spurred him on. Rancey's fury was contagious. Toxie directed Rancey where to go, and when they got there Toxie got out of the car. When he came back he was carrying two five-gallon cans. "Open the trunk," he told Rancey. At an all-night filling station, Toxie filled the cans, one with diesel fuel and one with gasoline.

Hidden in the woods on a hill above the Landing, the two waited for the last customer to leave. At 2:05 a.m. the last employee locked up the Landing and left for the night. After making a drive by to check everything out, Toxie told Rancey to turn in and pull around to the back. Toxie opened the trunk and removed the cans. Handing the keys back to Rancey, he told him to start the engine and keep it running. First, Toxie cut off the gas main to extinguish the pilot lights inside, then he set the cans down at the door and kicked the door panel with his steel-toed boots. On the second kick the door broke open and Toxie was inside. He went straight to the kitchen and doused the floor with diesel fuel and then poured all but a little of the gasoline on top of it. Then, he turned on the natural gas jets of the stove. Finally, he poured a tiny trail of gasoline as he returned, stopping only a few feet from the car. He turned the gas main back on and, after getting inside, he rolled down the window, looked over at Rancey and said, "You ready?" Rancey raced the engine, Toxie lit the match and threw it. The kitchen that had been soaking up grease for 40 years, exploded into flames.

Screaming sirens from the local volunteer fire trucks racing up the highway woke Clay and Khaki from their sleep. When they looked outside it seemed the whole world was ablaze. Larkin and Brian were already on the scene when Clay and Khaki drove up. Larkin was hysterical as she stood helplessly watching the flames ravish her Landing. Brian could not console her and stood by her in total disbelief.

Despite their efforts and even with a lake full of water only yards away, the volunteer fire fighters lost their battle. By daylight a pile of smoking rubble and ashes was all that was left of Larkin's Landing.

CHAPTER TWENTY-NINE

RAY JEAN HUX cried and listened as her 15-year-old sister relayed all of the vulgar details of how Toxie raped her. When she told how he had bitten her breast, Ray Jean burst into tears again. How many times he had bitten her before with no regard to the pain he was inflicting.

"I'm so glad you told me," she said gently to her sister when the girl finished her story.

"I couldn't live with it any longer. I feel so guilty."

Ray Jean took her in her arms, "You have nothing to feel guilty about, and don't worry about Toxie. He's not going to hurt you or anyone else ever again."

It was not an empty promise. She had thought about how she would do it hundreds of times before. Now, after hearing what her sister said, she knew that the time had come. She picked up her purse and told her sister to come with her. They drove to Wal-Mart, and inside Ray Jean pushed her buggy to the hardware section. A sales clerk cut three lengths of chain to her specifications. Next, she picked up three padlocks. Then, a roll of duct tape. At the drug department she pulled from her purse a prescription for sleeping pills and had it filled.

Leaving Wal-Mart, the sisters drove to a pawn shop where Ray Jean purchased a pair of handcuffs. "Are they strong?"

she asked the owner.

"Sure. They are the ones the police use," he told her.

"Good," she said.

Toxie came home a little after five. He was surprised to see Ray Jean's sister there. She had not been back after the rape. He leaned back in his recliner and ordered Ray Jean to bring him a quart of beer from the refrigerator. As soon as she left to get it, he looked over at her sister and whispered, "You must have gotten a little horny, huh?"

The girl turned her head in disgust.

Ray Jean brought the quart of beer back, opened and ready to drink, but not before she had loaded it with the powder of a half-dozen sleeping pill capsules. Toxie was in a deep sleep before the conclusion of *Hard Copy* on the television. Ray Jean shook him, "Wake up," she said. No response. She shook him again. He was out.

She brought out her bag from Wal-Mart. She fastened the handcuffs around his wrist, then padlocked a piece of chain around each foot. Quickly, she took the third section of chain and connected the feet and the handcuffs and, with one swift jerk, tightened the chain and padlocked it. Just as she had rehearsed so many times in her mind—Toxie was hog-tied. Toxie moaned but did not come out of sedation. Ray Jean's sister covered Toxie's mouth with duct tape and, before the next television commercial, Toxie Hux slept in his fuzzy white recliner, bound and captive.

It was almost ten p.m. when Toxie finally began to rouse himself. He jerked around but was helpless. Ray Jean slowly rose from her chair and turned off the television. Then she sat down again and began a long recitation of the things she had held inside herself for years. The years of abuse and beatings were all recounted for Toxie, and she ended with the rape of her sister. Then Ray Jean told Toxie how he would pay for his transgressions. This was the part she had anticipated with the most delight. Toxie jerked and moaned as she talked, pleading and then threatening with his eyes.

It was after one a.m., when she was certain that her closest neighbors were asleep, that she went outside and backed Toxie's pickup truck to the doorstep of the trailer. She reached underneath the mobile home and retrieved two boards to make a ramp from the truck's tailgate to the step's landing.

Inside, the two sisters jerked Toxie out of his chair. He hit the floor with a loud thump. They pushed and pulled on his body until they reached the front door and, with some effort, rolled him up the ramp and into the truck's bed. Ray Jean covered him with a sheet, anchored it with bricks and closed the tailgate. The last thing she loaded was a gas can.

Ray Jean's sister drove her car and followed the pickup as Ray Jean pulled out of the yard. Ray Jean took the back roads to Felder's Ridge, her sister still following closely behind. At Fire Tower Road she turned in on the gravel and drove to the same place where weeks earlier Toxie had killed Sugar Red.

Without hesitation, she got out of the truck and pulled the sheet off Toxie. Reaching for the gas can, she said, "You love to burn folks out and you love fire, Toxie. You evil son of a bitch, that's how you're going to hell." She doused the gasoline over Toxie, poured some in the cab and made a trail. From a safe distance she took a Bic lighter and lit it.

As the two girls sped away, Toxie's truck erupted in a fireball. On the highest elevation in Topisaw County, Toxie Hux's body crackled in the flames.

CHAPTER THIRTY

ARL BRADY SCANNED the classified ads of *The Times Picayune* looking for what he already knew was a pipe dream. On a lieutenant's salary, a Porsche, even an old one, was definitely out of the question. There were still mortgage payments, braces for his youngest daughter and a tuition bill each month from the private school she attended. Still, as he did every morning, he searched. Something with a Metairie address looked good and he circled it with his pen. Maybe, he thought, at noon he would ride out and take a look, kick the tires and tell the owner he would have to think about it. His morning ritual was interrupted by an officer from Vice standing over his shoulder. "Brady," he said, "what if I told you I could make your day?"

"How?" Carl asked incredulously.

"The stripper from the show bar wants to see you. I think she's ready to talk."

"Du Boise?" Carl asked, folding his paper.

"You got it."

Carl Brady stepped into the interrogation room. Barbara Ann Jones a.k.a. Sandra was wringing her hands between smokes. Carl had her folder in his hand. "Well, Mrs. Jones, I believe you have finally made it. You're going to be able to retire from Bourbon Street and the entertainment industry and enjoy the state's hospitality for the rest of your life at Angola State Prison." The detective was being condescending and she knew it. He lit a Marlboro and handed it to her. "You want to talk to me?" he asked.

"I need a fix," she replied. "Get me to Charity Hospital. I've gotta have help. I'm freakin' up the wall."

"I'll help you, Barbara Ann," Carl said in a pastoral tone, "but first I need you to help me."

Barbara was swinging her crossed leg rapidly. "Help you how?" she said.

"I need help with something nasty," Carl said, "something I know you didn't have anything to do with."

"Like what?"

"Like Du Boise and a pop job in Mississippi."

Barbara Ann scratched her head. "I don't know what you are talking about," she said.

"I believe you do," Carl insisted.

"So, what if I could remember something about that?" she said.

"Then I would say you got smart."

"How smart?"

"Smart enough to get you to Charity and smart enough to say Vice put the finger on the wrong person."

Barbara Ann pulled her hair back with her hands. Carl Brady knew from years of experience that the moment had come. He leaned forward, right up against her face. "Barbara Ann," he said, "if you have something to say, say it now or I'm going to walk out of here."

Barbara Ann sat silently. Carl stood up. She turned her head and looked away. Carl walked toward the door. "I don't have time for this," he said.

"Wait," she said. "I want to deal."

Carl returned to the table and sat down. "What have you got?" he asked.

"No," Barbara was firm. "What do I get?"

Carl lit another cigarette and handed it to her. "You give me Du Boise wrapped tight, and you walk."

Barbara Ann Jones inhaled deep and blew the smoke out in intermittent puffs. "Call me a lawyer," she said, "you got a deal."

The pro bono lawyer sat beside his client as she began to belch the story. "The Albino liked to talk about it when he was high," she said. "He told how the newspaper woman pled for her life. He had said that when he actually pulled the trigger that there was no sound. There's this void and then a rush that fills up your body."

Carl grew weary with the fluff. "What have you got?" he demanded.

Barbara Ann had now gained control of the interview and she knew it. "You're uptight," she said to the detective. "When's the last time you had a good blow job?" Barbara Ann did not hold out any longer. "In my closet," she said, "is a black tote bag. What you are looking for is in it, and the Albino is at 522 1/2 Dauphine."

Carl Brady pulled his car to a stop at the fifth block of Dauphine. He and his partner walked up to a stacked duplex and started up the stairs to the second story. Both men had their weapons drawn. Lyrics and music from the opera *Tosca* came from an open window of the second floor. Carl proceeded cautiously upward, advising his partner to stay back. When they reached the door, Carl knocked. "Police!" he said. "Open up." There was no response. Carl reached for the door knob and twisted; it was not locked. As he eased the door open, Feret Du Boise was sitting on an antique sofa, stoned out of his mind. There was no effort to resist, and he did not speak as they arrested him and read him his rights.

CAPTAIN RICHARDS with the Camellia City Police

Department was lacking in "good ole boy" personality. He never talked about hunting or dogs and did not own a pickup. His reserved nature was often misread as conceit. Richards was a by-the-book professional who had come up through the ranks, gaining the respect of his fellow officers as he went. He was proud of his uniform, kept it spotless and, from his days as a rookie, kept his black boots shined to perfection. The Vassar Lawrence murder was committed in his city and he had jurisdiction. It was Captain Richards that Carl called when he had Feret Du Boise in custody. Captain Richards listened as Detective Carl Brady spoke. "Captain," Carl said, "we have Feret Du Boise in custody."

"That's certainly good news," the captain replied.

"We also have the murder weapon, a razor and the clothes he wore when he murdered Vassar Lawrence."

"Excellent," Captain Richards was beaming.

"There's more," Carl said, "He's willing to sign a confession if he can cut a deal."

"What's he got?" Richards asked.

"He'll give you Rancey James."

Captain Richards was more than pleased. "When can we get him?"

"Anytime."

"We're on our way."

The captain went into his chief's office with the good news. "Chief," he said, "we're going to wrap up the Vassar Lawrence murder. Carl Brady has her killer in custody in New Orleans. The break we've been waiting for has finally come."

24 hours later, Captain Richards spotted the white Cadillac he had been looking for cruising down Davenport Avenue. He turned on his blue lights and Rancey James pulled over to the curb. "Sorry, boys," he began as the captain and a lieutenant walked up to the car, "I didn't realize I was speeding."

"Get out of the car, Rancey," the captain barked. Rancey did not respond. "Get out now!" Richards ordered.

The lieutenant had his weapon drawn and pointed in Rancey's direction. "What the hell?" was all Rancey could say before Richards cut him off. "Put your hands on top of the car." The lieutenant cuffed him. "You're under arrest for conspiracy in the murder of Vassar Lawrence." Then Richards read him his rights while the lieutenant frisked Rancey. He immediately found the .38 revolver in Rancey's back pocket. In less than 20 minutes Rancey James, the .38 revolver, and the white Cadillac were in police custody. Rancey rode to the station in the back seat, cuffed but confident that Ash Walker would have him back on the street by noon.

CHAPTER THIRTY-ONE

O N TUESDAY MORNING, while Rancey was being arrested, Rose Bower called Clay with an urgent message that she needed to see him. As he drove into Camellia City, Clay thought that Rose must have found out something about where Earl was staying.

Rose greeted him at the door and took him back down the same dark hallway that led to her den. She picked up a letter on her desk and handed it to him. "This was in the mail this morning," she said. The envelope was addressed to her and there was no return address on it. The note inside read, "Rose, I'm sending a box for you and one for Clay Brady. Please call him when they arrive, but don't open the one with his name on it. I'm o.k. Love, Earl." Clay looked up at Rose and asked, "When do you think they will arrive here?" Rose smiled, "The UPS delivered them a while ago. That's when I called." She walked over to a couch and picked up a package and handed it to him. "Do you want me to open it here?" he asked. Rose thought a minute, then answered. "No, I have a feeling I don't need to know what's there. But you might want to see what was in my box."

Proudly, she handed Clay a blue rectangular presentation box trimmed in gold. Inside was Earl Bower's Silver Star award from the United States Army. Clay kissed her on the cheek, thanked her and hurried out to get in his Jeep. The package from Bower contained a metal World War II ammunition box. He unlocked it and lifted the lid. A note in Bower's handwriting read, "Brady, Enclosed you will find the life insurance I took out for myself. These have kept me alive for 53 years, and now they will be the proof you need for your story. There are 1,059 of them... they are the dog tags taken from the 344th infantrymen that were killed in the massacre, though I know I didn't get them all. The bodies are buried in the bottom of an old salt mine owned by Ash Walker. The mine is located near the old Camp Middleton site beside the railroad tracks that run down to the river. Look for a group of deserted tin buildings. You will never hear from me again. Don't try to find me. The death gods are closing in. Earl."

IN HIS PRIVATE OFFICE across town at the *Chronicle*, Ash Walker listened as the man sitting in front of him brought him up to date.

"They know everything, then?" Ash asked.

"Yes."

"And Khaki Woodson is an agent for the FBI?"

"Yes. I know it for a fact."

Ash Walker handed the man an envelope filled with money. "What are you going to do with that?" he asked.

"I'm going to buy that camp on Lake Mary and a bass boat."

"You should be comfortable when you retire with what you will have from the state and what you have gotten from me over the years. How many years has it been?"

"At the end of this term, 16 years," Dallas Dawson replied.

"I still can't believe that Brady has spilled everything out to you like he has. He seemed too smart for that."

"It's the oldest mistake in the book," the Topisaw County

sheriff said, "he substituted emotion for reason from the moment I told him I was a friend of his brother's. Once you have someone's confidence, the rest is easy no matter how smart they are."

"Do you think they will run before we can kill them?"

"No, not until he finds the bodies, and he can't do that."

"Right."

"Even if he runs, all I have to do is call Carl and he'll tell me where they are hiding."

"You've got all the angles covered."

"I think so," the sheriff answered, "do you want me to kill them? It would be easy."

"No. Since Woodson is with the FBI, we will need one of Colonel Bradford's boys. All Bradford will have to do is pick up the phone and tell the director that one of his own agents has gotten into the Defense Department's sticky business, and the Bureau will be forced to look the other way."

"They would do that?"

"Yes. It happens from time to time."

Ash changed the topic of conversation. "What about Rancey James? Do you think he will talk?"

"I don't know. He's a loose cannon."

"Like not getting rid of that pistol?" Ash asked.

"Yeah. That's really put me in a bind. I can drag my feet a while longer, but I will have to charge him with Parker's murder sooner or later."

"The truth is, Rancey could turn pigeon at any minute," Ash said. "Where is he now?"

"After the city finished questioning him, they sent him to my jail."

"Still held without bail?"

"That's right."

"Then I think we have a problem. What can we do about it?"

Dallas thought for a moment. "What about a heart attack? He can have one by tonight."

"That would be perfect."

"You would be surprised at what you can accomplish when you have the coroner in your pocket."

"What will that heart attack cost me?"

"Don't worry. You'll never miss it."

"You got a deal. You take care of Rancey and I'll take care of Brady and Woodson."

As soon as Sheriff Dawson left Ash Walker's office, Ash picked up the phone and called Washington. Colonel Bradford answered. "What have you got?" he asked curtly.

"Brady knows everything."

"Are you sure?"

"Yes. Sheriff Dawson told me. He's just left my office and I've paid him off."

"Good."

"There's more. Brady has an FBI agent working with him."

"Who?"

"Khaki Woodson."

"Then you're not going to be able to handle this at your end."

"Right, that's why I'm calling you. I need the best man you can send."

"You got it. What about Rancey James, how's that going?"

"Dawson's going to kill him."

"I'll have one of my men in your office tomorrow by 11 a.m. to meet with you and Dawson."

Bradford hung up the phone and walked down the hall to find Bob Kruger. When he found him, his orders were clear and to the point. After a short briefing on the situation in Mississippi, Bradford said, "I want you to go to Camellia City and close the Evangeline File. Walker, Dawson, Brady and Woodson. All of them."

CLAY SPED DOWN the back roads going to the Camp
Middleton site described in Earl Bower's note. Twice he
stopped and pulled off the road making certain that he was
not being followed. He referred to his county map to find
the road he was looking for next to the river. As he
approached it he thought of Parker and Proby Lewis. When
he reached the railroad tracks, he took a road that ran along
beside the tracks until it ended ahead of him. Through the
trees he could see the buildings that Bower described. He
also recognized them as the same ones Parker had pointed
out when they flew over the base with Brian months ago.
He put his pistol in his back pocket and started walking
toward them. They were surrounded by a ten-foot chain link
fence and the gate to the entrance was locked. There were
no signs of activity. Clay scaled the gate ignoring the "No
Trespassing" sign and dropped to the gravel on the other
side. When he got closer he could still read the badly weath-
ered black letters painted on the side of the building that
spelled out, "The Evangeline Salt Company."

The building where the mine shaft was located was easy
to find. Although it was locked, Clay was able to see through
a window. Inside, the building was filled with cables, pulleys
and metal superstructures that had once been used to raise
and lower an elevator. The actual opening of the subterranean shaft had been sealed off with large sheets of welded
iron plates. Clay was expecting someone to walk up at any
minute, but he saw no one. There was nothing to indicate
that anyone had been there for a long time.

When Clay got back to his Cherokee, he referred again to
his map. It was just as he had suspected. The Evangeline Salt
Company was just across the state line. It was not in
Mississippi, but in Louisiana. That's even better, he thought.
Carl is personal friends with a federal judge. Maybe he could

get the search warrant they needed.

Brian was at Larkin's house when Clay returned to the lake. Clay said, "Come down to the cabin with me. I've got something to show you."

The two men spread the dog tags out on the floor and looked at each name and number. "So, the bodies are in the salt mine," Brian repeated as Clay told him the story. "Let's go out there and take a look."

"I've already been," Clay said.

"There's something I've never asked you," Brian said, "how did the military cover up that many dead soldiers? I mean, how did they handle it with their families?"

"It's all in the Evangeline File," Clay explained. "Khaki told me. First, they falsified the morning reports of the 344th which contained roll call rosters and pay roll. Then, letters were sent to the next of kin stating that their son or husband had been killed in the line of duty and that the body could not be recovered. If a soldier from Flagstaff, Arizona were killed, as was one in Lubbock, Texas, the odds of the two families comparing notes would be virtually impossible."

"And the families bought that?"

"There is no indication that they didn't. Death was such a common occurrence during wartime; different rules applied," Clay explained.

Brian nodded in agreement, "Particularly in the case of World War II, the war was clearly justified, and the war effort was paramount for the entire country. Families of soldiers always dreaded—but on some level almost expected—the telegram of notification from the War Department."

"Right," Clay continued, "Who would question missing remains? Remember, too, that during this era, people had an unwavering faith and trust in the government."

"They had little or no reason to disbelieve what was coming out of Washington," Brian said.

"That's true," Clay went on, "It wasn't until Vietnam and Watergate that Americans really began to doubt and question what the federal government was telling them."

"What about the other soldiers of the 344th—didn't they ask what happened to their buddies?" Brian wondered.

"Especially during a war, soldiers were moved and transferred all the time, usually with no notice. It wasn't a soldier's place to ask questions of the Army, only to follow orders. In fact, questioning orders could get you branded a traitor," Clay explained.

"Now that you have found all the missing pieces to the story, you must be pleased," Brian said. "You can wrap this thing up and go on with your life."

"It's not going to be that easy. This story, as sensational as it is, will be only another example of man with his finite mentality attempting to solve his differences with violence. The same dilemma is being played out on the streets of Camellia City today as we speak. Not much has changed, has it?"

"You mean the race thing?"

"Yes," Clay answered, "that's part of it. Before I came back to Camellia City, I was sick of all the talk of multiculturalism and diversity. I felt like I had no connection or need to be connected to those ideals."

"But this has changed your mind about that?"

"Yes. After coming back home, I realized that I must deal with this ideology. It's like a horse's head sitting on a banquet table. You can't ignore it. And that was what I was trying to do."

Both Brian and Clay realized that this was the most serious conversation they had shared during their long friendship. "I know that Parker's death had a tremendous impact on you and your feelings about race," Brian said slowly.

"Yes, it did. Without Parker I might never have seen the

bigger story. The challenge, as I see it, is to cultivate and write about a lasting spirit of hope that can overcome hatred and prejudice."

"What's next?" Brian asked.

"I plan to wrap up this investigation tomorrow. I'll send the newspaper story to Adrian by e-mail. Khaki and I will store all of the physical evidence of the investigation in her mini storage, which will now include these dog tags. I'll call Carl and get the ball rolling for a search warrant for the mine, and then Khaki and I will get out of Dodge."

"She's going with you then?"

"Yes."

"Does she know about your escape plan?"

"Only that we may be leaving at any moment. I didn't tell her where we were going or how, in the event she should be held hostage."

"And, if something should happen to you?" Brian asked.

"Then I know you would follow the plan and get her to safety. Brian, I think you and Larkin should get out of here as soon as possible. Things are going to heat up here when they realize that we are gone, and it's only logical that they will put the squeeze on you to find out where we are."

"When do you think you can return to the States?" Brian asked.

"Once the story breaks, it should all be over very soon. I'm thinking we should be back in a month or so."

Brian said, "I've leased a condominium in Point Clear, Alabama. It's right on the water and I think Larkin will love it. She really needs to get away. She hasn't been herself since the fire."

"Maybe when all this is over she can rebuild the Landing."

"I've suggested that, Clay, but she says it would never be the same."

Clay and Brian talked until Khaki and Larkin found them at

the cabin. After bringing Khaki up to date, Clay put the ammo box away and changed the subject. Larkin was quiet, too quiet, and he wanted to cheer her up. For the last time they would spend a perfect summer night at Dixie Springs— just the four of them cooking steaks, riding on the barge and enjoying each other's company. The only thing missing were the neon lights from the Landing that had always reflected so beautifully in the water.

CHAPTER THIRTY-TWO

C LAY KISSED KHAKI goodbye as she left for work. "Are you sure this is what you want to do?" he asked. She had written her resignation to the Bureau and was planning to mail it today.

"Positive," she answered, "Unless, of course, you don't want me to go with you." They both laughed. "See you this afternoon," she said. "What about going to Skinney's for some ribs?"

"That sounds good to me," Clay agreed.

On her way into Camellia City, Khaki took the last of the sensitive material and the ammo box full of dog tags to her mini storage for safe keeping. She stopped off at the post office on Walker Avenue and dropped her letter of resignation into the out-of-town slot.

Clay sent his finished newspaper story for *The New York Times* to Adrian's e-mail along with full details of where the bodies were hidden. Then he called Carl and told him everything. His brother was, as usual, concerned about his safety first. "When are you getting out of there?" he asked.

"In the next few days," Clay promised.

"Then I'll have everybody on standby."

"Good, we'll be giving you the word soon."

"You know that they have arrested Rancey James?" Carl

asked his brother.

"No, I didn't, but that is the best news I've heard."

Carl asked about Khaki and, once again, urged his brother to be careful, then hung up.

AT 8:35, BOB KRUGER'S flight landed at Keesler Air Force Base in Biloxi. Kruger had dark black eyes that sank into a hatchet face and black hair that he wore in a crew cut trimmed on the sides high and tight. He wore a collarless shirt, sport coat, dress slacks and loafers. Underneath his sport coat in a shoulder holster was a nine millimeter Sig Sauer automatic pistol with silencer attached. It was loaded with ten 115 grain hi-shock jacketed hollow-point cartridges that had a first shot kill ratio of 90%.

In an unmarked car he headed north to Camellia City. At eleven o'clock he pulled around to the back of the *Chronicle* and stopped at Ash Walker's private entrance. Dallas Dawson opened the door when he knocked. Ash Walker was leaning back in an expensive leather chair. "How's Bradford?" He asked as he stood up to meet the DIA agent. Bob Kruger made very little small talk with the two men before he asked them how he could find Clay Brady and Khaki Woodson. Dallas drew him a map showing how to find Lake Dixie Springs and Clay's cabin and then gave him directions to Khaki's apartment in town. Kruger slowly folded the piece of paper and opened his coat to place it inside a pocket. In one split second motion his weapon was drawn and he had fired twice. Ash and Dallas fell to the floor. The agent rolled both bodies over face down and fired twice more, shooting both men in the back of the head. The muffled, silenced shots went unheard over the noise of a running press. Kruger stepped over the bodies and picked up Ash Walker's phone. He punched in Lieutenant Colonel Bradford's number, and when the colonel answered he said, "Walker and

Dawson are dead. I'll call you when I've taken care of Brady and Woodson. I'm on my way there now. These gentlemen were kind enough to give me directions." Bradford said, "Just to make sure there's no slip-up, I'm sending in a back-up from Keesler."

KHAKI LEFT EARLY for lunch and drove to her apartment. When she opened the door she saw the light flashing on her recording device. The chilling call from Kruger to Bradford left her frozen with fear. There was no way to know what time the call was made. It might already be too late. She tried to call Clay, but there was no answer. Then the flight mechanism in her brain kicked in, and she grabbed the bag filled with clothes and cash that she had long ago withdrawn from her account anticipating this moment. She pulled her pistol from her bag and ran for the car. In seconds she was flying down the interstate on her way to the lake to warn Clay. This is what Khaki had feared most. She knew the DIA involvement meant all stops had been pulled out this time.

At the lake, Clay was sitting on the pier taking a break enjoying a glass of iced tea. He was looking across the lake when suddenly everything grew quiet. No birds were chirping, no squirrels barking, nothing but an uneasy silence. It was like the silence he had experienced at Buck Snort with Dallas Dawson when the hawk appeared out of nowhere for the rabbit. The hairs on Clay's neck began to prickle... and he turned around to see the human predator standing right behind him with his weapon drawn. Clay recognized the tell-tale military haircut and knew instantly who it was.

"Get up," Kruger said. Clay did as he was told.

Kruger was going to shoot him on the spot when he heard a car driving up. "Don't move," Kruger said. Kruger looked out on the lake toward the deep end in the distance and quickly studied the situation. "Get in the boat," he ordered and pointed to Larkin's barge tied up at Clay's pier. Clay walked to the barge and stepped in, the DIA agent right behind him with the gun. "We're going out there," Kruger said, motioning with his head toward the control valve and deep water. Clay cranked the engine, praying for another boat to be on the water, but he saw no one. The lake was deserted as the barge headed for the deeper water with Kruger standing behind him holding the gun. Clay knew this was going to be a one-way trip for one of them. As they neared the concrete platform of the control valve, Kruger carefully knelt down and picked up a length of nylon ski rope on the barge's deck and examined it. "Tie up over at that platform," he said. Clay knew at once what Kruger was thinking. He would kill Clay and tie his body around the concrete pilings.

Clay's mind was clear. Despite the fear for his life, he knew that he had only one desperate chance. It was a calculated risk and he would probably get shot in the process, but he had no choice but to take it. As they drove close to the platform, he throttled back on the engine and started coasting in just as Kruger directed. When he was only a few feet away, he jammed the throttle forward, crashing the boat into the concrete pilings. Kruger was caught off guard and fell forward. Clay swung for the hand with the gun as hard as he could and the gun broke free, flying across the tiled floor of the barge into the water. As quick as a cat, Kruger had regained his balance and moved in on Clay fast. A right smashed across Clay's face, then a left, then another. Clay swung back landing a blow to Kruger's mid-section. It was like hitting an anvil. Kruger was smirking with delight. The agent landed two more lightning fast jabs to Clay's face, brutally punishing him. The last blow opened a nasty gash over Clay's left eye and blood began to hamper his vision. Clay was not as skilled as his adversary, and he knew that this mil-

itary machine would beat him to death if the fight continued. Kruger was standing near the knee-high rail of the barge
and, with the fury of a cornered wild animal, Clay lunged as
hard as he could in a flying tackle. Both men fell overboard.

Clay was still locked around Kruger's waist as the water
closed over them. They were plunging deeper in the water,
wrestling around the mechanism of the control valve. Clay's
lungs began to hurt as they sank deeper. He broke away from
Kruger and started to kick for the surface, but Kruger
grabbed his foot and pulled him back deeper. They were
under the concrete pilings and Kruger pulled harder, maneu-
vering Clay deeper toward the sucking sound of the iron
grate around the valve. Clay was running out of breath. He
recoiled into a fetal position, with Kruger still holding on to
one of his feet, and kicked with all of his might into Kruger's
head. Kruger's head shot backward and slammed into the
valve rigging; the hand on Clay's foot turned loose and he
was free. He kicked diagonally upward until he broke the
surface. Treading water, he waited for Kruger to pop up
somewhere around him but, when he did not, Clay pulled
himself up to the barge and lay there breathless. There was
still no sign of Kruger.

After a few minutes, Clay went back over the side. He had
to be sure. He went straight down among the concrete pilings 20, 25, 30—and then he saw him. Kruger was suspend-
ed in the water. His feet were touching the metal grate, his
arms were outstretched like someone in a free fall bungee
jump. A ribbon of black inky substances oozed from the back
of his head. A piece of sharp rebar had punctured his head in
the struggle. Lt. Col. Bradford's best agent swayed in liquid
space at the bottom of Lake Dixie Springs. Clay shot back to
the surface before his lungs exploded. He would make one
more dive before he left the scene, this time with the rope
that he would use to tie the agent securely to the metal grate.

Khaki was watching helplessly from the pier as the drama unfolded. Brian heard her screams for help and joined her to watch the two figures in the distance. It was impossible to tell who was climbing back on the barge from where they stood, and they waited in terror until they could recognize Clay's broken, swollen face. Clay jumped off the barge and tied it up. Khaki was crying in his arms.

"Clay, they're going to kill us," Khaki said, following him up the path.

"No, Khaki. No, they're not."

She told him what she had heard on the tape.

"They killed Walker and Sheriff Dawson?" Clay asked in disbelief.

"Yes, that's what he told Bradford, and a back-up team is on the way from Keesler."

"Every minute counts, then. Let's get out of here, Brian."

The plan had been rehearsed many times in their minds, and it began to play out for reality this time. The call to Carl advised him that they were in an emergency situation and would have to leave at once. Soon the helicopters would be arriving from Keesler.

Larkin quickly loaded the Miata and headed to Point Clear. Clay changed into dry clothes, grabbed a tote bag with cash and clothes and reached for his laptop computer. Very shortly, Brian, Clay and Khaki were lifting off from the lake in a float plane Brian had brought the week before, headed to Springfield, Louisiana, only 18 minutes away. When Brian's plane touched down on the Tickfaw River, Charlie Albert was waiting to pick them up. Charlie owned the Blood River Landing on the Tickfaw River, and he also owned a fast boat that was the envy of racing enthusiasts around New Orleans. He was considered by most to be the most daring adventurer in the area. Twice he had taken his 35-foot cigarette boat, *Blood River*, to the Peninsula of Yucatan...once on a $1,000 wager. His maritime heroics had earned him the nickname, "Dundee Charlie." *Blood River* was already rigged with a 450-gallon gas tank. Carl had known Charlie for years and was certain that, with his expertise and equipment, Clay and Khaki would be in good hands. Charlie could get them to Mexico if every other part of the plan fell through.

Charlie was waiting for them in the boat with the twin 450 horse power marine engines idling. The master of *Blood River* was smiling and jovial. He wore shorts and a black muscle shirt. Wrapped around his head was a long do-rag with a pirate's skull flowing in the wind. "Let's boogie," he said as Clay and Khaki climbed aboard. "Get into the cabin and out of sight." The pirate of the Tickfaw looked at his watch. He had to cover 89 miles in less than two hours to make his prearranged rendezvous.

ON THE MISSISSIPPI coast two hours earlier, Carl had reached the other player in his escape plan. He found Captain Blanchard and *The Lottery* at the Bay St. Louis Yacht Club where he had just dropped off a charter. For weeks he had been prepared for Carl's call. There were clothes, personal items and provisions that would carry Clay and Khaki to safety, all carefully stored on his sailboat.

CHARLIE PASSED the *no wake* zone at Tin Lizzy's Landing and gunned his engine. The 35-foot beauty skimmed across the water at 70 miles an hour. He zipped past the Prop Stop and entered Lake Maurepas. The flashing red buoy #6 winked at him as he passed by. Five miles later he slipped underneath the bridge at Manchac and set a 100-degree course headed for Lake Ponchartrain. There was still a lot of water ahead of him before he would reach the Gulf of Mexico. The afternoon sun was hot, but the water was smooth and nice. Charlie was making better time than he thought. One hour and 30 minutes later, he carefully negotiated the treacherous jetties of the Mississippi Sound. Then it was on to Braton Island. It took one hour and 58 minutes to reach his rendezvous point at an abandoned Texaco oil rig #68 in the blue deep waters of the Gulf. When he got there, *The Lottery* was tied up beside it, waiting.

Clay and Khaki thanked Charlie and said goodbye. He smiled, "When you guys get back, look me up," he said. "Just look for the hottest boat on the river. That will be me." He waved goodbye and pressed his throttle forward.

Captain Blanchard welcomed the two aboard. Khaki still did not know their destination. She had begged, but Clay had repeatedly put her off, saying only, "I'll tell you later." The threesome cast off and, after setting the sails, Khaki and Clay returned to the cockpit. Blanchard was at the wheel. "Tell me, Captain, what will our heading be?" Clay asked.

Blanchard replied. "170 degrees due south. That will take us directly to the island of Cayos Cachinos."

Khaki shrieked and jumped with delight. "You're a rat, Clay Brady!" she teased.

"We have a long voyage ahead of us," the Captain said. "You sailors get comfortable. There is champagne and Russian caviar in the galley below."

It was dark when Clay and Khaki returned to the cockpit. They were rested from their ordeal. Khaki had cleaned the cut over Clay's eye and put a bandage on it. As *The Lottery* sails captured an uncommon northeast wind, they sat and talked.

"When you sell your book and the movie rights, you will have more money than you can spend," Khaki said.

Clay corrected her. "We will have more money than we can spend."

"And what will you do with it all?" Khaki playfully asked.

"Well," Clay pondered the question for just a moment.

"Well, I guess Carl will get that Porsche he's always wanted."

"And with that kind of money you could go anywhere in the world. Where would you go, Darling?"

Clay looked at her lovingly, "Home, Khaki. I would want to go home."

EPILOGUE

CARL BRADY STARTED putting it all together before *The Lottery* reached the Yucatan Peninsula. He had convinced a Louisiana federal judge to issue a warrant to conduct a search of the Evangeline Salt Company above and below the earth for the remains of soldiers of the 344th Infantry Regiment. The governor sent a unit of National Guardsmen to the parish to secure the premises until such a search could be conducted. A mining engineer had been hired to repair and restore the elevator at the salt mine. When it was ready, he, along with Carl and the sheriff of Tangipahoa Parish, descended the 792 feet into a shaft. Through a tunnel filled with briny tasting air, they followed a trail of bloody footprints and stains that long ago dried to a black, crusty substance. At the end of the trail, they stood at the entrance to a crystal chamber with walls as clear as glass. There were stacks of M-1 rifles and, beyond them, their lights illuminated the bodies: rows and rows of bodies.

Brass belt buckles now had a patina, and the bloody, bullet-riddled olive drab uniforms had turned to sepia. More than 50 years of entombment in an airtight salt chamber left the cadavers almost perfectly preserved. Their skin, once dark, had turned an unusual shade of blue, giving the appearance of thick leather stretched over bone. Eyes as black as marbles stared into nothingness. Still cast on their faces were the grotesque expressions of terror.

IN WASHINGTON at the Pentagon, Lt. Col. Lee Bradford was categorically denying the accusations that were fired at him from Ed Bradley and a producer from *60 Minutes*.

"Clay Brady is a sensationalist, prejudiced against the military by the loss of his father in Vietnam," he said. "His suspicions," he continued, "are based purely on a southern myth."